THE STORY OF THE NATIONS

THE CRUSADES

THE STORY OF THE LATIN KINGDOM OF JERUSALEM

BY

T. A. ARCHER

AND

CHARLES L. KINGSFORD

D1640159

NEW YORK

G. P. PUTNAM'S SONS

LONDON: T. FISHER UNWIN

PREFACE.

The present volume bears the sub-title, "The Story of the Latin Kingdom of Jerusalem," in order to make it clear at the outset that we are here concerned only with the Crusades which are Crusades in the proper sense of the word. With the Fourth Crusade, the Latin Empire of Constantinople, and still more with those developments, or perversions of the Crusading idea, which led to the so-called Crusades against the Albigensians and the Emperor Frederick, we have nothing to do. In making the story of the Latin Kingdom of Jerusalem the main thread of the narrative, stress has intentionally been laid on an important if comparatively unfamiliar side of Crusading history. The romance and glamour of Crusading expeditions has often caused the practical achievements of Crusaders in the East to be overlooked, or underrated. Yet it is through the history of the Kingdom of Jerusalem, that the true character and importance of the Crusades can alone be discerned.

A brief explanation of the circumstances under which this volume has been written appears to be required. When ill-health made it impossible for Mr. Archer to contemplate the completion of his own work, his material was placed in Mr. Kingsford's hands. The preparation of this material for the press involved not only much condensation and re-arrangement of the manuscript, but also the filling up of some considerable gaps. It would be almost impossible to satisfactorily divide the responsibility for a work produced under such circumstances, and in point of fact there is no single chapter to which both authors have not in some degree contributed. The book therefore appears, without further comment, under their joint names.

The circumstances of the present series forbid that constant citation of authorities in notes, which might otherwise be desirable; but the fact

i

that the narrative has in the main been compiled from the writings of contemporary historians, will, it is hoped, have given it some merit of freshness, even though the conclusions arrived at may often not differ materially from those of other writers. Whatever claim of originality is thus put forward for the present volume, is made in no spirit of detraction from the advantage, which has in places been derived from freely consulting previous workers in the same field.

In the matter of chronology the conclusions propounded by Mr. T. A. Archer in an article in the *English Historical Review* for January, 1889, have now been adopted without further argument. In the spelling of proper names, those forms which common use has made familiar have been preserved, whilst in the case of persons and places which would be novel to most readers, the endeavour has been to give the simplest form consistent with accuracy. It may, perhaps, be well to observe that the *j* in names like Kilij, Javaly, Sinjar is to be pronounced like *j* in judge.

"And I began to talk with the Most High again and said:

"O Lord, that bearest rule, of every wood of the earth, and of all the trees thereof, thou hast chosen thee one only vine: And of all the lands of the whole world thou hast chosen thee one pit; and of all the flowers thereof one lily; And of all the depths of the sea thou hast filled thee one river; and of all builded cities thou hast hallowed Sion unto thyself; And among all the multitudes of people thou hast gotten thee one people: and unto this people, whom thou lovedst, thou gavest a law that is approved of all."—II. Esdras, c. 5.

THE CRUSADES.

I.

INTRODUCTION.

"Reft of thy sons; amid thy foes forlorn,
Mourn widowed Queen, forsaken Zion, mourn."
HEBER, *Palestine.*

§ 1. *The Age of the Pilgrims.*

THE history of Syria is, to some extent at least, a synopsis of the history of the world; and the land itself is a palimpsest, from which the records of later civilisations have failed to obliterate entirely those of earlier times. Syria, indeed, is marked out by nature as a meeting-place of the nations. Westward it looks towards Europe, the adopted, if not the original, home of the Aryan race; to the east, across the desert, lies the great river on whose banks grew up that ancient Akkadian culture, which has bequeathed us much of our most familiar knowledge. In the south its inhabitants were brought into contact with the immemorial civilisation of the Nile; and in the north with still more mysterious races, of whom even modern research has as yet but little to tell.

No wonder that Syria has been the battlefield of the dominant powers of the world. Babylonians, Hittites, Egyptians, Assyrians, Persians, Greeks, and Romans, each in their turn were lords of part, if not of the whole, of Syria. Yet later this land beheld the struggle of Heraclius with Chosroes, of Mohammedan with Byzantine, of Turk with Saracen, and Crusader with Turk—all phases in the immemorial conflict of East and West.

1

But Syria has been something more to the world than this. Through the enterprise of the Semitic inhabitants of her coast, the germs of Babylonian culture were carried to the Aryan races of the West. Then, when her commercial mission was over, she fell beneath, first the Greek, and afterwards the Roman, and through their double agency imparted to the world that spiritual life which had found its cradle in the uplands of Palestine. So beneath the shadow of the "Pax Romana" this land became the centre towards which all nations of the Western world turned in pious aspiration.

There is no decisive evidence as to the exact date when the custom of pilgrimages to the Holy Land first obtained in the Christian Church. To the early Christians Jerusalem may well have seemed the city of the wrath rather than of the love of God. To them it was rather the scene of the death than of the resurrection of Christ, and its sacred associations were perhaps obliterated in horror at its profanation with heathen worship under the Roman name of Aelia Capitolina.

But when Christianity found a champion in Constantine the Great, Jerusalem began to raise its head among the cities of the world. The piety of this Emperor or his mother, Helena, built churches on the traditional scenes of Our Lord's birth and burial; traditional only, since the almost coeval legend of the Invention of the Cross shows clearly that all exact knowledge had been lost. Constantine himself is credited with the intention of a visit to the Holy Land, and from this time we can trace the history of the sacred pilgrimages from century to century. That emperor was yet alive when a pilgrim from Bordeaux made the journey by land to Jerusalem, and left a record which still survives. In the Holy City he saw the pool of Solomon, the pinnacle whence Satan tempted Christ to throw Himself, and the little hill of Golgotha, which was the scene of the Crucifixion. At other places, too, he notes with care whatever events in Scripture history had made them famous. Clearly men were already seeking to identify the chief scenes of the sacred

2

narrative, although in their credulity they were ready to accept whatever absurdities invention might offer; such, for instance, as the sycamore tree into which Zacchaeus had climbed.

By the end of the fourth century the practice of pilgrimages had so much increased as to give rise to the custom of collecting alms for the relief of the poor at Jerusalem. It was well, contended St. Jerome, that men should reverence holy shrines and relics. That saint himself, when forced to leave Rome, made his home in the Holy Land, and there his noble patroness, Paula, came to see him, and visit in his company Elijah's tower at Sarepta, the house of Cornelius at Caesarea, Jerusalem, Bethlehem, and Hebron. Paula herself wrote afterwards to her friend Marcella: "We do not doubt that there are holy men elsewhere than here, but it is here that the foremost of the whole world are gathered together. Here are Gauls and Britons, Persians and Armenians, Indians and Ethiopians, all dwelling in love and harmony." In Jerome's time Jerusalem already possessed so many sacred places that the stranger could not visit them in a single day. A hundred and fifty years later, after the city had been adorned by the splendid buildings of Justinian, they cannot have been less in number.

Early in the seventh century Jerusalem was plundered by Chosroes the Persian, and the Holy Cross carried off to a strange land, whence it was rescued a few years later by the victorious armies of the Emperor Heraclius. But already a power was rising which was to overthrow Persian and Roman alike. Even before Heraclius attained the zenith of his fortunes the flight of Mohammed from Mecca had marked for the world of Islam the beginning of a new era. No language can give an adequate idea of the fervour of the adherents of the new creed. Mohammed was hardly dead before his followers had conquered Syria and Egypt, overthrown the Persian monarchy, and founded an Arab empire. A century later, despite countless schisms, the new religion had made its influence felt from the banks of the Indus to those of the Loire.

3

For a moment in 717 it had even seemed that both the Roman civilisation and Christian faith must perish from the shores of the Bosphorus. But a deliverer appeared in the person of Leo the Isaurian, who with his successors, if unable to prevent, could at least take vengeance for, the inroads of the Mohammedans.

But the early enthusiasm of the new faith soon began to wax cold, and by the middle of the tenth century the Mohammedan world was in its turn tending to dissolution. The provincial governors rendered a merely nominal allegiance to the Caliph, whilst the schism of the Sunnites and Shiites had put on ever new forms, and from a rivalry of faith had produced a rivalry of temporal power. The vast body of Sunnites reverenced the orthodox Abbaside Caliph at Bagdad; though in Spain a rival dynasty of Omayyad princes established the Saracen Caliphate of Cordova. Yet a third Caliphate of Shiites has a more important bearing on Crusading history. Towards the end of the ninth century one Abdallah, the son of Maimún, established a new sect of Mohammedanism, which absorbed the Ismailians (a division of the Shiites). His doctrines spread rapidly, and above all in Northern Africa, where, in 973, his descendant, Moizz-li-dinillah, conquered Egypt, and became the first of that line of Fatimite Caliphs who ruled in the valley of the Nile for over two hundred years. Moizz became master of Syria also, and both he and his successor, El-Aziz, showed themselves very friendly to the Christians. Indeed the Ismailians, by the very nature of their creed, which taught that absolute truth could only be attained by slow degrees, and lay concealed under many forms of faith, were bound to display a tolerance strange to the ages wherein they flourished.

During all these centuries Palestine had lain subject to the Mohammedan power. It was one of the first of all the Saracen conquests, achieved in the time of Omar, the second Caliph, whilst the new faith was yet in the first flush of its vigour. Yet none the less, there seems to have been little or no cessation in the stream of pilgrims from

4

the West. The site of the Temple was, it is true, covered by a splendid mosque, but the Holy Sepulchre had been preserved to the Christians through the forbearance of Omar, who refused to enter its precincts lest, after his departure, his infatuated followers should claim possession of a spot whereon their Caliph's foot had rested.

Among the first of the pilgrims to the Holy Land during the time of the Mohammedan domination was a certain French bishop, Arculf. Arculf told the story of his travels to Adamman, Columba's successor at Iona, and by this means it came to the knowledge of our own historian, Bede. Arculf spent nine months at Jerusalem; there he saw not a few novelties that had escaped previous travellers; the lamps that, flashing from the glass windows of the Church of the Ascension on Mount Olivet, shone out through the night over the hill slopes to the eastern walls of the city; the linen cloth which had wrapped the Saviour in His tomb; and the lofty column erected on the spot where the newly-discovered Cross restored the dead youth to life. Arculf likewise visited Jericho, and bathed in the milk-white waters of Jordan. Then he journeyed north, and on his way saw the locusts on which John the Baptist had fed, and the three Tabernacles that now crowned the mountain of the Transfiguration. Afterwards he visited in turn Damascus and Tyre, Alexandria and Constantinople, whence he returned by sea to Rome, and so to his native France.

There are few or no traces of the pilgrimage of our English ancestors to the Holy Land during the first centuries after their conversion. For them it would seem that the nearer splendour of Rome had more attraction than the remote squalor of Jerusalem. In one instance, however, the Roman pilgrimage was but the first stage in the journey of an Englishman to Jerusalem. St. Willibald was a kinsman of Boniface, the Apostle of Germany. Educated in the monastery of Bishop's Waltham, in Hampshire, Willibald as he grew to manhood was seized with the desire to visit the Holy Land. Accompanied by his father and

5

brother, Wanebald, he travelled across France and into Italy. There his father died at Lucca, and at Rome Wanebald fell ill of a fever. Willibald then continued his journey with two comrades, and reached Palestine by way of Sicily, Ephesus, and Cyprus. They landed at Tortosa, and so journeyed to Emesa, where they were thrown into prison as spies. At length a Spaniard, whose brother was chamberlain to the Omayyad Caliph, Yazid II., took pity on them. The master of the ship in which they had come from Cyprus was brought before Yazid, who asked whence the strangers came. "From the land of the sunset," was the reply, "beyond which we know not of earth but only waters." "If this be so," burst out the Caliph, "why punish them? They have done us no wrong; set them free." Thus Willibald and his comrades were released, and so went on to Damascus, and thence to Cana, Mount Tabor, and Tiberias. Willibald spent a considerable time in Palestine, and made four separate visits to Jerusalem. In the Holy City he purchased some of the costly balm for which Jericho was famous. This balm was so precious that its export was forbidden; but Willibald hid his treasure in a vessel partly filled with petroleum, so that when he embarked at Tyre the strong-smelling oil threw the custom officers off the scent. From Tyre Willibald went to Constantinople, and thence, after two years, to Rome. He had been absent ten years, and now retired for a like period to Monte Casino, which he only left to join Boniface in Germany. By Boniface he was consecrated Bishop of Eichstadt, and after holding that see forty-four years, died in 786.

Less than half a century later the monk Fidelis related in the presence of Dicuil the Irishman how he had sailed up the Nile and visited the pyramids, standing afar off like mountains, and longed to search for the wheels of Pharaoh's chariots in the Red Sea. Whether or how Fidel is reached Palestine Dicuil does not tell.

At the end of the century the great Emperor Charles, whom legends long after represented as a Crusader before the Crusades, opened up

6

fresh communications between the East and West. When his political ambitions bade fair to involve him in conflict with the Emperor of the East, he found a useful ally in the great Abbaside Caliph Hárún-el Rashid. Hárún received the Frank ambassadors with kindness, and sent their master many presents, including his only elephant, Abulabaz, which Charles had desired to possess. Beyond all else he is said, by a contemporary writer, to have granted the great Emperor the Holy Places at Jerusalem. It is certain that, in the latter years of Charles's reign, a colony of French monks was established on Mount Sion. To this community, Charles himself gave a copy of the Rule of St. Benedict, and a letter is still preserved, wherein the monks complain to Charles that they had been ejected on Christmas Day from the church at Bethlehem.

The almsgiving of the great Emperor, which extended to Carthage and Alexandria, did not neglect Jerusalem. More than fifty years later Bernard of St. Michael's Mount, was lodged in the Holy City, "at the hospital of the most glorious Emperor Charles, wherein are received all Roman-speaking pilgrims, who come to that place out of religion." In Bernard's days parts of Southern Italy were subject to the Caliph of Bagdad, and at Tarentum he found six Saracen ships crowded with Christian captives, intended for the slave markets of the East. Thirty days' sail in one of these ships brought Bernard and his companions to Alexandria. There they found their letter of recommendation from the Saracen governor of Bari useless, and they had to pay thirteen-pence each for fresh passports. These latter only carried them to Babylon of Egypt, where a like payment had to be made before they could proceed in safety to Jerusalem. In the Holy City Bernard saw the noble library, which Charles had founded in the Virgin's Church, hard by the hospital. For a description of the Holy Sepulchre, he refers his readers to Bede; but he saw or heard of a wonder concerning which Bede is silent. "We must note that 'Kyrie Eleeson' is sung until an angel comes and lights the lamps above the Sepulchre. From the flame thus kindled, the patriarch gives a light to the bishops and the rest of the people, so that each may have a light to himself in his own home." This is often but perhaps wrongly said to be the first allusion to the "Miracle of the Sacred Fire," which fraud or superstition from that day to this, with hardly a break, has continued to perpetuate at our Lord's Tomb on every Resurrection Eve. After visiting Bethlehem and other places in the neighbourhood, Bernard went back by way of Rome to his monastery of St. Michael in Brittany (*circa* A.D. 870).

From the above narratives it is plain that during the seventh, eighth, and ninth centuries no insuperable obstacles barred the way of pilgrims from the West. The old path to the Holy City along the great roads of the Empire, through Constantinople and across Asia Minor to Antioch was, it is true, now closed; closed it may be from the very days when the Huns made themselves masters of the Danube valley. Probably, however, the pilgrims made their journeys as before; there was no breach of custom, but merely a change of route. The strange concessions which Mohammed made in favour of the "Peoples of the Book," ensured Christian pilgrims from any violent persecution. Willibald, apart from his imprisonment, was not ill-treated at Emesa, and no doubt in the days of Charles the Great, the pilgrim's condition would be improved. Indeed, Bernard found a market-place attached to the Emperor's hospital at Jerusalem, apparently for the special use of pilgrims.

But Bernard pays a higher tribute to the good order and religious moderation which characterised the Eastern Caliphate in his days. At Beneventum the Christian folk had murdered their own prince, and destroyed all Christian law, till Louis, grandson of Charles the Great, introduced some kind of discipline. Worse than this, the roads leading to Rome were so thronged with banditti, that no one could reach St. Peter's in safety, unless he belonged to a large and well-armed party. This state of misrule Bernard contrasts with the peace prevailing in the Mohammedan lands through which he travelled. "I will tell you how

Christians hold the law of God in Jerusalem, and in Egypt. Now the Christians and the pagans have peace one with another, in such wise that, if on my journey the camel or ass that bore my little property were to die, and I were to leave all my chattels there with none to guard them, while I went to another city, on my return I should find everything untouched. But if in any city, or on any bridge or road they find a man journeying, whether by day or by night, without some charter and seal from the king or ruler of the district, he is straightway thrust into prison till he can give an account of himself whether he be a spy or not."

This happy state of affairs continued with some intervals of disturbance till the early years of the eleventh century.

§ 2. *The Eve of the Crusades.*

At the end of the tenth century the great kingdoms of mediaeval Europe were assuming a definite shape. The sceptre of the Western Franks had passed from the hands of the degenerate descendants of Charles to those of Hugh Capet; from Hugh's accession the modern kingdom of France may be said to date, despite the limitations which the great vassal counts and dukes imposed on their nominal suzerain. In Spain the Christian kingdoms were growing daily at the expense of the decaying Caliphate of Cordova. In other lands the crown of Lombardy already was, and that of Burgundy soon was to be, annexed to the German realm. For the kingdom of the Eastern Franks had now, through the vigour of the three Ottos, entered on its more distinctively German phase. Yet further, the German kings had made good their claim to the imperial title also, and from the days of Otto I., it was the chief ambition of almost every German king to be crowned Emperor of the Romans; that ambition was destined to be fatal to German kingship, but in the tenth century it yet seemed that the union of the imperial and royal offices would bring strength to both. The papacy, that power whose enmity was to be the ruin of German king and Roman emperor alike, was at this period sunk in the lowest depths of insignificance and vice. From those depths first the Ottos and then the Henrys made a brave effort to raise it. But it was not till the days of Gregory VII. that the Popes learned the secret of their own strength, or the German kings the secret of their own weakness.

As the fateful year 1000 drew near, men's hearts began to fail them for fear. To their excited imagination, the Second Coming of the Lord seemed close at hand, and their forebodings were strengthened by the years of misery and famine which brought the tenth century to a close. This dread is marked in every aspect of life, and the very charters bear witness to its reality by their solemn opening "appropinquante termino mundi." The terror passed, but only to revive thirty years later as the thousandth anniversary of the Crucifixion approached.

When at length the cloud was lifted a spirit of piety seems to have seized upon all classes. The Peace of God was already formulated in Southern France; but of all the characteristics of the new era the most remarkable was the zeal for pilgrimages. No class and no sex was free from this passion. The same enthusiasm seized upon the mean and the mighty alike. "At this time," says a contemporary writer, "there began to flow towards the Holy Sepulchre so great a multitude as, ere this, no man could have hoped for. First of all went the meaner folk, then men of middle rank, and, lastly, very many kings and counts, marquises and bishops; aye, and a thing that had never happened before, many women bent their steps in the same direction." Happy circumstances opened up a long-closed pathway to the ardent pilgrims. For ages the land route to Jerusalem had been practically barred, and would-be travellers like Willibald or Bernard forced to sail across the Mediterranean to Ephesus or Alexandria.

But about the year 1000 the old route was opened up once more. The Huns had been converted to Christianity, and so Ralph Glaber a little later could write that pilgrims were forsaking the sea route and passing through Stephen's realm of Hungary because this seemed the safest road.

Of noble eleventh-century pilgrims a few call for special notice. Of all the counts of Anjou none bore a worse name than Fulk the Black. At length, after a life of bloodshed and battle, he was moved by the fear of hell to go as a pilgrim to Jerusalem. He returned somewhat softened, but once more his conscience sent him forth. At Jerusalem, so runs the story, he had to purchase an entrance for himself and his comrades; and to the Holy Sepulchre he was only admitted on promise of an insult to the cross of Christ, a hard necessity from which he escaped by a subterfuge. However he contrived to bite off a bit of the stone, which he brought home as a precious relic for his abbey of Beaulieu. Later on Fulk made a third pilgrimage, and died on his way back at Metz in 1040. In 1035 Robert the Magnificent left his duchy of Normandy and his young son the future conqueror of England, and went on a pilgrimage to Jerusalem, which he accomplished in safety. But on his way home he too fell ill and died at Nicaea, where he was buried in the Virgin's church.

Those princes who could not themselves go on the pilgrimage displayed their religious feelings by their habitual piety. Robert I. of France was more of a priest than a king. Richard II. of Normandy supplied to his namesake, the abbot of Grace Dieu, the funds which enabled him to go to Jerusalem, and between this prince and the monks of Mount Sinai a friendly exchange of gifts was maintained. William III. of Aquitaine (*ob.* 1029) won for himself the titles of "Father of the monks, builder of churches, and lover of the Roman Church." Every year he made a pilgrimage to Rome, or if circumstances prevented this then at least to St. James at Compostella. Duke William himself never

11

went as far as Jerusalem, but his trusty councillor William of Angouleme went there with many nobles and bishops passing through Hungary in the days of King Stephen. He left home on October 1st, reached Jerusalem in the first week of March, and by the third week of June was back in his own city of Angoulême. Other pilgrims of distinction were Earl Godwin's eldest son Swegen, whose uneasy conscience sent him to Jerusalem. Ealdred, Archbishop of York, went to Jerusalem in 1058, in such state as no other before him, and offered at our Lord's tomb a golden chalice of wondrous workmanship and price. Six years later Siegfried of Mayence and three other bishops led a motley crowd of seven thousand pilgrims to the Holy Land. Their gorgeous apparel excited the cupidity of the Saracens, and they fled for refuge to a fort, where they defended themselves during three days, but at last offered all their money in return for their lives, and admitted seventeen of the Arabs within the walls. The Arab leader unrolled his turban, and flinging it round Bishop Herman of Bamberg's neck exclaimed, "Thou and all thou hast are mine." This was more than the bishop could bear, and with a sudden blow he laid his captor prostrate. At this act of episcopal valour the Christians regained their courage, bound the Saracens who had entered the fort, and renewed the contest with those outside. At last the Saracen lord of Ramleh came to the rescue, and under his guidance the pilgrims visited Jerusalem in safety. But only two thousand lived to return to Europe.

We must now return to the course of events in the internal history of the East itself, and more particularly of Syria during the first three-quarters of the eleventh century. At the beginning of that era Jerusalem was subject to the Fatimite Caliph of Cairo. El-Hakim, the then Caliph, had succeeded as a boy of eleven in 996 A.D.; as he grew to manhood he seems to have developed a strain of madness, though it is difficult to trace the exact course of his actions, as told in the narratives of contemporary Christian and later Mohammedan writers. Like the other Fatimites, El-Aziz—El-Hakim's father—had been no bigot; but had a Christian for secretary, and a Jew for governor of Syria. El-Hakim did not share his liberality; first he put restrictions on Jews and Christians, then, according to Ralph Glaber on September 29, 1010, he ordered the destruction of the Holy Sepulchre itself Contemporary rumour ascribed this outrage to the artifices of the Jews, who persuaded El-Hakim, that unless he put a stop to the throngs of pilgrims he would soon find himself without a kingdom. False though the rumour was, it became the pretext for the widespread persecution of the Jews in Christian lands. Eastern historians, however, show that El-Hakim was the impartial oppressor of Jew and Christian alike, imposing absurd but harassing restrictions on the members of either creed. Later still his madness took a more serious form, and he allowed himself to be publicly declared the creator of the universe, until finally he was slain by order of his sister in 1021.

It was less than twenty years after the death of El-Hakim, that there appeared a new power in Western Asia destined to influence fatally the fortunes of Palestine. In 1038 Masud the Ghaznevid was defeated by the Seljukian Turks, who thereupon chose for their sovereign Toghrul Beg, the grandson of Seljuk, a Turkish chief who had adopted Mohammedanism and founded a principality in the neighbourhood of Samarcand. Toghrul rapidly extended his conquests over all Persia, and into regions further west. The effeminate Abbasides had long possessed but the shadow of power, and the reality now passed to Toghrul, who was eventually in 1055 invested with the dignity of Sultan or vicegerent for the Caliph in the orthodox Mohammedan world. Toghrul was succeeded in 1063 by his nephew Alp Arslan, under whose leadership the Seljuks conquered Armenia, and defeated the Emperor Romanus Diogenes at the great battle of Manzikert in August, 1071. As the fruit of this victory Alp Arslan acquired the lordship of Anatolia, and though he himself died within a year, the power of the Seljuks continued to progress throughout the twenty years' reign of his son Malek Shah. After the captivity of Romanus Diogenes, the Byzantine Empire became the prey of imperial pretenders, who appealed without scruple to the aid of Norman and even of Turkish arms. During this period Asia Minor was so ravaged by the Turkish hordes, that almost the whole peninsula was within a few years lost to civilisation. At the beginning of the reign of Alexius Comnenus in 1081, so far had the wave of conquest spread that the Turkish standards on the battlements of Nicaea were almost within sight of the Byzantine metropolis.

But the power of the Turks was not the only danger which threatened the empire of Alexius; the Normans, under Robert Guiscard, were at the same time cutting short his dominions on the shores of the Adriatic. Like his predecessors, Alexius had recourse to foreign arms for assistance and support. Chief amongst the mercenary leaders in the reign of Romanus had been the Norman Ursel, who was perhaps a far-off kinsman of our own English and Scottish house of Balliol. At the capital itself the Emperor maintained the famous Varangian guards, in whose ranks there served side by side with the countrymen of their conquerors, many English, who had fled their native land after the fatal day of Hastings. The employment of these mercenaries familiarised the Eastern emperors with the notion of deliverance through the prowess of Latin Christendom. Nor were the Latins without some feeling of sympathy for the affliction of the Eastern Christians. Pope Sylvester II.'s famous letter of appeal on behalf of Jerusalem, "the immaculate spouse of God," is possibly a forgery of the later eleventh century. It is, however, certain that seventy years afterwards the profound statecraft of Gregory VII. saw clearly the danger with which the advance of the Turks threatened all Christendom. In an urgent letter he called upon all Christian warriors to take up arms on behalf of Constantinople. But this appeal was not fruitful in important results, and even if Gregory

14

entertained any definite plan for uniting the West in defence of the Eastern Empire, the troubles of his later years prevented its execution.

Alexius I., however, seems to have hoped for some such aid. A letter purporting to be an appeal from him to Robert, Count of Flanders, brother-in-law of William the Conqueror, has been preserved in more than one form. As regards its actual wording it may be a forgery, but it certainly dates from the early years of the twelfth century and, as Robert had visited Constantinople whilst on a pilgrimage to Jerusalem, there is nothing improbable in the appeal. There is a pathetic ring in the Emperor's words as preserved in this letter: "From Jerusalem to the Ægaean the Turkish hordes have mastered all: their galleys, sweeping the Black Sea and Mediterranean, threaten the Imperial city itself, which, if fall it must, had better fall into the hands of Latins than of pagans."

The reference to Jerusalem is literally true, for since the victory of Manzikert, the Turks had conquered Palestine from the Egyptians. Tutush, brother of Malek Shah, had established himself at Damascus, and about 1092 granted Jerusalem to Ortok the Turk, from whose son Sokman, the Egyptian vizir El-Afdal captured it in 1096. But before the coming of the first Crusaders the East had obtained a temporary relief through the death, on the 18th of November, 1092, of Malek Shah, the noblest of the Seljukian Sultans, whose empire extended from the borders of China to the southern frontiers of Palestine. This vast inheritance was disputed for by Malek's children, and the consequent dissensions, by weakening the power of the Seljuks, made the progress of the first Crusaders from Nicaea to Jerusalem a comparatively easy task.

Reference has already been made to the definite shape that the kingdoms of Western Europe had begun to assume at the opening of the eleventh century. For four hundred years previously Europe had been devastated by three great plagues, against which, in her divided state,

15

she could make no effectual resistance. Yet it was, to no small extent, to the resistance offered to these three scourges that the feudal Europe of the Middle Ages owed its shape. Out of resistance to the Saracens arose the notion of religious war on a large scale; out of resistance to the Northmen rose the sense of national danger, which was ultimately to produce the sense of national unity; through resistance to the Hungarian invasion, the great rulers of the Saxon house made good their claim to the German kingship and all it brought in its train, the kingship of Italy, and the Empire of Rome.

But amongst all the incidents which these troubles gave rise to, there is none of such interest for our present subject as the settlement of the Normans in Southern Italy. An eleventh-century legend tells how forty Norman warriors, returning from a pilgrimage to Jerusalem, found the Saracens besieging Salerno. They eagerly offered their aid to Guaymar, the Lombard prince of the city; and, when success crowned their efforts, refused to accept any money payment for what they had done out of love for God. Historically speaking, the Normans seem to have established themselves in Italy towards the beginning of the eleventh century. The Greek emperors were then striving to recover the land from the Saracens and Lombards. The confusion was favourable to the new-comers, who further were aided by Melo, an Apulian rebel against the Emperor, and under their leader, Count Ranulf, the Normans fortified themselves near Aversa. Some years later the elder sons of Tancred of Hauteville, of whom the most famous were Robert Guiscard and Roger, came forward as chiefs of the new settlement. Robert obtained for himself the title of Duke of Calabria and Apulia, while Roger conquered Sicily from the Saracens. The conquerors were, however, eager to find a legal title for their authority. This they secured when, in 1053, they defeated and took prisoner Pope Leo IX., who was soon glad to purchase his release by the confirmation to the Normans of all their conquests past or yet to come.

The great and powerful Emperor, Henry III., died in 1056, leaving a little son—Henry IV.—a boy of six, whose infancy was to be the source of prolonged trouble. His subjects found in the weakness of a divided regency a fit opportunity for revolt, and hardly had the young king come to manhood when a yet greater danger appeared without Gregory VII. availed himself of the king's weakness for an unparalleled assertion of the superiority of the ecclesiastical over the civil power; nor did he scruple to support the rebellious nobles of Germany against their lord. Henry set up Guibert of Ravenna as an anti-pope, and when, in 1080, his opponent Rudolf of Saxony had fallen in battle, entered Italy and expelled Gregory from Rome. Henry was forced to retire by the approach of the Normans under Guiscard; but Gregory could not recover his city, and died as an exile at Salerno, leaving the contest to his successors—in full confidence as to its ultimate issue.

Indeed, despite the sadness of his last days, Gregory's labours had ensured the consolidation of the papal power. Popes Zachary and Hadrian I. had, it is true, played a great part in the days of Pepin and Charles. Nicholas I. (858-867) also had compelled Lothair to take back his divorced wife Teutberga, and established his authority in the Gallic Church despite the resistance of Hincmar of Rheims. But the ambition of such pontiffs did no more than furnish a foundation for the lofty and wide-spreading pretensions of a later age. The next century and a half forms the most degraded epoch in the papal annals, and it was Gregory who was the true creator of the mediaeval papacy. Only when Gregory's action had forced on a contest with the greatest temporal power of the age did the popes learn to perceive their own strength. It was that contest which gave to the popes their position as the spiritual heads of Christendom, and enabled them to preach with success the Crusade against the Saracen.

Gregory's ally, Robert Guiscard, had meantime prepared the road in another direction. In 1081 he had carried his arms across the sea and

17

was already master of Durazzo, when the news of Gregory's disasters compelled him to leave the conduct of the war to his son Bohemond. He was preparing for a second expedition against Constantinople itself, when death overtook him. He left his duchy to his son Roger, and his ambitious projects in the East to Bohemond.

Thus neither Robert nor Gregory lived to take part in the Holy War, for which they both had consciously or unconsciously laboured. Tradition, indeed, makes a simple hermit the prime mover in the first crusade, and to his history we must now turn.

II.

PETER THE HERMIT AND URBAN THE POPE.

"Bliss was it in that dawn to be alive,
But to be young was very Heaven."
WORDSWORTH, The Prelude.

THERE is little in the legend of Peter the Hermit which may not very well be true, and the story as it stands is more plausible than if we had to assume that tradition had transferred the credit of the First Crusade from a pope to a simple hermit. However, the full tale of Peter's visit first appears in the "Chanson d'Antioch," and in Albert of Aix, some forty years after the supposed event. In the more sober writings of contemporaries, there is no proof that Peter the Hermit stirred up Urban to his great achievement, nor indeed that he was present at the Council of Clermont at all. In Guibert of Nogent he appears as the apostle of one district of Northern France; and, though a contemporary chronicler seemingly takes him to the borders of Spain, it is more probable that his preaching and influence were confined to a very limited area.

To turn, however, to the picturesque narrative of the traditional tale. About the year 1092 Peter the Hermit, a native of Amiens or its neighbourhood, went on a pilgrimage to Jerusalem. Here his soul was stirred by the horrors that he witnessed, in the pollution of the Holy Places, and the cruel oppression of the native Christians and of the pilgrims from distant lands. The Patriarch, when appealed to by Peter, could only lament his own powerlessness and his dread of worse in store unless their brothers in the west should send them aid. At his entreaty Peter promised to rouse the princes of Europe to a sense of the sad condition of the Holy City. Before all else he bound himself to visit the Pope and enlist his sympathies on the same side.

Then, so runs the story, Peter left the Patriarch's presence, to spend the night in vigil at our Saviour's tomb. Weary with watching, at length he fell asleep. As he slumbered Christ appeared to him in a vision, and bade him hasten home to accomplish his task. But first Peter was to obtain from the Patriarch credentials for his mission: "So shalt thou make known the woes of our people, and rouse the faithful to the cleansing of the Holy Places; for through danger and trial of every kind shall the elect now enter the gates of Paradise."

At dawn Peter hurried to the Patriarch, and, after obtaining letters signed with the Holy Cross, went down to the coast and took ship for Italy. Urban proved a ready listener, and was easily induced to promise his aid. After more than one council in Italy, he crossed the Alps and gathered a great council at Clermont, where his exhortations stirred lords of every degree to bind themselves in a sacred mutual engagement to redeem the Sepulchre of Christ from the hands of the Mohammedan. Such is Albert of Aix's narrative, and despite some taint of legend it is no doubt true in the main.

Urban II., by birth a native of Rheims, and by breeding a monk of Cluny, had been advanced by Gregory VII. to be bishop of Ostia. Finally, in 1088, he became Gregory's second successor in the papacy and the inheritor of his struggle with the Emperor Henry. To this German trouble was added another scandal in France, where King Philip lived in open adultery with Bertrada de Montfort, the wife of Fulk Rechin of Anjou. In Lent, 1095, Urban held synod at Piacenza, where Philip's envoys attended to make peace for their lord; but a more remarkable embassy was that from the Emperor Alexius, pleading for help against the Turks. The church was not sufficient to hold the crowds that assembled, and mass was celebrated in the fields, where doubtless the multitude listened to the impassioned language in which the Eastern envoys appealed to their brethren of the West for aid against their pagan foes.

Urban at once displayed his interest in the proposal, and induced many to pledge themselves to such a holy service. A second council was then convened to meet at Clermont on November 18, 1095. In the Acts of this council it was declared that—"whoever shall have set out for Jerusalem, not for the sake of honour or gain, but to free the Church of God, may reckon his journey as a penance." The Acts contain no further allusion to the Crusade, but more than one contemporary historian has preserved what purports to be the very speech with which Urban kindled the hearts of the French warriors. These versions may be copies of encyclical letters from the Pope to the Churches of the West, or the compositions of the historians themselves. But in either case they represent the aspirations and breathe the spirit which impelled the first Crusaders to relinquish wife and child and home for the sake of Christ.

When the strictly ecclesiastical business of the council was completed, Urban preached to the assembled multitude, exchanging the language of the universal Latin Church for the French speech that had been familiar to him in his youth. To the French warriors the first truly French Pope could speak in his own and their mother tongue. He began by reminding them that they were of God's elect, set apart by a special providence from all other nations for the service of the Church. He painted in vivid colours the sad necessity that had brought him back to Gallic soil; he told how the cries from threatened Constantinople and down-trodden Jerusalem had long been ringing in his ears. It would take two months to traverse the lands, which the "accursed Persian race" had won from the Empire of the East. Within all this region the Christians had been led off to slavery, their homes laid waste, their churches overthrown. Could his hearers look on unmoved, when the heathen had entered into God's heritage? Antioch, once the city of Peter, was given over to Mohammedan superstition. Of Jerusalem it was a shame even to speak, but there were some there who had witnessed with their own eyes the abominations wrought by the Turks

21

in the very Sepulchre of Christ. Yet God had not in His mercy forsaken the land, and still repeated every Easter His miracle of the Sacred Fire.

Then Urban appealed to the proud knights standing by, and asked, how they were busying themselves in these fateful days, shearing their brethren like sheep, and quarrelling one with another. Yea! the knighthood of Christ were plundering Christ's fold. They were changing the deeds of a *knight* for the works of *night*. As they loved their souls let them go forth boldly, and quitting their mutual slaughter take up arms for the household of faith. "Christ Himself will be your leader, as, more valiantly than did the Israelites of old, you fight for your Jerusalem. It will be a goodly thing to die in that city, where Christ died for you. Let not love of any earthly possession detain you. You dwell in a land narrow and unfertile. Your numbers overflow, and hence you devour one another in wars. Let these home discords cease. Start upon the way to the Holy Sepulchre; wrench the land from the accursed race, and subdue it to yourselves. Thus shall you spoil your foes of their wealth and return home victorious, or, purpled with your own blood, receive an everlasting reward. . . . It were better to die in warfare than behold the evils that befall the Holy Places. Frenchmen recall the valour of Charles the Great and his son Louis, who destroyed the kingdoms of the unbelievers, and extended the limits of the Church. Valiant knights, descendants of unconquered sires, remember the vigour of your forefathers, and do not degenerate from your noble stock."

This challenge to Christendom to forget its private feuds in one great effort for God and Christ, this skilful allusion to the glories of the old Frankish race produced an instantaneous result. As the voice of the Pope died away there went up one cry from the assembled host: "Deus Vult! Deus Vult!" ("It is the will of God! It is the will of God!")

Then, raising his eyes to heaven, and stretching out his hand for silence, Urban renewed his speech with words of praise. "This day has been fulfilled in your midst, the saying of our Lord: 'Where two or three are gathered together in My name, there am I in the midst of them.' Had not the Lord been in your midst, you would not thus have all uttered the same cry. Wherefore I tell you it is God who has inspired you with His voice. So let the Lord's motto be your battle cry, and when you go forth to meet the enemy this shall be your watchword: *"Deus Vult! Deus! Vult!"*

"The vast concourse," says one who was himself present at this moving scene, "flung themselves prostrate on the ground while Gregory, a cardinal, made confession of sin on their behalf, and begging pardon for past misdeeds received the apostolic blessing." Then man after man pressed forward to receive his commission in the sacred service from the Pope's own hands. To each class was assigned its special share in the glorious work. But the old and feeble were dissuaded from an expedition wherein their presence was more likely to impede than to assist. No woman was to venture, unless in the company of husband or brother. Priests and clerks were not to start without the leave of their superior, nor any layman without the blessing of his priest. The rich were to aid in proportion to their wealth, and even to hire soldiers for the field. All these elaborate injunctions can hardly have been given out on one day: it is more likely that the historian is here speaking proleptically, for he certainly wrote at a date, when experience had proved the impossibility of conducting an unarmed rabble through so vast a space of unknown land. Of the warnings thus put into Urban's mouth few at the time could have seen the necessity.

The enthusiasm reached its height when the envoys of Count Raymond of Toulouse, declared that their lord, the most powerful prince of Southern France, had pledged himself to go on the Crusade. Not only would he conduct a mighty host from his own domains, but he was willing to give his counsel and wealth to all intending pilgrims. Moreover, it was announced that Adhemar, the bishop of Puy, would go with the lord of Toulouse, and so in their persons the people of God would find a new Aaron and a new Moses.

Urban himself was foremost in the work of distributing the crosses. All who took the cross did so of their own accord; there was no compulsion, but there must be no turning back. The renegade was to be shunned of all; he was to be a perpetual outlaw till waking to the true wisdom he undertook once more what he had abandoned so basely.

At length with the papal blessing all the laymen were dismissed to their homes. To confirm their good intentions, the Church promised her protection to the wives, children, and property of all who undertook the "Way of God."

The bishops and priests on their part went away to preach the new gospel each in his own diocese and parish. As the clergy uttered their exhortations, the laymen raised their voices in one great cry, doubtless, the same that had first made itself heard at the council Clermont: "*Deus Vult!*" Soon men began to seek for signs and wonders. Surely God must have given some foretoken of all that was to happen. Far away from Clermont, Bishop Gilbert of Lisieux, a philosopher, famous for his knowledge of astronomy and medicine, one of the physicians who had watched by the death-bed of the Great Conqueror, was looking out upon the starlit sky. The night was thick with falling stars, and as Gilbert watched, he expounded the significance of this marvellous sight to the servant who shared his vigil: "This prefigures the transmigration of many people from one realm to another. Many shall go forth and never return, until the stars return to their place in the sky, whence you now see them falling." Later, men saw the moon turn red and black at her eclipse, a sure sign of change in high places. Yet wilder stories spread abroad, and it was fabled that the Acts of the Council of Clermont became known within a few hours to the whole world; joy leapt up in the hearts of Christians, but fear and amazement fell upon the heathen dwellers in the East; for such a blast resounded from the heavenly trumpet that throughout all lands the enemies of Christ trembled and were afraid.

Raymond was the only great lord who had pledged himself to the Crusade at Clermont. But the enthusiasm was spread broadcast over Western Europe by the prelates, priests, and laymen as they returned from the great assembly.

A vivid picture of the intense excitement of the next few months has been preserved. In the highways and the cross-roads men would talk of nothing else; layman and priest alike took up the cry and urged their fellows to start for Jerusalem. The intending pilgrim gloried in his resolution, while his laggard friend took shame to himself for his sloth and slackness in the cause of God.

The last harvest had been a failure so complete that many of the rich found themselves in penury, while the poor were driven to feed on herbs and the wild roots of the field. Guibert of Nogent draws a vivid picture of these winter days, when all were sad with the prospect of approaching famine, save only the prudent rich man, who had long been storing up in the years of plenty, so to gather wealth in times of dearth. "It was a time," writes Guibert, "to gladden the heart of the miser as he added the price of his garnered grain to his precious hoard." And now just when the money-lender was rejoicing in hope of unexampled profit, his dream was rudely dissipated; Urban had spoken and Christendom was roused instead of the expected want, the markets were glutted; every one was eager to sell, few cared to buy. Before the council bread was scarce; after the council, though it was full winter, when stock had been killed off for salting, seven sheep were sold for fivepence.

As usual there was the crowd of greedy self-seekers only too eager to snatch a profit out of the enthusiasm of their fellows. "Yet, even these men," says a contemporary, "could not all hold out against the prevailing contagion. To-day a man might be seen chuckling over his friend's madness; to-morrow he might be seen acting the same part and selling all he had for a few trumpery coins."

It was in North-eastern France and on the lower Rhine that the popular frenzy first gathered head.

Eight months were to elapse before any of the great leaders started on the road, for many preparations had first to be made. But the wilder spirits could not brook delay, nor were there wanting men to set the torch to their enthusiasm.

In the long winter months the voice of one preacher was heard in North-eastern France urging men to fulfil the commands of God. This preacher was Peter the Hermit, and it is with the winter of 1095-6 that his historical career commences. From town to town he passed along walled round by a throng of eager devotees. "Never," says Guibert, "within our memory was any man so honoured." Of small stature, dark complexion, thin features, and if we may trust the evidence of romance, with a long white beard, he rode upon a mule, whence his followers plucked the very hairs as precious relics.

The exhortations of Peter and his fellows produced a marvellous effect. Guibert saw villages, towns, and cities emptied of their inhabitants as the preacher went along. This of course is the language of exaggeration, though it may possibly bear some relation to the truth, while Peter was passing through a district. But the real effect of his exhortations is to be seen in the expeditions that left France and Lorraine in the early spring of 1096.

The popular excitement, however, sank to lower depths than these. Madness, the near kinsman of enthusiasm and credulity, is often the slave of persecution. Whilst, on the one hand, crowds were starting for Jerusalem under the guidance of a mad woman, a goose, or a goat whom their frenzied imagination took to be the receptacles of the spirit of God, others made the movement an excuse for wanton rapine and murder. In Lorraine it was declared that a man's first service to God should be the destruction of the accursed race which had crucified the Lord. At Cologne the synagogues were destroyed, the Jews slaughtered, and their houses sacked. At Mayence the Jewish community vainly purchased the archbishop's protection and sought safety in his house. Even here they were not secure; at sunrise a certain Count Emicho led the rabble against them; the doors were broken open, and men, women, and children massacred without mercy, till in their despair the victims sought death at each other's hands.

The preaching of Peter the Hermit brought some fifteen thousand French pilgrims to Cologne about Easter 1096. Peter wished to stay and exhort the Germans also, but the French would not wait, and set out under the guidance of Walter de Poissi and his nephew Walter the Penniless. They journeyed through Hungary, where they were kindly treated by King Caloman, to Semlin on the Danube. Here the main body passed over to the Bulgarian city of Belgrade, but a small party remaining behind to purchase arms were plundered by the people of Semlin. Walter begged the Bulgarian chief to supply him with provisions, and on a refusal suffered his followers to pillage as they would. The Bulgarians then mustered in such force that Walter's host was scattered, and many of his followers killed. The stragglers, however, forced their way through the woods in eight days to Nisch, and there obtaining guides and food, made their way on to Constantinople, where they remained till Peter the Hermit and his contingent arrived.

Peter, with the German host which his eloquence gathered round him at Cologne, seems to have followed the same route as Walter the Penniless. Through Germany, Bavaria, and the modern Austria they passed in peace, some on foot, some floating down the Danube and other rivers in boats. At Oedenberg they reached the Hungarian frontier, and there awaited Caloman's permission to traverse his dominions. Thence they journeyed in peace and good order to Semlin. From the walls of that city they saw the arms of Walter's comrades hung as in derision.

27

This sight moved them to take vengeance, the horns blew to arms, the standards were advanced, a dense rain of arrows was poured in upon the city, and the Hungarians were driven from the walls. The citizens for the most part sought refuge in a lofty fortress, while the pilgrims occupied the town, in which they found an abundant supply of food and horses. After a stay of five days the Crusaders crossed over to Belgrade, the inhabitants of which town had fled in terror at the news of Peter's success. At Nisch the Bulgarian prince Nichita granted them a market, but, when he heard that some unruly Germans had fired seven mills on the river, at once bade his subjects make reprisals. Peter, who had already started with the main host, returned at the news, and a general conflict soon ensued. The Crusaders were scattered, their baggage lost, and Peter's own treasure chest with all its wealth fell into the hands of the Bulgarian prince. A few of the fugitives gathered under Peter's leadership on a neighbouring height, where one by one the stragglers joined them till seven thousand had re-assembled. Then they renewed their march, and at last, on August 30, 1096, they reached Constantinople. There Peter had an interview with Alexius, who advised him to wait till the great Crusading armies should arrive. But certain unruly Lombards set fire to some buildings near the city, and stripping the lead from the churches sold it to the Greeks. Annoyed at such disorder Alexius urged that they should pass over to Asia. Peter and Walter were accordingly carried across to Nicomedia, whence they proceeded to Civitot, a city on the coast. Here the Emperor's ships supplied them with abundance of food, and they stayed in all for two months.

Some of the Germans, however, led by one Reinald, left their fellows and made an expedition towards Nicaea. Near that city they seized a deserted fortress, called Exerogorgo, wherein they were presently besieged by Kilij Arslan, the Sultan of Rum. The sufferings of the Christians were intense, for there was no drinking-water; in their

28

anguish men drank the blood of their horses, some sought to procure a few drops of water by letting down their girdles into the foul fishponds, others dug pits in the earth, and endeavoured to obtain relief by covering their limbs with the moist soil. After eight days Kilij Arslan captured Exerogorgo, and moved on against Civitot. Peter was away at Constantinople seeking aid from the Emperor, and Walter was unable to control his motley host. The Sultan surprised the Christians as they lay asleep in their camp outside the walls of the town. Walter was slain, and numbers of his followers ruthlessly massacred, three thousand of them, however, found shelter in a roofless fort close by. The Turks, unable to effect an entrance, kindled a fire against the walls, but the flames, so runs the contemporary story, were driven back by the wind into the faces of the assailants. In this fort the fugitives maintained themselves, until Peter persuaded Alexius to send a body of troops to the rescue, whereupon the Turks withdrew with their spoil and their captives.

A second host of Germans started for Constantinople under the leadership of a priest named Gotschalk. They were well received by Caloman, whose kindness they requited in the usual way, by plunder and drunken disorder. Their conduct so angered the king that he ordered the pilgrims to be disarmed, and then the enraged Hungarians massacred the defenceless host, till, as it is asserted, the whole plain was covered with corpses and blood. Folkmar, a priest, led a mixed host through Bohemia with similar results. A fifth army under Count Emicho included some warriors of renown, but met with no happier fate. They besieged Meseberg, on the Leitha, and Caloman had prepared for a flight into Russia, when a sudden panic fell upon the invaders. The Hungarians took fresh courage and the blood of their foes soon reddened the rivers. A few of the leaders, including Count Emicho, escaped into Italy or to their own homes, but the mass of the pilgrims were slain or drowned: "Thus is the hand of the Lord believed to have been against these pilgrims, who had sinned in His sight, and slain the Jews, rather for greed of money than for justice of God."

III.

THE FIRST CRUSADE—THE MUSTER AND THE MARCH TO ANTIOCH.

Ἕσπερε νῦν μοι Μοῦσαι Ὀλύμπια δώματ'δώματ'ἔχουσαι,

ὅίτινες ἡγεμόνες Δαναῶν καί κοίρανοι ἦσαν.

Iliad II.

"Tell me, now, ye Muses that dwell in the halls of Olympus,
Who were the chiefs of the Greeks? what were their leaders' names?"

No sovereign prince of Western Europe took part in the first Crusade, nor did any prince of the second rank start before the summer of 1096. The intervening time was spent in negotiations to secure a free passage and plentiful provisions on the way to Constantinople. For there seems to have been no real thought of proceeding to Jerusalem by sea; men shunned the horrors of a Mediterranean voyage, and the conversion of the Huns had reopened the earlier track, by which the Bordeaux Pilgrim had journeyed to the Holy City. The numbers of the first Crusade, though perhaps grossly exaggerated, were too great to admit of a united progress through Central Europe. The main hosts of the Crusaders accordingly set out in five distinct bodies, under different leaders and by different routes. The first started in August, 1096, the last did not join its fellows till they were camped round Nicaea in the following summer.

First marched the Teutonic host, under Godfrey of Lorraine, who was now some thirty-five years old. His father Eustace II. of Boulogne had accompanied William on his expedition to England, and even before then had played a prominent, if not an honourable, part in English politics. Through his mother Ida he was, perhaps, descended from

31

Charles the Great; and claimed the duchy of Lorraine, which was confirmed to him while still a youth by the Emperor Henry IV. His early manhood was spent in war and politics; he fought for Henry against Rudolf and Gregory, and when ill of a fever at Rome vowed to make a pilgrimage to the Holy City. Historically speaking before the first Crusade Godfrey figures as a somewhat turbulent noble of no particular piety. His grandfather, Godfrey the Bearded, Duke of Lorraine, had been one of the sturdiest of the rebels against Henry III.; even in an age of violence men stood aghast at the daring of the man who had burnt the great church of Verdun to the ground. His grandson too, for all his later piety, could war upon the Bishop of Verdun in defence of what he deemed his rights. But in the next century men loved to think of Godfrey of Bouillon as marked out from his very infancy for his high career.

When Godfrey reached Oedenberg, on the borders of Hungary, he found his further advance stopped; for Caloman, angry at the injury already done to his kingdom, would not grant a passage till Godfrey had paid him a visit of reconciliation. Finally Godfrey's brother Baldwin, with his wife and children, were given as hostages, and a peaceful compact made with the King. "So day after day in silence and peace, with equal measure and just sale, did the duke and his people pass through the realm of Hungary."

Shortly after they had crossed the Save, the Greek Emperor's envoys met the duke, promising to supply his men with provisions if they would refrain from plunder. Nor did Alexius fail to keep his promise, for there was no lack of corn, wine, and oil for the leaders, while the common folk had full liberty to buy and sell. But at Philippopolis news came how Hugh of Vermandois was a captive in Constantinople. At first the duke had no thought of vengeance; but when the envoys, whom he sent to petition for the count's release, returned with a blank refusal, Godfrey gave orders to lay waste the surrounding country. A second and more friendly message from Alexius induced him to stay his hand and advance towards Constantinople. He pitched his tents outside the city, where he was welcomed by Hugh and his fellow captives; but by the advice of the French residents in Constantinople he refused the Emperor's invitation to enter the city, and rejected all presents, lest they should be poisoned. Alexius, in return, forbade his people to supply the Crusaders with food; nor was it till Baldwin, brother of Godfrey, took to plundering that the prohibition was withdrawn.

In the latter part of the eleventh century the coast of the Bosphorus beyond the Golden Horn to the Black Sea was bordered for some thirty miles with the palaces of the Byzantine nobles. Alexius, eager to have the Crusading host removed as far as possible from Constantinople itself, persuaded Godfrey to take up his winter quarters in this favourable district. To this Godfrey assented, but still refused the Emperor's solicitations for a personal visit. When Alexius had resort to actual violence, the Crusaders returned to their old position before Constantinople, and the Emperor was soon compelled to come to terms. A peace was patched up, and after the Emperor's son John had been given as a hostage, Godfrey visited Alexius in his palace. A little later, perhaps on the 21st of January, 1097, by the Emperor's request, Godfrey led his troops across to Asia.

Bohemond and his uncle, Count Roger of Sicily, so runs the contemporary story, were laying siege to Amalfi, when news came that innumerable Frankish warriors had started on the way to Jerusalem. Bohemond inquired of the messengers, "What are their weapons, what their badge, and what their war-cry?" "Our weapons," was the enthusiastic reply, "are those best suited to war; our badge the cross of Christ upon our shoulders; our war-cry *Deus Vult! Deus Vult!* " The piety or cupidity of the warlike Norman was aroused at this answer. He tore from his shoulders his costly cloak, and with his own hands made of it crosses for all who would follow him in the new enterprise. His example proved contagious, and nearly all the knights offered their services to Bohemond, so that Count Roger returned to Sicily almost alone. With Bohemond went his cousin Tancred, destined in later days to be lord of Antioch, and to find immortal honour in the great poem of Tasso.

Bohemond crossed to Durazzo about the end of October, and two months later had reached Castoria, where he spent the Christmas, and then proceeded on his way to Constantinople. He seems to have been well-supplied with provisions on the route, and kept good order on the march. At Rusa, on the 1st of April, he received an invitation to Constantinople, and leaving his troops under the care of Tancred, hurried forward with only a few attendants. Alexius knew Bohemond's measure, and by the promise of a princely lordship in the confines of Antioch prevailed on him to take an oath of fidelity.

The third host marched under Raymond of St. Gilles, and comprised all the men of the Langue d'Oc. Those of the Langue d'Oil had gone before, and under the guidance of Hugh, Count of Vermandois, had been the first of all the Crusaders to take the field. "Hugh," writes a contemporary, "was first to cross the sea to Durazzo, where the citizens took him prisoner, and sent him to the Emperor at Constantinople." How he was released from his captivity we have already seen.

Raymond had been merely Count of St. Gilles, but through the death of his elder brother, while on a pilgrimage to Jerusalem, had become in 1093 Duke of Narbonne, Count of Toulouse and Marquis of Provence. He was older than the other Crusading chiefs, being now past fifty years of age. In his company was the Papal legate Bishop Adhemar of Puy, and under his banners went many noble knights of Southern France. "It was already winter when Raymond's men were toiling over the barren mountains of Dalmatia, where for three weeks we saw neither bird nor beast. For almost forty days did we struggle on through mists so thick that we could actually feel them, and brush them aside

34

with a motion of the hand." So writes a contemporary, who had shared in all the horrors of this painful march. Raymond, with that careful consideration for the weak which seems to have marked his character, did his best to hold at bay the rude natives, who dogged his rear athirst for the plunder of the sick and old; as a deterrent he cut off the noses, hands, and feet of his captives, blinded them, and in this plight sent them back to their comrades. At Scutari Bodin, the King of the Slavs, promised them an open market. "But this was fancy only; for we repented of the peace we had sought for, when the Slavs once more began to rob and slay in their wonted manner." At last they reached Durazzo, "where," writes Raymond's biographer, "we believed that we were in our own country; for we believed that Alexius and his followers were our brothers and allies." The Imperial friendship proved, however, but a broken reed; "right and left did the Emperor's Turks and Comans, his Pincenati and Bulgarians, lie in wait for us, and this though in his letters he spoke to us of peace and brotherhood." However, despite such experiences and the consequent warfare, this host at last made its way to Rodosto, whence Raymond, at Alexius's bidding, hurried on to Constantinople. Raymond, unlike Bohemond, Godfrey, and Robert of Flanders, would take no oath to the Emperor. "Be it far from me," were the words of his proud humility, "that I should take any lord for this way save Christ only, for whose sake I have come hither. If thou art willing to take the cross also, and accompany us to Jerusalem, I and my men and all that I have will be at thy disposal."

While at Constantinople Raymond received news that during his absence the Emperor's troops had attacked his men. In his wrath it is said that he invited the other Latin chiefs to join him in the sack of Constantinople. Bohemond, however, was staunch to the Emperor, and even gave himself as a hostage that Alexius would recompense the count if it should prove true that the Imperial troops had done him injury. Godfrey, too, refused to bear arms against a brother Christian, and so Raymond had to endure his wrong as best he might. Nothing could induce him to become the Emperor's liegeman, but at last he swore to do Alexius no harm to his life or honour, and not to suffer any such wrong to be done by another. "But when he was called on to do homage," says Raymond of Agiles, "he made answer that he would not, even at the peril of his life. For which reason the Emperor gave him few gifts." Yet Raymond's oath proved of better worth than that of those who had sworn more. Anna Comnena perhaps writes by the light of later events, but her words are very precise, and apparently refer to this time: "One of the Crusaders, the Count of St. Gilles, Alexius loved in a special way, because of his wisdom, sincerity, and purity of life; and also because he knew that he preferred honour and truth above all things."

The last of the great hosts did not start till September or October, 1096. At its head was the Conqueror's son, Robert of Normandy, and with him went his sister's husband, Stephen, Count of Blois and Chartres; his cousin, Robert of Flanders; his uncle Odo, the turbulent Bishop of Bayeux, and a goodly host of warriors from the lands of Northwest France. They passed through Italy, at Lucca received a blessing from Pope Urban, and so by way of Rome came to Bari.

Winter was come when Robert of Normandy reached this town. The prospect of the stormy Adriatic determined him to spend the winter in Calabria; where as head of the Norman race he might look for lavish hospitality from the children of those Normans who had conquered Sicily and South Italy. But Robert of Flanders bade defiance to the winter storms, crossed the Adriatic, and appears to have reached Constantinople a little before Raymond. The great majority of those who remained behind suffered terribly; Robert enjoyed his ease in Italy or Sicily, but his humbler followers found it hard to support themselves in so unexpected a delay. "Many," says Fulcher, "of the commoner sort became disconsolate, and through fear of want sold their bows. Then, taking up their pilgrims' staves once more, they returned meanly to their homes. So they became vile before God and man, and the thing was turned to their shame." Of the prelates, Odo died at Palermo and was buried there.

By the end of March, 1097, Duke Robert and Count Stephen were ready at Brindisi, and fixed their departure for Easter Day, the 5th of April. The sinking of a large vessel laden with four hundred pilgrims seemed to augur ill for the success of the expedition. But when more than one of the bodies thrown upon the beach was found to be marked with a mysterious cross, the incident was turned to a happy omen. "However," says Fulcher, "some being of a less robust faith were greatly perturbed with fear, and went back home, saying they would no more venture themselves on the treacherous waters. The rest of us placing our trust in Almighty God, launched forth on to the deep amid the blare of many trumpets, and the breath of a gentle breeze."

Four days later they disembarked near Durazzo, and thence made their way across Thessaly to Salonica and Constantinople. Fulcher relates that "the Emperor would not let us enter the city lest we should do it harm;" but the new-comers were not indiscriminately excluded, and it was doubtless the tales of his luckier comrades that filled Fulcher with admiration: "Oh! how great a city it is; how noble and comely! What wondrously wrought monasteries and palaces are therein! What marvels everywhere in street and square! Tedious would it be to recite its wealth in all precious things, in gold and silver, in divers shaped cloaks, and saintly relics. For thither do ships bring at all times all things that man requires."

So one by one the varied hosts made their way to Constantinople. The successive arrivals of such numerous bodies of men, extending over nearly the whole of a year, may well have excited a feeling of dismay in the Eastern Emperor and his subjects. Almost all contemporary writers go further, and accuse Alexius of an actual breach of faith; nor were their charges entirely devoid of foundation. Yet so far as the providing of actual supplies was concerned Alexius seems to have kept his word in the main. We read how Bohemond's army marched "through overmuch plenty from villa to villa, from town to town, and from fortress to fortress;" at Philippopolis Duke Godfrey found an abundance of things necessary for eight days; and at Salonica Duke Robert and his comrades pitched their tents before a city abounding in all good store.

But the hordes of Peter the Hermit and Walter the Penniless can have known little of discipline, and even in the more regularly constituted hosts it was impossible that the chiefs should maintain strict authority. It was perhaps still more impossible for Alexius to have arranged the commissariat without a flaw, and possibly his authority did not count for much in cities remote from the capital. "At Castoria," says Bohemond's chronicler, "the inhabitants would not assent to a market, for they feared us greatly, deeming us no pilgrims, but a people desirous to waste their land, and slay them." Afterwards this same host was eager to attack a certain fortress, for no other reason than that it was full of all manner of good store. Bohemond refused, as much, we read, from love of justice as from loyalty to the Emperor. But even Tancred did not take so strict a view of what good faith meant.

Mutual distrust soon breeds open discontent, which is the speedy harbinger of open war. Nor was Alexius without justifiable suspicions of more than one Crusading chief; he can never have forgotten how within the last few years Bohemond and his father had waged war on the Empire. Byzantine duplicity was only too ready to suspect Norman guile; might not Bohemond, after all, be using the Crusade as a cloak for his own designs against the Imperial city? Such at least was the suspicion of the Byzantines a few years later, when they could interpret the events of the eleventh century by those of the early twelfth. "Some of the Crusaders," writes Anna Comnena, "were guileless men and women marching in all simplicity to worship at the tomb of Christ; but there were others of a more wicked kind—to wit, Bohemond and the like: such men had but one object—to get possession of the Imperial city." Such plans as these, if they ever existed, Alexius was bound to resist to the utmost, but his hopes went much further. He remembered that the Empire, which he ruled, had once stretched to Antioch and the Euphrates, nay, even to Jerusalem itself Might he not turn the Crusade to his own advantage, by its aid beat back the invading Turks, and recover for the Empire all that Frankish valour could wrest from Saracen hands? This was what Alexius had in view, and it was possibly by his insistence on this, that he sowed the first seeds of permanent distrust between himself and his so-called allies.

In all his actions Alexius had but one aim: he was resolved to give the Crusading hosts no facilities for their journey through Asia Minor until the leaders, one and all, had taken an oath of fealty to him. They must promise too that whatever conquests they might make elsewhere on their own account, everything that had once belonged to the Empire should revert to it again. Doubtless he would grant them out in fiefs to the Frankish warriors, but he must at least be over-lord. Godfrey was first to take this oath, but it was uncertain whether the other leaders would consent to follow his example; the bargain seemed dishonourable, and they suspected some hidden trap. But at length the Emperor won his way. We have seen how Bohemond was bribed by the promise of a vast principality, and how Raymond, at first inexorable, eventually yielded so far as to take the oath in a modified form. In the end Tancred was the only Crusader of the first rank who escaped the oath, and that only for the time. "He came," says his biographer, "to get himself a kingdom, should he find himself a yoke?" So Tancred would not approach Constantinople, but crossed the Hellespont in disguise, whilst Bohemond had to excuse his conduct as best he might. After the fall of Nicaea, Bohemond brought his kinsman back to Constantinople, and Tancred then took the oath, but refused all the Emperor's smaller gifts, hoping for a splendid tent, "turreted like a city, and a load for twenty camels." This Alexius refused to give him, making a few wholesome remarks on his covetousness, and Tancred accordingly returned in dudgeon to Nicaea.

The first exploit of the Crusaders after they were all mustered in Asia Minor was the siege of Nicaea, which city they reached on May 6th. The first attack on the city failed, and then came news that Kilij Arslan was approaching with an army of relief On Saturday morning, May 16th, his troops were pressing down upon the city, when fortunately Raymond of St. Gilles and Adhemar of Puy arrived to join their comrades. It was a glorious day for the Crusading armies, and their first battle with the enemy resulted in a complete victory. "The Turks rushed to war, exultingly dragging with them the ropes, wherewith to bind us captive. But as many as descended from the hills remained in our hands; and our men cutting off their heads flung them into the city, a thing that wrought great terror amongst the Turks inside."

After this victory the siege was renewed with fresh vigour, and when, early in June, Robert of Normandy and Stephen of Blois, arrived the whole city was at length encompassed, except on one side, where a lake afforded means to go out and come in. It was plain that Nicaea would never be taken till this entry was closed. Envoys were sent to seek aid from Alexius, and through his assistance vessels were brought overland from the sea, and launched upon the lake. It seemed now that the city must fall; and all were looking forward with eagerness to the plunder, which was to repay them for their labour. But the Turks preferred to fall into the hands of Alexius, and just when the Christians were hoping to capture the city the Imperial banners were seen floating from the walls. Still though Alexius had thus forestalled his Frankish allies he was lavish of his gifts among them. "To our leaders," says Fulcher, "he gave gold and silver, and raiment; and among the foot-soldiers he distributed brass coins that they call Tartarons." No generosity, however, could quite satisfy the greed of the disappointed soldiery. What, they angrily demanded, had become of the gold and horses of the conquered? Where was the hospital that Alexius had promised to build for the poorer Franks? So also says Raymond of Agiles—"Alexius paid the army in such wise that, so long as ever he lives, the people will curse him, and declare him a traitor."

The siege of Nicaea thus ended, the Crusaders started on their way to Antioch on June 29th. Whether by accident or design they divided into two parts; with one went Raymond, Adhemar, Godfrey, and Robert of Flanders; with the other Bohemond, Tancred, Hugh the Great, and Robert of Normandy. At evening on the following day Bohemond found himself beside a little stream. The heights around were thronged with thousands of Turks, and a hasty order was issued to pitch tents. The night passed in anxious expectation, till in the early morning of July 1st, the horn gave the signal to resume the march. An hour or two later the scouts of the two armies came to close quarters; Bohemond ordered a halt, the baggage was stacked, and a message sent to call up the other host of the Crusaders. Then the knights dismounted, and Bohemond bade them be of good cheer, and keep the foe at bay, while the footmen guarded the tents.

It was a day of heroic deeds; "the very women were a stay to us," writes Bohemond's eulogiser, "for they carried water for our warriors to drink, and ever did they strengthen the fighters." At last, hemmed in by thousands of Turks, Bohemond himself was losing heart, and his men giving way, when Robert—mindful, perhaps, how his father turned the day at Hastings—bared his head to view, and urged his comrades to stand firm. The battle was resumed with vigour, and as the other Christian leaders came up, the Turks were driven back, and fled leaving their treasures behind them. Victory had been snatched out of the very jaws of defeat, and well might the Christian warrior write: "Had not the

Lord been with us in this battle, and sent us speedily another army, none of our men would have escaped."

Such was the fight at Dorylaeum, the first pitched battle between the Crusader and the Turk. Fable or superstitious enthusiasm soon cast a halo round the fight. "A wondrous miracle is reported to have taken place," writes Raymond of Agiles, "but we did not behold it; for it is said that two knights of wonderful appearance, and clad in shining armour, went before our army and pressed the enemy in such wise as to leave them no chance of fighting." A few years later men told one another with awe how St. George, St. Demetrius, and St. Theodore, came forth from the mountains on white horses, bearing white banners in their hands, and dealt deadly blows against the infidels.

From Dorylaeum the Crusaders plodded on over the rugged table-lands of Asia Minor, through a waterless and uninhabited region, "whence we scarcely issued with our lives." Survivors related to Albert of Aix, the story of their terrible march across the mountains. Men, women, and horses, perished of thirst in the heat of the hot July sun. Pregnant women dropped down by the way to give birth to their hapless offspring before their time; men marched along with open mouths, hoping thus to cool their parched throats by even the slightest breath of air. The hawks and dogs, which accompanied the chiefs to the war, died in the hands of their attendants. At length a stream was reached; there was a general rush to gain the bank; men and cattle unable to restrain their desire drank themselves to death.

Over the rough mountains the Crusaders passed into the pleasant valleys near Iconium, where the friendly inhabitants taught them how to carry water in the skins of the country. At Heraclea now Erkli, Tancred and Baldwin left the main army, and, by the famous "gates of Judas," passed into the Cilician plains. This they did in order to conquer on their own account, nor were they the only chiefs who at this time left the army for such a purpose. Raymond, Bohemond, Godfrey, and the two Roberts, for some unexplained reason, turned north towards Armenia; but at length the main host of the Crusaders, under their command, pitched its tents before the walls of Antioch on Wednesday, October 21, 1097.

IV.

THE FIRST CRUSADE—THE FIRST FRUITS OF CONQUEST: EDESSA AND ANTIOCH.

"The true old times
When every morning brought a noble chance,
And every chance brought out a noble knight."

TENNYSON.

§ 1. *The Conquest of Edessa.*

WHEN Tancred entered Cilicia, and pitched his tents outside the walls of Tarsus, that city, like many other towns of Asia Minor and Syria, though mainly inhabited by Christians, was held by a garrison of Turks. The citizens were eager to obtain Bohemond's protection, and in his absence Tancred was only too ready to become their lord. The Turks were on the point of surrendering, when Baldwin's host appeared on the neighbouring mountains. The Turks, mistaking this force for allies of their own, refused to keep their engagement. The new-comers then joined the Normans in prosecuting the siege, but Baldwin, jealous of Tancred's success, presently induced the citizens to transfer their allegiance to him. Tancred was too weak to resent such injustice, and withdrew to Adana, where Welf the Burgundian gave him a kindly welcome.

A little later the Turks surrendered, and Baldwin, leaving a garrison at Tarsus, started eastwards in his turn once more. Tancred who was now at Messis, beheld with indignation his rival come again to pitch his tents outside the city. Was he always to yield his conquests to the greed of Baldwin? So at their chief's bidding the Norman knights attacked the new-comers, but only to meet with a repulse. Next morning each army began to regret such a violation of their pilgrim's vows, and peace was restored. Baldwin then went off to seek fresh adventures in Armenia, whilst Tancred proceeded by the coast towards Antioch.

Among the cities of Armenia proper, none was more famous than Edessa, celebrated in Christian legend for its king Abgar, and for the tombs of the apostles Thomas and Thaddeus. At this time it was ruled by an Armenian prince called Thoros, who, though nominally subject to Alexius, had much difficulty in maintaining himself against the conquering Turks. Almost all the Armenian lands had fallen into the possession of the infidels, and it was only here and there that a remnant of that powerful nation still maintained themselves in their ancient home. Others had already commenced that obscure and mysterious migration, which, before the close of the next century, was destined to establish a new kingdom of Armenia on the shores of the Mediterranean.

Such a state of confusion offered not merely great facilities, but some justification, to Frankish conquests. Nor were the Franks long before they availed themselves to the full of their opportunities. Baldwin was led by the advice of Pakrad, an Armenian, who had joined the Crusaders at Nicaea, to seek a field of conquest in Armenia. His fame reached Thoros at Edessa, and a message soon came to beg his assistance against the Turks beyond the Euphrates. Baldwin accepted the invitation with alacrity; with eighty knights he crossed the great river, and was received within the walls of Edessa to the sound of trumpets. Thoros welcomed him kindly, but presently, growing jealous of Baldwin's popularity, refused to pay the promised wage. The twelve senators, who seem to have formed an aristocratic curia in Edessa, then begged their governor to fulfil his bargain, and so retain this illustrious warrior for service against the Turks. Thoros yielded to their persuasion and adopted Baldwin as his son; after the manner of their race and country, he and his wife in turn took the count beneath their shirts, and pressed him to their naked breasts. This curious ceremony completed,

Baldwin started on an unsuccessful expedition against Balduc, the Turkish ruler of Samosata. On his return he found the people of Edessa eager to have him for their prince. Treachery was at work, and on the Sunday and Monday before Easter, 1098, Thoros and his adherents were attacked, and the prince imprisoned in his own citadel. Baldwin seems to have been a party to the tumult; but at least he may be credited with a sincere desire to save his benefactor's life. He counselled Thoros to abandon all his treasures, and swore to secure him a safe retreat to Melitene. But Baldwin's promises were in excess, either of his powers or his intentions. Once more the people rose up against their ancient prince. Trembling for his life, Thoros attempted to let himself down from a window by a rope. His attempt was detected and in a moment his corpse, riddled with arrows, was flung out into the square.

Baldwin was now lord of Edessa, but it was by a precarious tenure; for the Turks were close at hand, and his own troops few in number, whilst he had already learnt how little trust could be reposed in Armenian fidelity or valour. Yet for all this he held himself as proudly as if he had an army of Franks at his back. Balduc sent offers of tribute, and in return for a talent of gold Samosata was left in Turkish hands. "But from that day," writes Albert of Aix, "Balduc became Baldwin's subject, a dweller in his house, and one among his friendly Gauls."

Baldwin's next conquest was Saruj, a town a few miles south of Edessa, which was surrendered by its Armenian ruler and entrusted to Fulcher of Chartres. He then sought to make his rule more pleasing to his subjects by taking an Armenian wife; for his English wife, Godwera, who accompanied him on the Crusade, had died a few months previously at Marash. Baldwin now married a niece of the Armenian prince Constantine the Rupenian, by which alliance he strengthened himself both among his new subjects and against his Turkish foes. Still his position was very insecure, and he could render no help to the great army of the Crusaders, and indeed was himself besieged for forty days by Corbogha, when the Mussulman prince was on his way to Antioch. He did, however, contrive to send large store of provisions to his brother Godfrey, whilst the Armenian mountains furnished many of the Crusaders with a refreshing scene of adventure during the weary months of the siege of Antioch. Such hospitality was, however, a great strain on Baldwin's resources, and the consequent oppression excited a rebellion in Edessa. Although this movement failed, the renewed extortion for which it furnished a pretext alienated many of Baldwin's best friends, and so the position of the Franks in Edessa was, from the first, one of danger and difficulty.

§ 2. *The Siege of Antioch.*

Antioch on the Orontes was by far the most famous of the sixteen cities founded by Seleucus Nicator in honour of his father. Within four centuries of its creation it was the third city of the Roman world, the central point of all the Hellenic east. Later it became the seat of one of the four great patriarchates, and the birth-place of the golden-mouthed preacher of the Eastern Church. Justinian surrounded it with a girdle of enormous walls, which after the earthquakes and sieges of thirteen centuries, still bid defiance to the wasting power of time. It was taken by the Saracens in 635 A.D., recovered under Nicephorus Phocas in 968, and again lost to the Seljuk Soliman in 1084.

At the present day Antioch, lost in its gardens and orchards, occupies but a small portion of its ancient extent. Now, as of old, the city lies on the south bank of the Orontes, beyond which there stretches northwards to the foot of Mount Amanus a wide and level plain; on the south the precipitous hills ploughed with deep ravines run down from the mountains of Ansarieh to within half a mile of the river. The modern Antioch is huddled together in one corner of the narrow space that lies between these hills and the Orontes; but in the eleventh

47

century the southern walls of the city were built along a ridge of the hills which rise in that quarter to a height of several hundred feet above the valley, and are cleft by a deep and narrow ravine, down which a mountain torrent ran northwards through the city to the Orontes. On the more westerly half of the range rose the citadel; the other portion also was secured by a castle. The whole circuit of the fortifications may have enclosed an area of some four square miles. Within its course were included four gates: on the west, the Gate of St. George; near the north-west angle, a gate which led to a stone bridge over the Orontes; on the north-east, the Gate of St. Paul; and on the south, at the deep ravine, the Iron Gate. Besides these there were numerous smaller gates at comparatively short distances apart.

Such was the city that the Crusaders sat down to besiege in October, 1097. Orders had been issued that all the predatory bands were to gather together, but even in their fullest strength the Crusaders were all too few for the task before them. Yet a contemporary, who should have had special opportunities for knowledge, asserts that the host consisted of three hundred thousand armed men; whilst within the walls there were but two thousand choice horsemen, five thousand mercenaries, and some ten thousand footmen. Finding it impossible to invest efficiently the whole circuit, the Crusaders directed their first efforts to the north-eastern portion of the walls. Bohemond pitched his tent furthest south, on a rock opposite the castle; a stone's throw off and nearer the city wall was Tancred. Then came Duke Robert of Normandy and Robert of Flanders; near the Dog gate were stationed Raymond and Bishop Adhemar; Godfrey and his fellow Teutons were posted before a gate which in William of Tyre's days was still called the Duke's gate.

It was Wednesday, 21st of October, 1097, when the Crusading army encamped before Antioch. For fifteen days no Turk dared issue from the city, but the Armenians and Syrians came out daily to the camp, pretending friendliness to their fellow Christians, but in reality seeking intelligence for the besieged. Presently the Turks began to make sallies in every direction, whilst their friends in Harenc also pressed the besiegers hard. As Christmas drew near, the Crusaders felt the first touches of want: "We did not venture abroad, nor could we find aught to eat in the land of the Christians; for none dared enter Saracen land without a great host." Bohemond and Robert of Flanders led out a large force to forage, but they gained little booty, and the Turks seized the opportunity to make a sudden sally, wherein they slew many knights and footmen. From this moment the Armenians and Syrians ceased to bring provisions to the Christian camp, and transferred their services to the besieged.

As the new year advanced on things grew worse and worse. There was no provender for the horses, and two solidi would scarcely purchase a man's food for one day. There were signs in heaven above, and in the earth beneath; the earth trembled, and red lights burnt in the northern sky at night. Terror seized upon the bravest hearts; Bohemond declared that he could not stay to see his men perish. Godfrey was ill, and so also was Raymond. The leader of Alexius' Greek auxiliaries urged his Latin colleagues to retire, and it seemed that there was no hope but to abandon the siege. Then came news that a vast host of Turks was advancing from the east. Bohemond's warlike spirit was roused, and at his own suggestion he led out one half of the host to battle, while the other half remained to keep watch on the city. Starting late at night, at early dawn he came upon the Turks encamped on either side of the river. But despite this advantage the battle at first went against the Christians, till the reserve under Bohemond's own banner restored the day. Then the Turks were routed, their camp plundered, and Bohemond returned with a hundred heads as a trophy of his valour. This was on Tuesday, February 9, 1098.

The Crusaders now determined to build a fortress on the height above Bohemond's camp, hoping thus to check the constant sallies from the city. Another castle was to be built on a little hill near the bridge over the Orontes. During a temporary absence of Bohemond, the Turkish commandant sent out his troops across the bridge, and closed the city gates behind them, bidding them conquer or die. It would have gone hard with the Christians, but for a valiant knight, Isuard of Gagia, who with a hundred and fifty footmen made a desperate onset on the Turks, and drove them back to the bridge to find that Bohemond was returned. The narrow causeway was crowded with horsemen, and the walls of Antioch were thronged with Christian women eager to behold the destruction of their Turkish tyrants. "We overcame the enemy, and flung them into the river, where they received everlasting damnation, and rendered up their wretched souls to Satan. If by chance any strove to climb on to the piers of the bridge, or to swim ashore, our men slew them from the bank. Twelve emirs and fifteen hundred of a meaner sort fell upon that day." On the morrow the Turks came out and gathered their dead for burial; but the Christians broke into the cemetery, flung the corpses into a ditch, and carried off the heads as witness to the number of those slain. Then the besiegers renewed the building of the castle, and when it was finished entrusted it to Count Raymond to guard.

During all these months it would seem that Bohemond had been in negotiation with the besieged. He had further obtained a promise from all the other chiefs, except Raymond, that he should be lord of the city when captured. Now, after having arranged with a certain Emir, Pyrrhus or Firuz, for the betrayal of the city, Bohemond prevailed upon the chiefs much against their will to promise Antioch to the man, who should succeed in taking it.

Once sure of his reward Bohemond revealed his plan. A night was fixed for the surrender, and on the preceding day a part of the Christian army went foraging so as to throw the enemy off their guard. At midnight a little band gathered below the Gate of St. George, and there waited for the signal. At last a messenger came to bid them stay till the passing of the watch, which every night made the circuit of the walls lamps in hand. Dawn was breaking before the wished-for sign was given, and Bohemond ordered his men to advance. They found a ladder ready, and sixty men ascended and seized the three towers of which Pyrrhus had charge. When Bohemond learnt that the towers were in the hands of his men, he advanced with the remainder; in their exultation the Christians crowded on to the ladder, which broke beneath their weight. It was a desperate moment for the few, who were now left alone upon the walls; it was still too dark to see clearly, but at last they felt their way to a gate, broke it down, and so let in their comrades. As the morning sun rose, the Christians from their tents against the eastern walls saw Bohemond's banner floating on the hill. There was a general rush forward, the other gates were burst open and the city won. There was riot everywhere, and forgetful of their God men gave themselves over to banquets, and the blandishments of pagan dancers.

Hardly had the Crusaders taken Antioch, when on June 5th the scouts of Corbogha's army appeared before the city. He drove the Crusaders before him within the walls, and even gained possession of the citadel. From this vantage ground the Turks pressed the city hard. All day the Christians strove to bar their progress, and at night rested among the corpses of their comrades. As Corbogha's host closed round the city on the south, the hearts of the besieged began to fail. Men turned their thoughts to flight, and under the cover of darkness let themselves down by ropes from the walls. The panic affected even the noblest; the Grantmaisnils—Alberic and that Ivo whose turbulence a few years later won him an evil fame in English history—escaped over the hills to the port of St. Simeon, and put out to sea. Scarcely any event made such an impression as this cowardly flight: the recreant nobles are spoken of with scorn as "rope-dancers," and as men who were everywhere called infamous and held up to shame and execration. But there was one deserter of still more importance even than these. Stephen of Chartres, son-in-law to the great Conqueror, had made his failing health an excuse for retiring to Alexandretta before the fall of Antioch. The besieged Christians sent him daily messages for help, and at last he mustered heart to scale a height whence he could look down upon the innumerable tents that filled the plain of Antioch. The sight was too much for his unwarlike mind; panic seized him, and he hurried back to his own camp eager to escape the coming doom. Departing northwards he met Alexius, who was marching with a great army to assist the Crusaders. The Emperor was only too glad for an excuse, and despite the expostulation of Bohemond's brother Guy, Stephen and Alexius shortly went back to Constantinople.

Meanwhile the state of Antioch grew daily worse. "We, who remained," writes Tudebode, "could not hold up against the arms of those within the castle, and we built a wall between ourselves and them, and watched it day and night." Hunger came as the climax of their ills; those who had money might purchase a small goat for sixty shillings, or a horse's head for three; the poorer folk fed on any garbage they could find, on boiled fig-leaves, or ox-hides softened in water. Even the greatest nobles were reduced to beg for the commonest necessities, and but for his successful mendicancy Robert of Flanders would have been horseless on the day of the great battle.

For nearly a week the fight had raged hotly along the southern wall, and things were at their very worst, when the madness or enthusiasm of a poor Provençal brought hope and ultimate victory. It was early on Wednesday, June the 9th, as Count Raymond and Adhemar were sadly gazing at the enemy's stronghold, that one Peter Bartholomew appeared before them with a strange story. St. Andrew had revealed to him in a dream the hiding-place of the very lance, wherewith the Roman soldier had pierced the side of Christ. He was bidden to reveal this vision to Raymond and Adhemar, but feared to approach men so noble. Twice was the vision repeated, and twice he failed to obey the apostle's command. He had even fled from the city, and set sail for Cyprus, but a storm drove him back to Mamistra, whence he had now made his way to Antioch. At first this strange tale received little credence. "The bishop thought it empty words; but the Count believed, and entrusted Peter to the care of his chaplain Raymond." Such is the account which Raymond of Agiles gives of the famous legend of the Invention of the Holy Lance.

Confirmation soon followed, for that night as a priest named Stephen was watching in St. Mary's Church, Christ Himself appeared to him, and promised aid within five days. These visions had come at the darkest hour of the Crusaders' fortunes; it was on the previous night that the Grantmaisnils had fled, and it was even rumoured that all the great leaders were meditating flight. In such a strait it is no wonder that policy or superstition inclined the Crusaders to look for aid from a supernatural quarter.

The five days passed, and early on the morning of the 14th of June, Raymond of Agiles and eleven others went to the Church of St. Peter. From morn to eve they dug without reward; as each withdrew in weariness fresh workers took their place. "At last, seeing that we were fatigued, the young man who had told us of the lance leapt into the pit, all ungirt as he was, without shoes and in his shirt. He adjured us to call upon God to render us the lance for our comfort, and our victory. At last the Lord, moved by such devotion, showed us the lance. And I, who have written these things, as soon as ever the blade appeared above ground, greeted it with a kiss; nor can I tell how great joy and exultation then filled the city."

By this time Corbogha must have changed the siege into a blockade. What happened during the ensuing fortnight we cannot precisely tell. Perhaps these were the worst days of the famine, during which the

Crusaders hoped against hope for the coming of Count Stephen, or the Emperor Alexius. It would, however, seem that the time was partly spent on fruitless negotiation. The Christians offered to stake the issue on the valour of six or three chosen champions from either side; but this and other offers were rejected with disdain. So at length the Crusaders determined on action, and in the morning of Monday, 28th of June, issued to the attack. A gentle rain was falling with the dawn of day, and to their pious feelings it seemed like the dew of God's blessing.

They marched in six battalions; first were Hugh the Great, Godfrey and Robert of Normandy; fourth was Adhemar bearing the Holy Lance, and leading the men of Provence, Count Raymond being left behind to watch the citadel; fifth went Tancred and the men of Poitou under Gaston de Béarn; last was Bohemond with the horseless knights. Many bishops and priests accompanied the army with crosses in their hands; whilst others from the city walls called down God's blessing on the departing host. "As we marched from the bridge towards the mountains it was a toilsome journey," writes Raymond of Agiles, "for the enemy strove to hem us in. Yet though we of the bishop's squadron were hard pressed in the fight, thanks to the Lord's Lance none of us were wounded, no not so much as by an arrow. I, who speak these things, saw them for myself, since I was bearing the Lord's Lance. And if any says that Heraclius, the bishop's standard-bearer, was wounded in this battle, let him know that Heraclius was straggling far from our ranks."

Meantime Corbogha dreamt of nothing so little as an attack. He was sitting in his tent playing at chess, when news came of the sally of the besieged. A fugitive Turk, who had escaped from Antioch, assured Corbogha that there was no cause for fear; but as the bishop's followers came in view, he added, "These men may be slain, but they will not be put to flight."

In strict truth Corbogha seems to have suffered the Crusaders to approach, in the hope of drawing them out from the city to battle in the open plain. He had despatched a force of Turks to make a circuit and take the Christians in the rear, warning their commander that a fire would be the signal that the main battle was lost. Perceiving these tactics, and fearing to be surrounded, the Crusaders organised a seventh squadron of knights, taken from the divisions of Godfrey and Robert, and placed it under the command of a certain Count Reginald. When the Christians came within range of the camp, Corbogha's men discharged their bows; but a violent wind destroyed the surety of their aim, so that they fled in panic, and Count Hugh on his arrival found none to oppose him. Bohemond was, however, hard pressed, and Hugh and Godfrey hastened back to give their aid where the real stress of conflict lay. Many deeds of valour were then wrought; but at length the signal of defeat was raised, and the Turks fled on all sides for the mountains. In their excitement the Christians imagined allies of no earthly mould. "For there came out of the mountains innumerable armies on white horses, and bearing white banners. And our men seeing this host, knew not who they were, till they recognised it for the promised aid of Christ. The leaders of this host were George, Mercurius, and Demetrius. These things are worthy of belief, for many of our men beheld them."

It was a day of glory for the Christian host. A half-famished and ill-equipped band had routed an immense army well provided with all warlike stores. "But the Lord multiplied us, so that in battle we were more than they. And returning to the city with great joy, we praised and magnified God, who gave the victory to His people."

V.

THE FIRST CRUSADE—THE CAPTURE OF THE HOLY CITY.

"Lay siege against it, and build a fort against it, and cast a mound against it; set the camp also against it, and set battering rams against it round about."—EZEKIEL iv. 1, 2.

THOUGH Antioch was at last secured, the Crusaders neglected to hurry on to Jerusalem, the goal of their ambition. Godfrey had learnt at Rome, fifteen years before, what dangers attended summer warfare in a hot climate. He therefore opposed an immediate advance, which, if undertaken promptly, might have brought about the fail of the Holy City without a siege, and the departure was accordingly postponed till November 1st.

This interval the chiefs devoted to conquest on their own account; each great lord offering pay to all who would enlist under his banner. To these months we must ascribe the acquisition of most of the fortresses between Antioch and Edessa, though only a few scattered incidents of this warfare have been preserved. Raymond Pilet, a follower of Count Raymond, took the castle of Tell Mannas, but failed in an attack on the more important town of Marra. The count himself captured Albara, and slew all the Saracens whom he could find, men and women, young and old. Then he sought out for his conquest a bishop who might convert it from a house of devils to a temple of the living God. The chief of Hazart, who was hard pressed by his lord, Ridhwan, the powerful ruler of Aleppo, appealed to Godfrey for assistance. When the proffered alliance had been accepted, the envoys, to the astonishment of the Christian bystanders, drew two pigeons from their breast, and despatched them as messengers of their success to Hazart. Godfrey summoned Baldwin from Edessa, and the two brothers then advanced to Hazart. Ridhwan, who was already encamped before the town, withdrew on their approach. Godfrey renewed his compact with the chief of Hazart, and gave his ally a wrought helmet of gold, a masterpiece of art, wherein his ancestor, Herebrand of Bouillon, had been wont to issue forth to battle. After this Godfrey, shunning the August heat, withdrew to the highlands of Armenia, where his brother gave him Ravendal and Tell-basher.

About this time the Christians at Antioch experienced a grievous loss. On August 1st, Adhemar, Bishop of Puy, "one dear to God and man, departed in peace to the Lord." On the night after his burial in the Church of St. Peter, the bishop appeared in a dream to Peter Bartholomew, in company with Christ and the Apostle Andrew. To Peter, Adhemar confessed that he had been led down into hell in punishment for his doubts as to the Holy Lance; but after his burial Christ had visited him in the flames, and brought him up to heaven, whence, Adhemar said, he now came to assure his former comrades that he would not forsake them.

In November, the chiefs began to assemble at Antioch. Bohemond was absent at first, and Count Raymond took occasion to protest against the bestowal of the citadel on the Norman chief to his own detriment. The other chiefs feared to offend either of these great lords, and so would make no decision. It seemed that the quarrel would prevent any further advance, when Raymond, with characteristic self-restraint, offered to waive the question for a time. If Bohemond would join in the march south, the count would leave the dispute to the judgment of their peers, always saving the fealty due to the Emperor. Bohemond agreed, and the two rivals were formally reconciled, although both thought well to fortify such parts of the city as they held.

When peace had thus been patched up, the army set out on its march. On Saturday, November 28th, Raymond made an unsuccessful attack on Marra, which, on Bohemond's arrival next day, was renewed,

57

but again to no purpose. Raymond, who often figures as the engineer among the Crusading chiefs, then built a great wooden castle. The huge machine overtopped the city walls, and defied all attempts to burn or crush it. The defenders of the city were driven from their posts by showers of stones, the Crusaders clambered up the walls, and the Saracens fled in panic. The Crusaders slew without discrimination, "so that there was no corner without a Saracen corpse, and one could scarcely ride through the streets without trampling on the dead bodies" (Dec. 11, 1098).

The capture of Marra led to a fresh quarrel between Raymond and Bohemond. The Norman mocked at the latest revelations of the Count's Provencal follower, Peter Bartholomew; he also refused to surrender his portion of the city unless Raymond would relinquish his share of Antioch. Raymond taunted his rival with greed and slackness in the fight; he wished to bestow Marra as a military fief on the Bishop of Albara. A further cause of discord was soon added. Bohemond urged that the advance to Jerusalem should be postponed till Easter; Christmas was close at hand, Godfrey and many knights were still absent at Edessa. The army, however, was in favour of advance, and with one accord appealed to Raymond to be their leader, if all the other chiefs should fail. After some hesitation Raymond agreed, and named a day for the renewal of the march. Bohemond thereon returned in wrath to Antioch. In the face of these troubles Godfrey was summoned from Edessa, and a conference of the chiefs held. Only a few supported Raymond, although these few included the two Roberts and Tancred. But news of the dispute reached those who were lying sick at Marra, and their indignation took a strange, though practical form. Rising from their beds they tottered feebly to the walls in eagerness to destroy a city over which their chiefs were quarrelling. Indignation gave them strength to drag huge stones from their places; and though the bishop's officers might stop the work of destruction for a moment, it was renewed as soon as they had passed by. "Those who dared not destroy by day pressed on by night; hardly a man was too weak to work at bringing down a wall."

At last the appointed day arrived, and despite all the opposition, Raymond and his followers marched out from Marra on January 13, 1099. The fear of the Christians had gone before them, and the rulers of the great cities along the Orontes were eager to purchase peace. In the valley of Desem, where the Crusaders, spent the Feast of the Purification (February 2nd), they passed a fortnight of ease and plenty. Then, having determined to forsake the straight road for Damascus, they crossed the Great Lebanon, hoping on the coast to hear news of the ships they had left in the ports near Antioch, and through this means obtain supplies from Cyprus. On Monday, February 14th, Raymond sat down before the stronghold of Arkah, a fortress situated on a steep and almost inaccessible hill, and surrounded with a double wall. Here the Crusaders were detained three months, finding in the neighbourhood ample scope for the foraging adventures, so dear to the eleventh-century knight. Moreover, the besiegers were in no lack of provisions, for these were brought in abundance by the Greek and Italian merchants to the seaports close at hand.

Presently there came a rumour that the Caliph of Bagdad was sending an immense host to raise the siege. In this peril Raymond appealed to Godfrey and Robert of Flanders, who were besieging Jebleh or Gibel. The northern army marched to Arkah only to find the rumour false. The new-comers openly charged Raymond with having invented the story, and murmured at his wealth, which they contrasted with their own poverty. The visions of Peter Bartholomew and others, which had not abated, were again turned to ridicule, the chief among the scoffers being Robert of Normandy's chaplain Arnulf, afterwards Patriarch of Jerusalem. Peter Bartholomew retorted, "Make me the biggest fire you can, and I will pass through its midst with the Lord's

59

Lance in my hand. If it be the Lord's Lance may I pass through unharmed; if not, may I be burned up."

On Good Friday morning, April 8th, forty thousand Crusaders gathered to see the ordeal. In front of them were two parallel piles of dead olive branches, fourteen feet long by four feet high, and only one foot apart. "When the fires were kindled, I, Raymond, spake before the whole multitude: 'If God hath spoken to this man face to face, and if the blessed Andrew showed him the Lord's Lance as he slept, may he pass through the fire unharmed; but if the thing be a lie, let him be burned up together with the Lance that he holds.' And all the people answered, 'Amen.' Now the fire blazed so fiercely that it occupied the space of twenty cubits, nor could any man approach it." Then Peter Bartholomew, clad only in his tunic, knelt before the Bishop of Albara, received the Lance, and manfully entered the fire. Some fancied that they saw a bird fluttering over his head, but the great mass of the people do not appear to have seen anything miraculous; though, as Raymond remarks, "There was a multitude present, and all men cannot see everything." As Peter issued from the flames he was greeted with loud cries of "God aid him." Such was the popular enthusiasm that he would have been torn to pieces, had not Raymond Pilet forced a way through the thronging multitude, and carried Peter off in safety.

Peter died within a few days, and the ordeal, as might be expected, only served to confirm the believers and the incredulous each in their own faith. For while his supporters declared that he passed through the fire comparatively unhurt, and owed his wounds to the unruly crowd, his enemies asserted his death to be due to the effects of the ordeal itself Even Raymond of Agiles had to confess that "there was some sign of burning about him," though qualifying his admission by adding that his wounds were great.

Easter passed and Arkah was still untaken. There were two parties among the Crusaders; some urged that the host should await the coming of Alexius, who had promised to join them by midsummer, others pointed to the harvest, which was already ripening in mid-April, and were for proceeding to Jerusalem with the new crops. The latter counsels prevailed, and on Friday, May 13th, the host departed from before Arkah, and marched along the coast to Caesarea. There they celebrated Whit-Sunday, and thence, turning inland, marched to Ramleh.

At Ramleh the Crusading chiefs held a council of war. Some advised that they should strike at the very heart of Mohammedan power, and leaving Jerusalem on one side, march south for Alexandria and Babylon; thus they would conquer a great kingdom, and Jerusalem would then fall without an effort. Others asked how a host which numbered only fifteen hundred knights could conquer vast nations, if it were too feeble to take the capital of a province like Jerusalem. Finally, the latter prevailed, and the march for the Holy City was resumed. Many eager for present gain hastened to set their banners on the neighbouring strongholds and homesteads, others mindful of Peter Bartholomew's advice, refused to think of such earthly things while nearing the goal of their desire. "These, to whom the Lord's command was dearer than lust of gain, advanced with naked feet, sighing heavily for the disdain that the others showed for the Lord's command."

It was June 6, 1099, when the Crusaders arrived before the Holy City. During the course of the few preceding years, Jerusalem had once more passed into the hands of the Egyptian Caliph, who had been in negotiation with the Crusaders for more than two years before. Alexius had pointed out the advantages to be gained from an alliance with the Egyptian Caliph, who as head of the Shiites would willingly co-operate against the unorthodox Turks. During the siege of Nicaea, the Crusading chiefs had sent an embassy to the Caliph, and during that of Antioch had received one in return. Later when the Caliph found both Turks and Christians bidding for his friendship, he had compromised matters by offering to admit three hundred unarmed pilgrims into Jerusalem. "But we laughed this proffer to scorn, hoping for God's grace, and threatening that unless he gave us up Jerusalem for nothing, we would lay claim to Babylon."

The Crusaders were too few to encompass Jerusalem entirely; but so far as possible they distributed their forces over the whole circuit. Robert of Normandy camped on the north, by St. Stephen's Church, and near him was his namesake from Flanders. Godfrey and Tancred besieged the city from the west. Count Raymond stationed himself on Mount Sion to the south. Eastward, by Mount Olivet, the Crusaders kept no watch, for the city was impregnable on that side, where the strong walls of the Temple enclosure rose abruptly from the deep valley of Jehoshaphat.

After some days of preparation the Crusaders on June 14th delivered an assault, which almost succeeded, but they could not secure any permanent advantage. Then, as the days crept on, hunger and thirst made their appearance in the besiegers' camp. The chief water supply was the little fountain of Siloe, which, bubbling up only every other day, was but a doubtful blessing; for as soon as it began to flow, men and animals crowded to the waterside in such numbers that they trod one another to death, and at last the spring was entirely choked with the corpses of men and animals. Raymond of Agiles draws a fearful picture of the things he saw: "Near the fount lay many weak folk, unable to utter a cry for the dryness of their tongues; there they remained with open mouths, and hands stretched out to those whom they saw had water. Horses, mules, and oxen, lay rotting where they had fallen, till the stench of the decaying flesh became abhorrent to the camp." Afterwards, when water was discovered a few leagues distant, the Saracens lay in ambush among the mountains to plunder the cattle as they were being driven to drink.

Food also was running short, when fortunately news came that nine Christian ships had put in at Jaffa. With early dawn on Friday, June 17th, Raymond Pilet started with a band of a hundred knights to convey the provisions to the camp. The seamen at Jaffa welcomed the Crusading warriors with a feast, and they spent the night together in careless glee. In fancied security they kept no watch, and at dawn they awoke to find themselves surrounded by their enemies; but they contrived to unload their cargo, and carry it up to the camp, though the ships fell into the hands of the Saracens, except for one that had been cruising outside, and which escaped back to Laodicea.

The danger of famine was thus averted; but fresh trouble arose through the outbreak of the old quarrels once more. Some grudged Raymond his post on Mount Sion; others blamed Tancred because he had set up his banner over the Church of the Nativity at Bethlehem; others again began to talk of electing a king for the yet uncaptured city. With the old quarrels the old visions also began to multiply; Adhemar of Puy appeared to Peter the Hermit, and promised that the city should fall, if the host encompassed it barefoot during nine days. The bishop's brother, Hugo, took up the cry; a council was called, and the chiefs, admitting that they had been lax, agreed to work and pray henceforward with more vigour and concord. A general reconciliation was proclaimed; processions were to make the circuit of the walls, and every effort was devoted to the construction of the great engines necessary for the siege. The lack of wood for this last purpose had been among the most pressing difficulties of the besiegers; Tancred, while prowling about the mountains, had discovered four choice beams in a cave, but this was as nothing to the amount required, and there was no nearer source of supply than the groves at Nablûs some thirty-six miles off. Robert of Flanders superintended the work of felling the trees, and protecting the timber on the road, and so at last two wooden castles were constructed; one by Godfrey on the north, the other by Count Raymond on the south.

While these works were in progress, the other half of Adhemar's injunctions was not forgotten. It was probably on Tuesday, July 12th, that the Crusaders made their grand procession round the city. The whole army, so far as it was possible, marched slowly from St. Mary's Church on Mount Sion to St. Stephen's on the north-east. At their head went the white-stoled priests and bishops barefoot, and cross in hand, chanting hymns and praying as they went for the fall of the city. The Saracens clustered on the walls to see the novel sight, and as the Crusaders made their first halt near St. Stephen's, mocked them with derisive shouts and gestures. "Moreover, in sight of all the Christians, they kept beating the most holy crucifix, whereon Christ shed His blood for the redemption of mankind, crying out in the Saracen tongue: 'Franks, it is the blessed cross.' "On the Mount of Olives, where a small church marked the place of Christ's ascension, Arnulf, afterwards Patriarch of Jerusalem, preached a sermon, while the Saracens ran up and down the opposing height, brandishing their swords in futile anger at the foe. Thence again the Christians started in procession to St. Mary's monastery, in the valley of Jehoshaphat, and by this route returned at length to Mount Sion.

The Saracens within the city on their part were not idle; they had strengthened their walls, and raised the height of their towers. But the native Christians in Jerusalem kept the Crusaders informed of all that went on. On Wednesday, July 13th, the attack was commenced on every side, and continued next day, but without any decided success. On the Friday the Saracens attempted to fire Godfrey's castle, which, through the fracture of one of its wheels, was fixed at a little distance from the walls, unable to advance or to withdraw. The defenders further protected the walls from the assaults of the ram by hanging out sacks stuffed with straw. But the Saracens were driven from the walls by continual volleys from the stone-slingers; the straw sacks were set ablaze by fire-bearing arrows; the scaling ladders were placed against the walls; the drawbridge lowered from the castle, and Jerusalem was won. Bernard of St. Valery, a surname afterwards very glorious in Crusading history, was first to leap upon the battlements, and as his comrades followed him the Saracens fled in panic before them to the Temple of Solomon.

Meanwhile, in the opposite part of the city, Raymond had met with less success. He had built his castle with the aid of the Genoese sailors who had lost their ships at Jaffa. After breaking down the outworks (*antemuralia*), and filling up the foss (*vallum*), he found the Saracens on the walls had ten times as many engines as he could bring against them. It was the ninth day of which Peter had spoken, and though the Crusaders were not working as they should have done, this was doubtless due to the spells of two Saracen witches upon the wall. A stone silenced their iniquitous incantations, but even this brought no relief, and at noon the wall was still unshaken. The chiefs were already meditating the withdrawal of the engines, when suddenly the count's men caught sight of a strange apparition. Far away on the Mount of Olives stood a knight waving his shield in triumph. It was a sign that the city had been forced from the other side. "Who this knight was," says Raymond of Agiles, ever ready to believe in a miracle, "we could never find out." But his meaning was understood at once, and the Provençal soldiery returned to the assault with renewed vigour.

Jerusalem had at last been taken, and was to fare as captured cities only too often did in mediaeval warfare. The words of an eye-witness paint the horrors of the day in general terms without any attempt at detail—"When our men had taken the city with its walls and towers, there were things wondrous to be seen. For some of the enemy, and this is a small matter, were reft of their heads, while others riddled through with arrows were forced to leap down from the towers; others, after long

65

torture, were burnt in the flames. In all the streets and squares there were to be seen piles of heads, and hands, and feet; and along the public ways foot and horse alike made passage over the bodies of the dead." Tancred burst into the Temple, and tore down the golden hangings from the walls—seven thousand marks in weight. He was, perhaps, of a more pitiful turn than most of his compeers, for he offered to protect such as took refuge in Solomon's Temple. But even his charity could only offer a reprieve, and not a full pardon. Weary with slaughter the Christians at length turned their thoughts to sacred things, and went in tearful procession to the Holy Sepulchre. But early next morning their sterner mood revived; the rumour went about that Tancred had been luring the fugitives to their destruction, and the Crusaders armed themselves anew to the work of death. Every one was eager for blood: some stationed at a distance shot the hapless Saracens with their arrows; others scaled the roof of the Temple itself and massacred both men and women with the sword. Raymond alone seems to have felt an honourable compassion for the conquered; he offered life to those who had taken refuge in the Tower of David, and on their surrender, suffered them to depart unharmed to Ascalon.

This terrible slaughter "filled all the city with dead bodies," and the first work of the conquerors was to cleanse the streets of the impurity which might breed a plague. The surviving Saracens were compelled to carry the dead outside the walls, where they were "heaped up in mountains," to be presently destroyed by fire. "Such a slaughter of pagan folk had never been seen or heard of; none knows their number save God alone."

VI.

GODFREY DE BOUILLON.

"He was a very parfite gentil knyght."

CHAUCER.

EIGHT days after the capture of the Holy City, the Crusaders met to elect a king (July 22nd). Few, however, of the great chiefs were willing to accept so barren and laborious an honour. The object of their expedition accomplished, all were eager to return home; so to one after another was the crown offered in vain. Raymond of St. Gilles, if we may trust his biographer, refused to bear a king's title in the Holy City. "Robert of Normandy's refusal," writes an almost contemporary English chronicler, "aspersed his nobility with an indelible stain, to which not reverence, but sloth or fear impelled him." At last Godfrey de Bouillon was persuaded to accept the headship of the conquered city. But he, too, refused to wear a crown in the city where our Lord was crucified, and so does not figure among the kings of Jerusalem. He contented himself with the modest title of Baron of the Holy Sepulchre, even after he had practically become king of a new realm.

After a temporal head, it was necessary to elect a spiritual one. There were many claimants for the office, but finally the choice fell upon Arnulf, chaplain to Robert of Normandy, According to Raymond of Agiles, he was as yet only a sub deacon, and a man of loose life, whose notorious amours were the theme of popular songs in the Crusading camp. Ralph of Caen, on the other hand, speaks in no mean terms of his literary taste. Arnulf had been tutor to the Conqueror's daughter, Cecilia, and followed Odo of Bayeux on the Crusade. He was chief of the disbelievers in the Holy Lance, and narrowly escaped murder at the hands of the Provençal count's emissaries; when the Holy Lance was discredited he had a golden crucifix made to take its place as an object

67

of devotion. His influence had grown as that of Raymond's followers diminished, and he had been chosen to preach the sermon on Mount Olivet on the day of the great procession round Jerusalem. Such was the man who was first elected to the Latin Patriarchate in the Holy City.

Immediately after the capture of Jerusalem, Tancred and Count Eustace started north to secure Nablûs. Meantime at Jerusalem a quarrel broke out between Godfrey and Raymond, who refused to surrender the Tower of David. When Godfrey wrested the stronghold from the Bishop of Albara, to whom it had been entrusted, the count indignantly declared that he would go home at once. But first, in accordance with the injunctions of Peter Bartholomew, Raymond and his company made a pilgrimage to the Jordan. There his followers, unable to find a vessel, launched their lord on a boat of wicker-work; and then flinging off his worn-out garb, dressed him in new apparel. "This," said Raymond of Agiles, "we did in accordance with our instructions, but we know not why the man of God bade us act so."

In August, there came news that a great Egyptian army was mustering at Ascalon. Tancred and Eustace were called back in haste, while Godfrey and Robert of Flanders marched out from Jerusalem. Robert of Normandy and Count Raymond refused to move without more certain information, but on a message from Godfrey that, "if they wished to share in the battle they must come quickly," they also set out, leaving Peter the Hermit at Jerusalem to organise processions and prayers for their success. On the 11th of August, the united host advanced towards Ascalon.

The Egyptians never dreamt of danger from so weak a foe, and rested idly in their tents, since the soothsayers forbade them to give battle till Saturday, the 13th of August. The Christians advanced in nine battalions: on the left fought Duke Godfrey; on the sea by the right, Count Raymond; while in the centre rode the two Roberts and Tancred.

From the moment when the Crusaders caught sight of their adversaries each standing with his skin of water hung round his neck, there seems to have been no doubt as to the result of the battle. It was rather a massacre than a conflict; some threw themselves into the sea, others buried themselves in the earth, "not daring to rise up against us, and our men cut them down as a man fells animals at the shambles" (Friday, Aug. 12, 1099).

The honours of the day seem to have belonged to Robert of Normandy, who slew the standard-bearer with his own hands. The standard with its golden apple and silver shaft, he purchased for twenty marks of silver, and gave to the Holy Sepulchre. The booty was immense, and when each had taken what he desired, they returned with joy to the Holy City, their camels and asses laden with biscuits, flour, wheat, and all things needful. "Wherefore there was such plenty that one could buy an ox for eight or ten coins, a measure of corn for twelve, and a measure of barley for eight."

Not even the unity forced upon them by the late danger could entirely reconcile Godfrey and Count Raymond. The count had accepted from the citizens of Ascalon the offer of their allegiance; but the chiefs declared that the possession of that stronghold was essential to the royal power. Truly or falsely—for the story is told in too many ways to be entirely true or entirely false—Raymond is alleged to have given back the town to the Egyptians rather than suffer it to pass into Godfrey's hands. It was with difficulty that the two leaders were kept from open warfare through the intervention of Robert of Flanders.

Many of the leaders now started homewards through Northern Syria. So great was the terror produced by the victory of Ascalon that the Egyptian garrisons at Acre, Tyre, and other towns received them kindly. Laodicea which Bohemond, with the aid of the Pisans and Genoese, was endeavouring to secure for himself, was put into the hands of Count Raymond, who thus obtained some consolation for his previous disappointments.

Godfrey meanwhile led his whole force against Arsuf, but after a prolonged and futile siege he was forced to go into winter quarters, and withdrew to Jerusalem. His return to the capital was hastened probably by the arrival of his brother Baldwin and Bohemond of Antioch. Fulcher of Chartres, who was present in attendance on Count Baldwin, has left a detailed account of this march, which furnishes a typical example of the perils besetting an eleventh-century pilgrimage.

The two chiefs started from Balunyâs, a little south of Jebleh, taking with them Bishop Dagobert of Pisa. Their united companies numbered some twenty-five thousand, including women and children. As they passed along the Saracens refused them food, and since there was no fodder for the horses, the pilgrims would have fared ill, but that in the tilled fields there were crops of what the common folk called "cannamelles." "These cannamelles are almost like reeds, and hence their name from canna (*a reed*) and mel (*honey*). Whence as I take it wild honey draws its name, for that it is cunningly confected from these." The hungry people managed to stay their pangs by sucking these reeds, but they were of little use as food. During four or five days also a ceaseless torrent of cold rain was added to their troubles. Fulcher says that on one day he saw several men and women, besides very many beasts, perish through the cold. Only twice in the long march did the pilgrims secure a market—at Tripoli and Caesarea. At last, on the day of the winter solstice, they reached Jerusalem. The Holy Sepulchre was visited, and Christmas Eve spent in vigil at the Church of the Nativity in Bethlehem. Even now, though it was nearly six months after the taking of Jerusalem, Fulcher was only too conscious of the offensive odours from the dead bodies of the Saracens. On January 1st the pilgrims started on their journey back; by the Jordan they cut their palm branches, and so returned through Tiberias, Banias, Tortosa, and Laodicea.

A little later Gabriel, the ruler of Melitene, applied to Bohemond for help against Ibn Danishmend. Bohemond, eager to extend his sway, accepted the invitation. On the road he fell into an ambuscade through the careless confidence of his men who, wearied by the heat, were marching without their armour. Most of the Franks were cut to pieces, and Bohemond himself with his cousin Richard were taken prisoners.

By this time Godfrey had forced Arsuf to surrender, and obtained a promise of tribute from the other cities along the coast, including Ascalon, Caesarea, and Acre, for "the fear of the most Christian duke fell upon all the lands of the heathen folk." Even the sheiks of the wild Arabian tribes begged for peace in order that they might have a market for their flocks. But neither Christian nor Saracen kept peace by sea; and while the merchants of Ascalon and Jerusalem passed to and fro from one city to the other, the Saracen warships scoured the Mediterranean, and the Crusading warriors cut off all vessels that brought up provisions from Alexandria and Damietta for the Egyptian cities along the coast.

Godfrey's next task was to fortify Jaffa, a town that was of extreme importance to the infant kingdom and for a double reason; it was practically the only harbour at which the Crusaders could disembark reinforcements from the west; it was also their base of supply since the Franks could not trust entirely to an alien race for their provisions. From this labour Godfrey was called away to assist Tancred, who was establishing himself near the lake of Tiberias. As he returned from this expedition along the coast towards Jaffa, a deadly sickness fell upon him, due, so it was declared, to poisoned fruit sent him by the Emir of Caesarea. At Jaffa he met the Venetian bishop and doge, who had lately arrived, but was too feeble to endure the excitement of a prolonged interview. The same night he grew worse, and feeling unable to bear the

71

bustle of a maritime city, had himself carried up to Jerusalem. He breathed his last on July 18, 1100, and was buried in the Church of the Holy Sepulchre.

Godfrey's death occurred three days after the anniversary of the capture of the Holy City. Under the later kings the two events were celebrated together, and the anniversary of the great duke's death was marked by the distribution of gifts in accordance with his will. Godfrey himself is one of the most remarkable characters to be met with in history. No other ruler, perhaps, combines so perfectly the religious and active elements in life. His history was soon surrounded with tales of wonder, so that he seemed to have been marked out from his earliest days for his sacred mission. His mother told how long before the First Crusade he had desired to make his journey to Jerusalem, not as a pilgrim, but at the head of an army. Yet he does not seem to have held the first place amongst the leaders, and the reason for his election must be sought in the jealousy between the men of north and south France. The fierceness of this feeling had everywhere been displayed in the quarrels between the followers of the Norman and Provençal leaders. Some compromise was necessary, and seeing that the Germans, as Ralph of Caen expressly says, had "stood outside the quarrel," it is little wonder that the choice fell on the great leader, whose engines had made the first breach in the walls of Jerusalem. Moreover, Godfrey, as a native of the French and Teutonic borderlands, was unlike most of the chiefs, familiar with both the French and German tongues.

Piety had always been a marked feature in Godfrey's character. Either this or his natural humility made him refuse to wear a golden crown of state in the city where his Saviour had worn a crown of thorns. He was fond of religious services, and even in the turmoil of the capture had stolen away to pray at the Holy Sepulchre. Yet there were harder elements in his character; he had sternly punished any lack of discipline among his followers, and shown himself merciless to his foes.

Still his short reign was so far as possible one of peace, and all the varied dwellers round Jerusalem mourned for his death.

It must have been within a very few years that Godfrey began to figure in contemporary song. Later he became the centre of one of the five great cycles of romantic literature. In the twelfth and thirteenth centuries the fame of Godfrey and the First Crusade rivalled the older legends of Arthur and Charlemagne, and he is named with them as one of the three Christian heroes who made up the number of the nine noblest. Slowly the floating mists of romance gather shape and substance round his name, not only from the true exploits of his Crusading life, but from others in which he had taken no part. Like the mother of Thomas a Becket, his mother was fabled to have been an Eastern princess, and his grandmother's name was associated with the old-world legend of the Knight of the Swan. Whatever its form his legend became one of the chief themes of mediaeval song. Ballads of the siege of Antioch cheered the camp fires of the warriors of the Third Crusade, and men almost forgot the miserable feuds which wrecked the fair prospects of 1191-2 in thinking of the self-denial, the devotion and the chivalrous valour of the great Crusaders of an earlier age.

Thus in little more than a year from the capture of the Holy City had the hero of the First Crusade passed away. Of the other great chiefs, Raymond, Bohemond, Tancred, and Baldwin alone remained in the East. The remainder had hurried home to meet with more or less tragical fates. Robert of Normandy reached his duchy just too late to secure the succession to England on the death of his brother William. Six years later his defeat at Tenchebrai consigned him to lifelong captivity, but even so his name was not forgotten in the Holy Land, where an illegitimate son of his, William by name, played a prominent part under Baldwin I. Robert of Flanders, like his cousin and namesake, reached home by way of Greek territories; eleven years later he was thrown from his horse and killed. Hugh the Great, who had been sent to

Constantinople after the fall of Antioch, shared in the disastrous expedition of nor and died at Tarsus. The recreant Count Stephen of Blois, driven back to the East by his wife's reproaches, took part in the same expedition, and was slain in the great battle of Ramleh (1102). This expedition, which ended so disastrously for the two French counts, must detain us for a little.

The conquest of Jerusalem kindled a warlike enthusiasm in many hearts which had been cold to the impassioned pleading of Urban and Peter. Amongst those who now took up arms was the powerful Duke William of Aquitaine. Religious feeling had not restrained him from the endeavour to turn Count Raymond's absence on the Crusade to his own profit. He is perhaps the first of all the Crusading chiefs who undertook the expedition in the frivolous spirit of the mere adventurer eager for some new thing. The details of this crusade, or series of crusades, are difficult to follow; but first of all a large and unruly horde of Lombards reached Constantinople, and after some riotous conduct, in the course of which they broke into the palace and killed one of the Emperor's pet lions, crossed the Bosphorus. At Nicomedia they were joined by Conrad the Constable of the Emperor Henry, and the two Stephens of Blois and Burgundy.

It was now Whitsuntide, 1101, and the Crusaders, eager to depart, begged Alexius for a guide. He offered them Raymond of St. Gilles, who was present at Constantinople. But when the time for departure arrived a feud broke out between the two divisions. Stephen of Blois was for following the old Crusading track through Iconium to Antioch. The Lombards, however, were seized with a wild desire to push across the highlands of Asia Minor to the realm of Chorazan, by which they probably understood Persia or the region of the Lower Tigris. There they hoped to rescue Bohemond from captivity or, happier still, to seize Bagdad itself. Others, among whom was Ekkehard, our chief authority for this expedition, took alarm at a reported speech of the Emperor

74

Alexius, to the effect that he would let the Franks and the Turks devour one another like dogs; these went by sea from one or other of the Greek ports, and, as Ekkehard says, "Through the Divine mercy, after six weeks we reached the haven of Jaffa."

Raymond threw in his lot with Count Stephen. Three weeks' march through a region of plenty brought them to Ancyra on June 23rd. Here they entered on a waterless and desert region, and from this point their steps were dogged by the Turks, who, shooting from a distance, picked out with their arrows the stragglers and weak. At last the whole rearguard, consisting of seven hundred Lombards, was cut off. Next morning there was a deadly panic, and only Raymond and the Duke of Burgundy volunteered to take the post of danger. Some three weeks later, when the Christians were already near Maresch, not far from Sinope, Raymond was defeated by the Turks, and on the next day rode off with his followers, leaving his fellow Crusaders to fare by themselves. The other leaders, infected by his example, fled in panic, leaving their goods and their very wives as a booty to the Turks. "Ah! what grief was it to see delicate and noble matrons carried off by impious and horrid men—men whose heads were shorn behind and before, whose beards were long and unkempt, and who were like to foul and unclean spirits in conduct."

The two Stephens, Conrad, and the Bishop of Milan got back to Constantinople, where Raymond also presently arrived by sea. The Count of St. Gilles found a general prejudice against him by reason of his alleged desertion, but he excused himself successfully to Alexius on the score of necessity.

Another expedition, under William, Count of Nevers, had reached Constantinople from Brindisi, and marched through Asia Minor in the train of Raymond and his fellows. Count William, with a scanty following, at length reached Antioch on foot, in the autumn of 1101.

Duke William of Aquitaine reached Constantinople a little later than the rest; with him came Welf of Bavaria, the Countess Ida of Austria, and, if we may credit Albert of Aix, 160,000 pilgrims of either sex. This expedition fared worse than their predecessors alike in Europe and in Asia. In the end many thousands were slain or carried off captive by Kilij Arslan. Welf went wandering over the mountains, and hardly escaped with his life; as for the Countess Ida, says Albert of Aix, whether she was carried off or trod to pieces under the feet of horses is unknown to this day; William fled with a single knight, and found shelter near Tarsus till Tancred came and escorted him to Antioch.

The remnants of all these expeditions met at Antioch in March, 1102. "Of so innumerable a host of God's people," writes a survivor, "alas! alas! we do not believe one thousand survived; and these we saw afterwards at Rhodes, Paphos, and other ports, hardly more than bones, but only a few at Jaffa."

VII.

THE LAND AND ITS ORGANISATION.

"A land of settled government,
A land of old and fair renown."
TENNYSON.

THE capture of Jerusalem and the formal constitution of the kingdom which took its name from the Holy City were hardly more than the first stage in the conquest of Palestine. Even at the time of Godfrey's death the Franks held little besides Jerusalem itself, together with the communications with the Byzantine dominions, which they had established in the course of their march south. Though Bohemond at Antioch and Baldwin at Edessa had already secured somewhat more extended sovereignties, the true period of conquest covered the reigns of Godfrey's first two successors. But indeed the whole history of the Frankish rule in Syria was so chequered, that its curtailment at the hands of the reviving power of Mohammedanism had already commenced in one quarter before it could attain its full extension in another. The death of Baldwin II. may be said to mark the moment of greatest extension, when in the words of Abulfaraj, "all was subject to the Franks, from the neighbourhood of Mardin to El Arish on the borders of Egypt." The present is, however, the most convenient place for a description of the territory of the Syrian Franks, always remembering that at no moment did its actual extent coincide with that which was theoretically theirs.

In its entirety the Frankish dominion should have included all the lands that lay between the sea on the west and the desert on the east. This region, taken as a whole, is one of well-marked characteristics, and, despite certain weak points, not ill-suited for defensive occupation. But, as we shall see, the Franks never did occupy it fully, and the neglect or incapacity to do so may without doubt be classed among the causes which prevented the Frankish principalities from maintaining a more permanent existence.

The extreme length of the Frankish territory from the Euphrates to the borders of Egypt was somewhat over five hundred miles. Its breadth, except in the far north, seldom exceeded fifty miles, and was for the most part much less. This extreme attenuation left a long frontier open to attack, and whilst the Mohammedans still held Damascus, Emesa, Hamah, and Aleppo the danger of attack was ever present. Otherwise, so long as the Franks retained their hold on Edessa and had Greeks and Armenians for neighbours in the north-west, the only serious danger would have proceeded from Egypt, a source of trouble to which the later Crusaders at least were keenly alive.

Physically speaking, the land consists of four longitudinal zones. The first is the plain country on the border of the Mediterranean, a region of sandy tracts alternating with wooded lands. This district, which extends to a width of some fifteen miles in the south, gradually narrows to very small dimensions in the region of the ancient Phoenicia, thus to continue to the head of the Gulf of Iskanderoun. In the kingdom proper the district is broken by the height of Carmel, but immediately to the north, in its turn, extends eastward over the fertile plain of Esdraelon. Behind the plain of the coast lies the mountain country which in Palestine proper consists of an undulating district of moderate elevation (1,500 1,800 feet); though with some more striking heights, as those on which the cities of Hebron and Jerusalem are situate, the one lying 3,000 feet, the other some 500 feet less, above the level of the Mediterranean. Behind the Phoenician coast lies the far loftier range of Lebanon, which is continued in the mountains of Ansarieh to the neighbourhood of Antioch. This mountain country rises for the most part gradually on the west, but on the east falls by a steep and rugged descent to the depression which forms the third zone. The valleys of the

78

Orontes, the Litany, and the Jordan, with the Wady-el-Arabah, form a long and deep trench extending in an almost straight line from Antioch to the Gulf of Elim, and broken only by Hermon and the highlands to the south of the Dead Sea. This trench formed the eastern limit of Frankish conquest except in the extreme north, where the county of Edessa spread to the Euphrates and beyond, and in the south, where it comprised the highlands to the east of the Dead Sea and reached to the Gulf of Elim. The fourth zone, that bordering on the desert, included the highlands of Moab and the Djaulan, together with the range of Anti-Lebanon and its eastern slopes. For the most part a high and bleak plateau, it comprises many well-watered and fertile spots, especially in the more northern part, where lay the great Mohammedan cities of Damascus, Emesa, Hamah, and Aleppo.

The Frankish dominions in Syria consisted of four main divisions—the kingdom of Jerusalem proper, the county of Tripoli, the principality of Antioch, and the county of Edessa.

Beginning with the north, we find in Edessa an extensive but ill-defined territory lying on both sides of the Euphrates. On the left bank, besides the proper district of Edessa, it extended northwards to the neighbourhood of Mardin, and in the south to the fertile region of Saruj. On the right bank of the Euphrates its chief territory consisted of the lordship of Joscelin of Courtenay, whose capital was Turbessel, now Tell-basher. The principal fiefs of Edessa were Hatab or Ain-tab, and Tulupe, Coris, Ravendal, Samosata, Bir, and Saruj. The Frankish settlers were not numerous, and confined themselves, as it would seem, to the towns and fortresses; even in Edessa itself they were but few in number. The mass of the population consisted of Armenians and Syrians, and the system of government appears to have remained almost purely Byzantine. Edessa, the capital, is identical with the Rohas of antiquity and the Orfa of modern times. Built on the banks of the Kara Tchai, at the foot of a hill called the Top Dagh, and dominated

79

by a strong castle, Edessa was at once a fortress and a great place of commercial transit. To the Franks it was of supreme importance as commanding the best route from Mesopotamia to Syria.

West of the county of Edessa lay the extensive principality of Antioch. Under the rule of its first princes Antioch was rapidly developed, till by 1130, the moment of its widest extension, it reached on the north-west far into Cilicia, and even included the towns of Tarsus, Adana, and Mamistra; but the conquests of John Comnenus in 1137 confined it within the river Jihun or Pyramus, and later on it was further circumscribed by the growth of the kingdom of Armenia. North-east it marched with Edessa, and south east included beyond the Orontes the territories of Albara, Apamea, and Marra, and, as we shall see, pressed hard on Aleppo itself on the west lay the sea, and south the mountain district of Tripoli. Within these limits were included a great number of dependent fiefs, chief of which were Cerep, Harenc, Hazart, Zerdana, and Marra. On the coast lay the important ports of Laodicea, and Soudin, or St. Simeon, at the mouth of the Orontes, which was the harbour of Antioch. The position of the capital has already been sufficiently described, and it is enough to emphasise here the importance of the principality as the earliest, and perhaps the most permanent, of all the Frankish colonies.

The county of Tripoli formed a strip of territory about a hundred miles in length, and extending from the sea on the west to the Orontes on the east. Its southern boundary was at the Nahr Ibrahim, a little to the north of Beyrout, and at the other extremity it approached to the neighbourhood of Markab. On the east lay the territory of the Assassins and the Mussulman principalities of Hamah and Emesa. Among its fiefs were Arkah, Botron, Jebeil, and Tortosa, and it also included the strong fortresses of Safed and Kerak or Krak des Chevaliers. The town of Tripoli in Crusading times consisted of the actual city on Mount Pilgrim and the more ancient city on a peninsula below. In the thirteenth century it was a great centre of commerce, famous for its schools and for its silk factories, that gave employment to four thousand artisans.

Edessa, Antioch, and Tripoli were all theoretically dependencies of the kingdom of Jerusalem. In Edessa the royal authority was secured from the day when its first count became the second king of Jerusalem. Antioch was to have been held by Bohemond as a dependency of the Byzantine Empire; but the conduct of Alexius gave the Franks a fair excuse for disowning his suzerainty. During the disasters which followed on the death of Roger in 1119, Baldwin II. was called in to defend the unguarded principality, and for some years the king was in fact its governor. In 1126 the second Bohemond married Baldwin's daughter, and on his death a few years later the king, as guardian for his grandchild, received the oaths of all the vassals high and low. From this time Antioch may be considered both legally and politically as a dependency of the kingdom of Jerusalem. Tripoli, as we shall see, passed into the same position, when Raymond's son Bertram appealed to Baldwin I. for aid against William Jordan, and became the king's man. Henceforward its allegiance hardly wavered, except when in 1122 Pons for a while refused obedience to Baldwin II.

The kingdom of Jerusalem properly so called extended along the coast from the Nahr Ibrahim to the Wady-el-Arish. The eastern boundary was formed by the valley of Baccar and the Ghor, or basin of the Jordan and Dead Sea. But in the north the fortress of Banias and the land of Soad lay east of this line, and in the south-east the Franks occupied the land beyond the Dead Sea, and as far south as the Gulf of Elim. The kingdom was divided into four great baronies and twelve lesser lordships. The first were:—(1) the county of Jaffa and Ascalon; (2) the lordship of Kerak and Montreal; (3) the principality of Galilee; (4) the lordship of Sidon. The lesser fiefs were Darum, Hebron or St. Abraham, Arsuf, Caesarea, Nablûs, Bessan or Bethshan, Caimont, Haifa, Toron and Banias, Scandelion, St. George or Lydda, and Beyrout.

The county of Jaffa and Ascalon stretched over the plain of Sharon between the sea and the mountains of Judah, and from the river Leddar to Darum and the desert of Sin. It included the fortresses of Ibelin, Blanchegarde, and Mirabel, and the towns of Gaza, Lydda, and Ramleh. Jaffa was erected into a county by Baldwin I. for his kinsman Hugh de Puiset. After the untimely fate of his son Hugh H., it passed into the royal hands to be revived by Baldwin III. for his brother Amalric, who was already Count of Ascalon. From this time the double county became an appanage of the royal house, and so was held by Guy de Lusignan and Walter de Brienne. The authority of the counts was, however, much circumscribed by the power of the great house of Ibelin. Balian the Bearded, founder of that house, appears in 1120 as Constable of Jaffa, and eventually became lord of Ibelin, Ramleh, and Mirabel. In later days his descendants accumulated many fiefs both in Jerusalem and Cyprus.

The lordship of Kerak and Montreal took its name from the two great fortresses in the land beyond the Dead Sea. Its peculiar importance lay in the fact that the rich caravans from Egypt to Damascus had to pass through its territories, and pay it toll. Its first lord was Roman de Puy, afterwards Fulk gave it to Payn, uncle of Philip of Nablûs. Philip's daughter conveyed it to Reginald of Châtillon, its last and most famous lord. This lordship included the maritime fortress of Elim or Aila, and was eventually united with the lordship of Hebron.

The principality of Galilee besides the district properly so called included the land of Soad beyond Jordan, and had Tiberias or Tabarie for its capital. It contained many important fortresses, such as Safed, La Féve, Forbelet, and Belvoir, and the towns of Nazareth and Sepphoris. Tancred was for a short time Prince of Galilee, afterwards it was held by Hugh of Falkenberg or St Omer, Joscelin of Courtenay before he became Count of Edessa, and William de Bures. Later it returned to the Falkenberg family, and in the thirteenth century passed by marriage to the Ibelins. On its northern borders lay the important lordship of Toron, whose rulers for four generations were called Henfrid, and were long constables of the kingdom.

The lordship of Sidon was bounded on the north by the Damour, on the west by the sea, on the east and south by the Litany. It included the strongholds of Beaufort and the Cave of Tyron, with the towns of Sidon and Sarepta. It was first granted to Eustace Grener, who was lord of Caesarea. Eustace married a niece of the Patriarch Arnulf; of his two sons, Walter became lord of Caesarea and Gerard of Sidon.

The immediate royal domain comprised, besides Jerusalem and its neighbourhood, including Nablûs, the two great cities of Tyre and Acre, the latter of which became in the thirteenth century the capital of the Latin colonies in Syria.

Of the city of Jerusalem itself detailed accounts from the hands of one pilgrim or another during the Crusading period are not wanting. Chief among these are the narratives of John of Wurzburg, who visited Palestine between 1160 and 1170, and one Theoderic, who came a few years later. But perhaps we can for the present purpose take no better guide than a Norman-French description of the state of the Holy Places and the city of Jerusalem as they were on the day that Saladin and the Saracens conquered them from the Christians. Mediaeval Jerusalem had four chief gates—David's gate on the west, the Golden gate on the east, and St. Stephen's and Sion gates on the north and south. The pilgrim who had arrived from Jaffa would enter by the first named, with the Tower of David on his right, and would soon reach Patriarch Street on the left, where the Patriarch had his palace, and which also led to the Church of the Holy Sepulchre and the Hospital of the Knights of St. John. David Street itself led into" Temple Street, and so to the Temple enclosure or Haram, wherein was the Templum Domini, together with the royal palace or Templum Salomonis, and the House of the Knights Templars. The Temple enclosure lay upon the eastern wall and the Golden gate opened directly into it. The northern gate, or St. Stephen's, was that by which the pilgrims who came up from Acre entered; from this gate St. Stephen's Street ran into the heart of the city. At its southern end, on the left, were three narrow vaulted ways, the Rue Couverte, where the Latin merchants sold cloth goods; the Rue des Herbes, which was the market for all vegetables, fruits, and spices; and the Rue Malcuisinat, where the hungry pilgrim could obtain his food. From this point two streets ran south to the gate of Mount Sion.

There were in the city of Jerusalem or its vicinity no less than thirty-seven churches, many of which, as those of St. Anne, St. Maria Majora, and St. Mary Magdalen, were built during the Christian occupation.

But churches are far from being the only buildings of the Crusading period which have survived. The Tower of David is the Castle of the Pisans erected early in the twelfth century, Tancred's Tower survives as the Kalât Jâlûd in the north-west angle of the present city, and the Malcuisinat is a Crusading erection which still forms the meat bazaar. But the zeal of the Crusaders devoted itself above all else to the glorifying of the Church of the Holy Sepulchre. The existing church is mainly their work, and until the great fire in 1808 stood practically uninjured. They gathered into one building all the sacred sites of Golgotha and the Resurrection, and adorned the new buildings with rich mosaics and enamels wrought by Greek artists. Within the church, near the Adam Chapel, were the tombs of the Christian kings from Godfrey to Baldwin V., which were much injured by the Charismians in 1244, and finally destroyed by Greek jealousy after the fire. Both the Templum Domini and the Templum Salomonis, or Aksa Mosque, were also altered and beautified in Crusading times; but much of the Christian work was defaced or destroyed when these buildings were restored to Mohammedan worship. But in both some mediaeval Christian work still survives, and among other remains in the Haram enclosure are those of the magnificent refectory of the Templars.

84

The organisation of the kingdom of Jerusalem was feudalism in its purest form, the great feudatories duly receiving and observing their rights and obligations. The collection of usages devised for its governance are known as the Assizes of Jerusalem, and give us our most perfect picture of an ideal feudal state. Not that they describe the kingdom as it ever actually existed, for indeed the Assizes only began to take their present shape when the thirteenth century was well advanced, and were the work not of the kings of Jerusalem, but of the jurisconsults of Cyprus. Chief among these lawyers were Philip of Navarre and John of Ibelin, nephew and namesake of the famous head of that house in the time of Frederic II. According to the story preserved by John of Ibelin, Godfrey de Bouillon, by the counsel of the Patriarch of Jerusalem and of the princes and barons, appointed wise men to make inquiry of the Crusaders from the various countries of Europe as to what usages prevailed in their several lands. The result of this inquiry was put in writing, and formed the basis of the "Assizes and usages which Godfrey ordered to be maintained and used in the kingdom of Jerusalem, by the which he and his men, and his people, and all other manner of people going, coming, and dwelling in his kingdom of Jerusalem were to be governed and guarded." Thus there were composed two codes, one for the nobles and the other for the bourgeois, which were deposited in a coffer in the Church of the Holy Sepulchre at Jerusalem, and from the place of the keeping called "Lettres du Sepulcre." The coffer was not to be opened except for the purposes of consulting or modifying the law, and that only in the presence of nine persons who were carefully specified, and of whom the king and patriarch were two. The laws thus carefully made were afterwards from time to time modified by Godfrey and his successors, and especially by Baldwin I. and Amalric I. On the occasion of the capture of Jerusalem by Saladin these two precious volumes were destroyed, and thus all written record of the legislation perished. But owing to the circumstance that the knowledge of the written law was not a matter of common property, there had grown up in the courts of the kingdom a body of usages and customs based upon oral tradition. These usages and customs were carefully collected by the great jurisconsults of the thirteenth century, and their writings formed the basis of the extant Assizes.

There are, however, in the Assizes certain salient features which may be safely ascribed to Godfrey or his immediate successors. Such are the prescription of constant military service—not merely for a fixed part of each year—and the rules intended to prevent the concentration of fiefs in a single hand, and to secure that each fief should be able to render its requisite service. These ordinances were very essential for the safeguarding of a conquered country, and though they failed in their purpose, the history of the kingdom illustrates well their necessity; their failure, inevitable though it may have been, was indeed a main cause of the downfall of the kingdom.

More important, however, in the present connection than the actual laws, is the system of government and organisation which was established. At the head of the kingdom stood the king, whose legal title was "Rex Latinorum in Hierusalem," King of the Latins in Jerusalem. Next to him in dignity came the Seneschal, whose duty was primarily to hold the king's sceptre on the coronation day, and to see to the due ordering of the coronation feast. He also owed services—somewhat like the English custom—at the four great annual feasts. As a great officer of justice the seneschal was supreme over all the bailiffs in the kingdom; he looked after the king's rents, and visited the royal castles, with power to appoint and remove the castellans; in the king's absence he presided at muster and foray. Second of the great officers was the Constable, who held the king's horse at the coronation, and, as head of the royal army, ordered the battle in the king's absence, and was responsible for the maintenance of military discipline. The Marshal assisted the constable on the coronation day, and was more or less subordinate to him in ordinary times. It was his duty to engage knights and sergeants for the royal service. The Chamberlain robed the king on coronation day, and had to see to the homage of the king's vassals. Other officers were the Butler, the Forester, and the Chancellor. The last, in this respect differing from the early English custom, often retained his post after he had been rewarded with one of the great bishoprics.

Similar functionaries existed in the great dependencies; Antioch had its own constable, marshal, and a special officer called "*dux*" or duke; whilst in a charter of Joscelin II. of Edessa, Robert the Constable, and Hubert the Marshal, appear among the witnesses. Even the smaller baronies within the realm of Jerusalem itself had each its own officials, who, as in the case of Galilee, attested their lord's charters. Every great baron would have his leaden seal, and it is perhaps with a touch of shame that Hugh of Ibelin borrows the seal of his lord Amalric because he "had no seal" of his own.

For the administration of justice there was at Jerusalem a High Court, over which the king himself presided, or in his absence one of the great officers. This court, intended in the first place to have jurisdiction over the great lords, gradually came to concern itself with all that related to the political and civil administration of the kingdom, and was, in fact, the king's Council of State. In the country generally the administration of law and justice was in the hands of certain of the lords who had, in technical language, the right to hold a court, coin money, and do justice. The lords themselves presided in their seignorial courts, where they dealt with criminal cases in accordance with the customs and laws observed in the High Court, to which they were subordinate. In addition to the High Court there was also established in Jerusalem and all other towns where the Frankish settlers were sufficiently numerous, Courts of the Burgesses. These courts were presided over by officers called Viscount, and were concerned with the civil jurisdiction. The viscount was the representative of the lord; his office was often hereditary, and in some cases, as at Nablûs, he was a man of noble family. In addition to his judicial functions the viscount had charge of the revenue, and through his assistant, who was called the "Mathessep," was entrusted with the police. Other courts were those of the *Fonde* for commercial jurisdiction, under a bailiff; of the *Chaine* for maritime business, instituted by Amalric I.; and the Syrian Court, or Court of the Reïs. No doubt the courts of the Fonde and the Reïs were largely governed by local custom, though the Assizes of the Court of the Burgesses were held to be of force in them. Wherever the Syrians were not sufficiently numerous to form a community under a Reïs, the Fonde constituted their special court. This elaborate organisation with its criminal, civil, and commercial jurisdiction, formed in its entirety a system that was superior to anything of the kind which then existed in the West.

The judicial institutions of the subordinate principalities closely resembled those of the kingdom proper. The Prince of Antioch had, like the King of Jerusalem, both his High Court and Court of the Burgesses. The Assizes of Antioch were, however, distinct; they served likewise for the kingdom of Armenia, and no doubt also for the county of Tripoli. Edessa also had, we may assume, a similar body of law, but its existence as a Frankish state was probably too short for the growth of an equally elaborate organisation.

As for the commercial colonies in the cities on the coast, they had special privileges and their own civil courts presided over by bailiffs, consuls or viscounts. But of these it will be more convenient to speak in a later place.

The pressure of warfare made finance a question of great importance in the Latin colonies of Syria. Baldwin I. was, as we shall see, much crippled by lack of money, and again in the last days of the kingdom its

88

rulers had to seek pecuniary aid from the West. There was, however, a regularly organised financial service, called "La Secrète," managed by a bailiff and a staff of clerks or writers. Chief among the sources of revenue were the customs; the Assizes of Jerusalem specify in articles on which duty was paid at Acre. Ibn Jubair thus describes a visit to that city in 1184: "On our arrival we were taken to the custom-house. Opposite the door there sat on a covered bench the clerks of the custom, who are Christians; they had ink-pots of ebony, gilded and handsomely decorated, and wrote in the Arabic language, which they spoke well. Their head, who farms the customs, is called simply their chief, and has to pay a very heavy sum to the government. The merchants deposited their goods in a store above the custom-house; private travellers were allowed to pass after an examination of their baggage. The officials did their work courteously and without violence or exaction." In addition to the customs there were market dues, and tolls on caravans levied by the various lords. Other sources of revenue were the monopolies on various industries, such as dyeing, tanning, brewing; the tallage paid by the native Syrians; a poll-tax on the Mohammedans and Jews. On special occasions also the royal treasury had resort to an extraordinary tallage; such was the great levy for the defence of the kingdom in 1183, of which William of Tyre has left a minute account. One per cent, on movables was to be paid by all who had property worth a hundred besants; those who had less were to pay one besant for hearth-tax; the churches, monasteries, barons, and their vassals were to pay 2 per cent, on their rents. The hearth-tax fell upon the country-folk, who dwelt in the casals or villages; the lord of each casal was to so apportion the tax that the rich should not escape, nor the poor be oppressed. Two treasurers were appointed at Jerusalem and Acre to see that the money was applied only to defence against invasion, and not to the petty business of the realm. The special character of this census was marked by a proviso that it was not to be taken as a precedent, and during its operation the ordinary tallages on churches and towns were to be suspended. We, however, hear of other extraordinary levies, as for the equipment of a fleet, and the building of walls and towers.

As might be expected from the circumstances of their origin, the Latin colonies boasted an ecclesiastical organisation not less elaborate than the civil. One of the first acts of the Crusaders was to establish Latin bishops in the conquered cities, following for this purpose the divisions of the ancient Oriental churches. At the head of the Latin hierarchy were the two patriarchs of Jerusalem and Antioch. Under the former were four archbishoprics of which Tyre and Caesarea were the chief, and nine bishoprics; under the latter four archbishoprics and seven bishoprics. In each patriarchate there were also numerous abbeys and priories of the Latin rite. In addition to these the hierarchies of the Armenian, Syrian, and Greek rites still subsisted. Despite their external divisions it is noticeable that the Christians were all animated by a very conciliatory spirit, which at one time promised to lead to a general reunion. For the rest it is enough to state that the powers and pretensions of the clergy were not less remarkable than those exercised or assumed by their Western brethren, and that from successive donations they acquired vast estates, not only in Syria, but also in every country of Western Europe.

VIII.

THE CONQUEST OF THE LAND—BALDWIN I. (1100-1118.)

"Baldwinus qui parum ab optimo, qui unquam fuerit, milite distaret."—WILLIAM
OF MALMESBURY.

THE succession to the kingdom was not allowed to pass undisputed
on Godfrey's death. Dagobert of Pisa, who had supplanted Arnulf in the
patriarchate, and whose ecclesiastical pretensions were of the loftiest
nature, dreamt that in Bohemond he might find a second Guiscard to
defend a second Gregory. But the Crusaders at Jerusalem refused to
recognise any lord except one of Godfrey's race. They held the Tower of
David against the patriarch, and summoned Baldwin of Edessa to come
and take possession of his rights. Baldwin accepted the offer, and
leaving Edessa to his cousin and namesake, Baldwin du Bourg, started
for Antioch on the 26th of September; thence, despite the opposition of
Dukak of Damascus, with whom he had to fight a severe battle in the
tortuous passes of Lebanon above Beyrout, he made his way to
Jerusalem. The magnificence of his reception in his new capital was
only marred by the hostility of Dagobert; there was, however, no further
opposition to his recognition as king.

But king though Baldwin was in name, he had yet to conquer his
kingdom. From the first he had to contend with two great obstacles,
lack of money and lack of men. The internal history of his reign is to a
large extent the story of how he overcame these difficulties.

On leaving Edessa Baldwin had only been accompanied by two
hundred knights and seven hundred foot, whilst three months later at
Jerusalem he could only muster another hundred knights. The
Mohammedans themselves do not seem to have ever collected large
armies, though they greatly outnumbered the Christians. Thus at Jaffa
in 1100 they were eleven thousand horse and twenty-one thousand foot

to two hundred and forty knights and nine hundred foot, and at Ramleh twenty thousand against two hundred. "To all," says Fulcher, "it appears to be a palpable and truly wondrous miracle that we could live among so many millions, making them our subjects and tributaries." Had Baldwin been dependent solely on the French and German soldiers who stayed with him in Palestine, he could not long have held his own. But aggressive operations on a large scale were almost uniformly carried out with the aid of Crusading fleets from Italy, England, or Norway. Thus two hundred ships under Harding the Englishman, Bernhard of Galatia, and Hadewerck the Westphalian, saved Baldwin from the consequences of his rash daring at Jaffa in 1102. An English and North German fleet helped him at the siege of Sidon in 1107, and the fall of that city three years later was due to the assistance of Sigurd the Norwegian. More important still were the services rendered by the Italians. The Genoese helped in the capture of Caesarea (1101), Tortosa (1102), Acre (1104), Tripoli (1109), and other places. The Pisans fought for Bohemond at Laodicea, and for Raymond's successors at Tripoli. The Venetians, who under their doge had met the dying Godfrey at Jaffa, were present at the siege of Sidon, and were the moving force at the conquest of Tyre in the next reign. All these allies reaped large rewards; Baldwin granted the Genoese streets in Jerusalem and Jaffa, together with their part of Caesarea, Arsuf, and other towns; the same king promised his Italian confederates one street in the towns they helped to conquer, and a third share of the booty; in 1124 the Venetians bargained for still higher privileges, and were promised a street, oven, and bath in every city whether belonging to king or noble.

In his early years Baldwin must have relied very largely on the members of his own and Godfrey's household. The need of supplying these and other mercenaries with money forced the king, on many occasions, to injustice and robbery. The easiest way of procuring funds was by taking tribute of the unconquered towns. Thus Godfrey had received tribute from Ascalon, Caesarea, and Arsûf; Baldwin himself raised the siege of Sidon for money in 1107. However, despite these and other payments, the king's impecuniosity brought him into serious conflict with the patriarch. Dagobert's pretensions had offended even the pious Godfrey, and his hostility to Baldwin was yet more bitter. It was only after long bickerings that Dagobert had consented to anoint the new king, and when a little later Baldwin demanded that he should furnish forty knights for the war, the patriarch treated his message with contempt. The indignant king broke into the patriarch's banqueting-room, and threatened to tear down the golden ornaments of the Sepulchre if his demands were not complied with. Dagobert unwillingly promised thirty knights, but soon after broke his word and fled to Tancred. Evremar, who then succeeded to the patriarchate, worked well with the king for a long time, but eventually lost the royal favour, and was in his turn supplanted by Gibelin.

Through his want of money Baldwin was frequently driven to have recourse to promiscuous plunder. In 1108 he made a night attack on the great Egyptian caravan beyond the Jordan, and carried off thirty-two camels laden with sugar, honey, and oil to Jerusalem. On another occasion William, bastard son of Robert of Normandy, brought a like benefit to the royal treasury. Worse still, after promising protection to the men of Tyre as they were carrying their treasures to Damascus for safety, the king adopted the base maxim that "truth need not be kept with unbelievers," and robbed them on the way. In 1113 Baldwin sought to improve his shattered finances in another manner, by marrying Adela, widow of Count Roger of Sicily. Albert of Aix draws a glowing picture of the state in which she reached Acre Her vessels were laden with gold and gems, while her own ship had its mast covered with pure gold. She brought a thousand skilled warriors to aid in the royal wars, and not content with helping her husband, she gave a thousand marks and five hundred besants to Roger of Antioch. But after three years, finding herself unable to live with the king, she returned home.

Baldwin's reign was one of continued activity; every year saw him engaged in fresh enterprises, and exploring fresh fields for conquest. His chief dangers lay on the south west and north east of his kingdom. In the former region he had to keep up a perpetual struggle with Ascalon, whence the Egyptian garrison sallied out by land or sea on every opportunity. Even before his coronation Baldwin had been compelled to lead an expedition against the town. In 1101 he had renewed the warfare with the cities of the coast. Chiefly through the valour of the Genoese seamen Caesarea was captured with but short delay. Thence a reported invasion called Baldwin south; it was not, however, for four months that the Egyptians took the field near Jaffa with eleven thousand horse and twenty-one thousand foot. To meet this host the king could only muster two hundred and forty knights and nine hundred foot soldiers; but, says Fulcher, "having God on our side, we did not fear to attack them." Three times the Christians were driven back, but when the king led out his fifth battalion in person, the Egyptians lost heart and fled before him. Abbot Gerhard, who this day bore the Holy Cross, told Ekkehard that the arrows fell around the king like snow, and everywhere the enemy melted from his face like wax (September 7, 1101). Undismayed at their defeat, the Egyptians renewed the war next year. Baldwin was then at Jaffa, whence the Aquitanian Crusaders, after spending Easter at Jerusalem, were on the point of departing. William of Aquitaine was already gone; the two Stephens, however, were still there, and those who but now were eager to depart, caught gladly at the chance of striking a last blow against the Saracen. But, though there were many knights in Jaffa, there were but few horses; and, as Baldwin would not wait to muster his footmen, he had no more than two hundred knights with him when he marched out to Ramleh. Despite the numbers of the enemy the Christians by the fury of their first onset nearly carried the day, but all to no purpose, for within one short hour they were in their turn routed or slain. Baldwin himself, accompanied by four knights, forced his way out of Ramleh, and after wandering over the hills came on the second night to Arsûf. Of his companions only one now remained, and the watchmen on the walls refused to believe that it was indeed their king till they had lit a torch, and thus recognised Baldwin as he stood with head uncovered. The two Stephens and many other knights were slain during the battle or after.

After this battle, Ramleh fell into the hands of the Saracens, and Jaffa was seriously threatened. Baldwin was in great anxiety, for the loss of that town would have involved the downfall of Jerusalem. By land he could not journey, but there was less difficulty by sea. At Arsuf he embarked on May 29th, with a certain English pirate, Godric by name, in whom we may fairly recognise our own English saint, Godric of Finchale. With banner displayed, he boldly sailed into Jaffa, despite the opposition of thirty Egyptian galleys that strove to bar his way. It was a daring exploit that only the urgent necessity could justify. The Saracens almost at once withdrew to a little distance from the walls. Reinforcements gradually arrived from Jerusalem and from Arsûf; and when in the early days of July the great fleet under Harding the Englishman arrived, Baldwin could once more take the field, and retrieve the disaster of Ramleh by a complete victory. Later in the year, when Tancred and Baldwin of Edessa had come to his aid, the king even felt strong enough to make an attack, though with little effect, on Ascalon itself Eight years later, Baldwin nearly secured, by the treachery of the governor, what he could not obtain by force. The governor was, however, slain by the townsmen, and Ascalon remained a constant source of anxiety for many years to come.

The years that followed the battle of Ramleh were chiefly marked by the capture of Acre and siege of Sidon. Further north the warfare with Damascus was waged by deputy rather than in person. When Tancred was called away to rule Antioch for Bohemond, Baldwin had conferred the lordships of Galilee and Tiberias on Hugh of Falkenberg, a warrior from North-eastern France. This Hugh had fought with Baldwin at Ramleh and before Jaffa in 1102. In his own lordship he imitated Tancred's example by a desultory warfare. After a raid in the summer of 1107, he had drawn off his booty as far as Banias, when the Turks came down upon him. Unarmoured and heedless of his numerical weakness, Hugh turned to meet them; an arrow pierced his breast, and he breathed his last in the midst of the foe. This disaster called Baldwin north, and gave the men of Ascalon a chance, which they were not slow to take advantage of. The lordship of Tiberias was now bestowed on Gervase, another French knight Gervase next year fell into an ambush and was carried captive to Damascus; Tughtakin, the atabek, demanded as the price of his release Acre, Haifa, and Tiberias. Baldwin, in reply, offered one hundred thousand besants, but he would give up no Christian territory, not even to release his mother's son. Gervase was shot to death at Damascus, and then the king restored his lordship to Tancred. During these years Tughtakin, though formidable in the north, had concerned himself little with the warfare in Southern Palestine; however, it was his intervention which saved Sidon in 1107, and Tyre three years later.

Towards the close of his reign, Baldwin was much occupied in Arabia. In 1115 he built the famous stronghold of Montreal, or Shobek, beyond the Dead Sea. In the following year he led two hundred knights yet further south, being anxious to gaze on the waters of the Red Sea, which he had not yet seen. They marched as far as Elim, whose inhabitants put out to sea in little boats on their approach. Fulcher, with the curiosity natural to him, eagerly cross-examined the travellers on their return home, and gazed in astonishment at the "sea-shells" and little stones which they brought back with them: "I questioned them closely, with eager heart, as to the nature of the Red Sea; for I had

96

hitherto doubted whether its waters were fresh or salt, and whether it was a pool or a lake—with exit and entrance like that of Galilee."

Baldwin's last years were filled with disasters. The years 1114 and 1115 were marked by great earthquakes. In 1117 a plague of locusts devastated the crops and vines. The following June saw a blood-red moon change to black; and in December there was an aurora borealis, so bright that Fulcher and his friends saw the surrounding country as clear as in the day: "We conjectured it to portend the shedding of much blood in battle, or some other speedily approaching disaster; but what is uncertain we commit with all humility to the Lord's keeping." A little later, Fulcher knew the true meaning of these portents; for next year there died Pope Paschal, King Baldwin, Adela his wife, the Patriarch Arnulf, and the Emperor Alexius.

Early in 1118, Baldwin determined to attack Egypt, hoping through a bold stroke at the heart of this wealthy kingdom to force Ascalon to submission. He plundered the city of El Farema, but could proceed no further. Some fish caught in the Nile disagreed with his digestion, and the consequent illness awoke the trouble from an old wound in his side. Unable to ride on horseback, his followers placed him in a litter; the horns blew the signal for retreat, and the little army turned slowly back towards Jerusalem. At El Arish Baldwin died; his body was embalmed and carried home to rest in the Church of the Holy Sepulchre by his brother Godfrey. It was Palm Sunday when the cavalcade, as it drew near the Holy City, met the solemn procession winding down in ancient fashion from the Mount of Olives to the valley of Jehoshaphat. The songs of joy were soon turned to the wail of woe, and Franks, Syrians, and even Saracens, wept for the fate of the great king.

Baldwin I. was, like Saul, of a very lofty stature; a man, brown haired and brown bearded, but with a somewhat white complexion. His nose was aquiline, his mouth peculiar, for the teeth in the lower jaw were drawn back. He was neither over-stout nor over-broad. His bearing betokened a man of dignity, and the "chlamys" hanging down from his shoulders stamped him as a person of importance, even to strangers. "He looked," says William of Tyre, "more like a bishop than a layman." His private life was licentious, though he had the prudence to keep this fact from the outer world. But he was a warrior *sans peur*, if not *sans reproche*, and was lavish in his generosity. He was indeed the very type of the twelfth-century knight-errant: eager after adventure, reckless of his own life, craving for excitement. His rashness more than once threatened not only himself, but his kingdom with ruin. He trusted in himself more than he ought, and lacked the "modesty" requisite for the prudent king and wise general. But from the pictorial point of view, no king in all history stands out in more glowing colours. We can see him striking down the Saracens at Ramleh; stripping off his armour to find it soaked and clotted with gore; mounted on his fleet Arab, "the Gazelle," wandering over the hills by midnight, and with the dawn standing beneath the walls of Arsûf; sailing on to Jaffa in his little vessel, with the royal banner displayed full in view of the hostile fleet. No obstacles could daunt his valour. Once, between Caesarea and Jaffa, he met sixty Saracen horsemen laden with spoil. Amongst their burden he espied the head of a Christian knight. This sight scattered all prudence to the winds; though he had but two horsemen with him, Baldwin attacked the Saracens and drove them back to Ascalon. His favourite sport was hunting, and it was while pursuing this recreation, in July, 1103, that he received from some Saracens, who lay in ambush, the wound that troubled him to his death.

Baldwin had been brought up as a priest, and even held preferment in the diocese of Cambray. But his later life belied the mildness of his youth, and showed little of the priestly spirit. He can hardly have been loved by the people of Edessa, and it is a speaking fact that his biographer and friend, Fulcher, refuses to say a word as to the means by which he became ruler of Edessa. But whatever his blemishes, he was a great warrior, a true knight-errant, with all the accomplishments and all the stains inseparable from his calling.

IX.

THE CONQUEST OF THE LAND—THE FRANKS IN NORTHERN SYRIA.

"Sciebant milites nostros esse probissimos bellatores, et mirabiles de lanceis percussores."—FULCHER OF CHARTRES.

WHEN Bohemond was taken prisoner by Ibn Danishmend Tancred left his lordship in Galilee and went north to rule Antioch for his kinsman in March, 1101. He acted with a vigour sprung from the desire to conquer on his own behalf against the day of Bohemond's release. Laodicea was captured from the Greeks after a siege of eighteen months, whilst Mamistra, Adana, and Tarsus were also recovered from the Emperor, into whose hands they had once more lapsed.

Alexius can hardly have regarded these proceedings with equanimity; and there is therefore less ground for distrusting the almost contemporary story that he endeavoured to get Ibn Danishmend's prisoner into his own hands. Bohemond, hearing of the offer, secured his own freedom by outbidding his would-be purchaser. Thenceforward he was the sworn foe of the Christian Emperor, and perhaps the half-ally and tributary of the Turkish lord; thus there came about a curious combination in which Bohemond and Ibn Danishmend were united against Alexius and Kilij Arslan of Rum.

It was early in 1103 that Bohemond was released. In the following year he was called to the aid of Baldwin du Bourg. That noble had received the county of Edessa when his cousin and namesake was called to the kingdom of Jerusalem; Joscelin de Courtenay, another cousin, at the same time obtained the second Baldwin's old territory to the west of the Euphrates. Edessa was as it were an outpost in the enemy's country, and its fields were exposed to yearly ravages. In the hope of preventing this constant loss Baldwin determined to garrison Harran,

100

and accordingly invited Bohemond, Tancred, and Joscelin to join in an expedition.

The feuds of the Turkish emirs left the Franks to pursue their conquests near the Euphrates with comparative immunity. The contest for the sultanate had continued till January, 1104, when Malek Shah's two sons, Barkiyarok and Mohammed, were reconciled and divided their ruined inheritance. In this time of confusion each emir had enough to do to hold his own, and had little time for concerting plans against the common foe. At Mosul, Corbogha had given place to Jekermish, while further north Sokman ibn Ortok held sway at Hisn Keifa. Further west things were in much the same state of disorder. Ridhwan, son of Tutush and nephew of Malek Shah, was prince of Aleppo, whilst Tughtakin ruled Damascus in the name of Ridhwan's nephew, son of his brother Dukak; Hems or Emesa was under an emir named Janch ed-Dauleh. On the coast the Egyptians were recovering much of their lost ground. In the absence of any real central power the Franks had full chance to spread and prosper; and, holding as it were the balance between the rival parties, were not slow to realise the strength of their position.

However, on this occasion Sokman and Jekermish abandoned their feud to rescue Harran. In a desperate battle outside that city Baldwin and Joscelin were taken prisoners, whilst Bohemond and his nephew fled to Edessa, where the Christians then chose Tancred for their lord. The battle of Harran had a disastrous effect on the principality of Antioch; the Greeks once more recovered Adana, Mamistra, and Tarsus, whilst Ridhwan on the south ravaged Artah and captured Kafer Tab. Bohemond declared his intention of seeking help across the sea, and accordingly, towards the end of 1104, left Syria never to return. Going to France, he married Constance, daughter of Philip I., and by his promises of rich fiefs induced many nobles to join him. With a large army he laid siege to Durazzo in October, 1107. A year later he was forced to return to Italy, and died in nil, leaving two sons by his wife Constance. Of these John, the elder, died young; the second, Bohemond, survived to receive his father's principality fifteen years later.

Tancred had been left to rule Antioch with disheartened subjects and an exhausted treasury; by skilful management he contrived to replenish his own coffers from those of the wealthy citizens, and by the example of his self-denial inspired his subjects with fresh confidence. His first exploit was to recover Artah and the neighbouring strongholds from Ridhwan. Thus he became the greatest lord of Northern Syria; he was master of Antioch, Tellbasher, and Edessa, whilst Aleppo itself could hardly have held out much longer but for the quarrels of the Franks and the coming of Maudud to Mosul.

Death and dissension worked also for Tancred in the ranks of his Mohammedan rivals. Ibn Danishmend and Sokman ibn Ortok both died in 1104-5; whilst, by the decease of Barkiyarok, Mohammed had become sole Sultan. Jekermish at Mosul had lost the vigour of his youth, and Ridhwan took advantage of his weakness to form a league against him; but the project was frustrated by the craft of Jekermish. In the meantime Mohammed had conferred Mosul on one of his own officers, Javaly Secava, who defeated Jekermish beneath the walls of the city. The citizens, steadfast to the end, appealed for aid to Kilij Arslan of Rum. Kilij Arslan relieved Mosul, but in June or July, 1107, was, through the treachery of his allies, defeated by Javaly near the river Khabur. Javaly then became lord of Mosul, to be supplanted a year later by the Sultan's brother, Maudud, with whom was soon afterwards associated his nephew, Masud.

On Maudud's approach Javaly took refuge with Il-Ghazi, lord of Mardin and brother of Sokman, but finding little support turned towards the Franks. He had the means of purchasing their support ready to hand in Baldwin of Edessa, who had become his captive on the fall of Jekermish. A bargain was struck, and Joscelin de Courtenay, who

102

had already been set free, came back as hostage for his overlord. Tancred would not surrender Edessa to its old lord, and Javaly, eager to score every point, released Joscelin also. Thereon Tancred called Ridhwan of Aleppo to his aid, and thus, near Tell-basher, a battle was fought, in which Mohammedan strove with Mohammedan, Frank with Frank. In the end Tancred was victorious. Javaly, driven from the field, made his way across the desert to Ispahan; winding-sheet in hand he prayed humbly for his life; Mohammed forgave him, as he could well afford to do, for Maudud had by now captured Mosul.

After the battle of Tell-basher Baldwin went back to Edessa, where he was soon threatened by a new and more serious danger. Early in mo Maudud appeared before his walls with an immense host. For a hundred days he pressed the city hard. King Baldwin of Jerusalem was appealed to for aid, but would not leave Palestine till he had taken Beyrout, which was on the point of falling. Directly he was master of the city the king gathered his army and crossed the Euphrates with eleven thousand men. With him came Bertram of Tripoli, the Armenian prince Kogh Vasil, and Tancred, who in such an emergency crushed down his feelings of hatred and jealousy. At their approach Maudud retired to Harran, "knowing that our knights were warriors of prowess and wondrous smiters with the lance."

A few days sufficed to garrison Edessa, and the royal army turned its steps homewards, followed however, by many Armenians who feared to stay in such an exposed city. At the Euphrates only two vessels were found wherewith to cross the river. Whilst some five thousand unarmed Armenians still remained on the left bank, the Turks suddenly appeared; what followed was a massacre rather than a battle. The river ran red with blood, and all the time the king's troops stood looking on from the opposite bank, grieving, but unable to lend any aid to their perishing comrades.

Meantime in Tancred's absence Ridhwan had broken the truce. Tancred on his return speedily compelled the emir to purchase peace at the price of twenty thousand dinars, and in a fresh invasion next year reduced Aleppo to a state of terror. The clamour of the unhappy Mohammedans reached the ears of the Caliph at Bagdad. Fugitives from Aleppo burst into the Great Mosque at Bagdad, and tore down the ironwork from the screen of the Caliph himself. About the same time, so an Arabic writer says, there came an envoy from Constantinople to Bagdad urging the Caliph to make war against the Franks. The populace in their fury crowded round the Sultan, reproaching him for his slackness in the service of God. "The very infidels," they said, "showed more zeal for the Holy War than did he."

This disturbance led in 1111 to a great expedition, which besieged Tell-basher under the command of Maudud. But dissension and death paralysed his efforts, whilst Ridhwan, after appealing to him for aid, shut the gates of Aleppo in his face.

Tancred continued his career of conquest at the expense of Aleppo. Early in 1112 he captured a fortress near that city itself, but died at the close of the year, on December 12th, whilst warring with the Armenian Kogh Vasil. Antioch should by right have gone to the young Bohemond; but the times were too troublous for a child of four or five to hold his own, and Roger Fitz Richard, Tancred's sister's son, succeeded with little opposition.

Maudud, after ravaging the neighbourhood of Edessa, gathered a great host, and in June, 1113, laid siege to Tiberias in Galilee. Baldwin summoned Roger to his aid, and himself started from Acre. The Turks drew the king into an ambush, and, according to the Arabic account, Baldwin was actually taken prisoner, but his ignorant captor, in greed for spoil, suffered his greatest prize to escape. The royal banner and tent were taken, whilst Baldwin, with the remnants of his host, took refuge on a neighbouring hill. There he was presently joined by the reinforcements from Antioch, but for six-and-twenty days he dared not move. Meanwhile the light Turkish horsemen were flying over all the land from Jerusalem to Acre. At last, when provisions began to fail, Maudud retired to Damascus (September 19th), intending to remain there till the spring. Soon afterwards, as he entered the mosque accompanied by Tughtakin, an assassin sprang out and dealt him several blows. The wounded prince was carried to the atabek's palace; recognising that his end was near, he refused all food, declaring that he desired to appear before God fasting. "Maudud," says a contemporary Christian historian, "was a man of great wealth and power. He was most famous among the Turks and subtle in his actions. But he could not resist the will of God, who, though He suffered him to scourge us for our sins, decreed that he should die a mean death, and perish by a feeble hand."

Rumour ascribed the crime to Tughtakin. Nor was the charge against the atabek confined to Mohammedan lands, for Ibn El-Athir had heard from his father that Baldwin in his indignation wrote to Tughtakin: "A people that is capable of destroying its mainstay, and of slaying him in the house of God, deserves to be cut off from the earth."

Ridhwan of Aleppo died soon after, on December 10th. The eunuch Lulu administered the government for ten months in the name of Ridhwan's young son. Alp Arslan. Then he slew his master, and set up his brother, Sultan Shah, a child of six, in his place. Aleppo was during this time in great distress, and Tughtakin would vouchsafe no aid. "Strange it was," writes the Arabic historian, "that among so many princes, none could be found to accept so rich a possession, and defend it against the Franks. But the princes wished to prolong the French occupation, so as to keep themselves in power." At last the Sultan despatched a vast army under El-Borsoki, the new governor of Mosul, with whom was associated Zangi, the future conqueror of Edessa.

Meantime there had been a general reformation at Antioch. The conscience of its citizens was awakened not less by the terrible earthquakes, which towards the close of 1114 shook the whole Levant, than by the approach of Borsac, lord of Hamadan, whom Mohammed sent in May, 1115, at the head of a fresh army to support El-Borsoki. At the patriarch's call, with bare feet and streaming eyes, they passed from church to church in long processions. Roger further made alliance with the discontented Mohammedan princes, Tughtakin, who feared to be punished for Maudud's death, and Il-Ghazi of Mardin, who in the previous year had failed in his duty to the new ruler of Mosul. Roger took up his position near Apamea, and sent for aid to King Baldwin and the Count of Tripoli. Borsac supinely let his opportunity slide, and with the arrival of the king and count retired without fighting.

But when Baldwin had gone home Borsac at once returned. Roger with his personal followers hurried out to Rugia. Next morning, as the ranks were being arrayed, Theodore de Barneville, one of Roger's scouts, rode up with a joyful countenance: the enemy were even then unfolding their tents in the valley of Sarmit, where the Franks had meant to camp. Roger bade his warriors quit them like men, and the Bishop of Jebleh, holding the cross in his hands, assured them of success. As he spoke the host fell on their knees and burst out with an unanimous cry, "Holy God, holy, mighty, and immortal, have mercy upon us!"

The Turks, in accordance with their usual custom, had sent on their baggage ahead. Behind came the troops marching hand in hand, and expecting no ill. Suddenly there appeared the flash of the white banners on the horizon, and before there was time to form their ranks the Christians had burst into the empty and defenceless camp. Each detachment of the Turkish army was cut off as it came up, and Borsac fled from the field to meet a peaceful death at home.

106

Roger returned with a vast spoil to Antioch. The streets were hung with silk and gold and flowers, as he passed in triumph to render thanks to God in the Church of St. Peter. "Hail, Champion of the Truth!" was the general cry, "May the enemies of God fear thee, and mayst thou have perpetual peace. Salvation and victory to thee throughout all ages! Amen!"

This victory gave the Franks the predominance in the northern parts of Syria. "They spread their arms to the east of Aleppo," says an Arabic historian; "they laid waste the province, and attacked Aleppo itself. That city would have been deserted had its inhabitants known where to find safety."

During the troubles that ensued on this defeat Lulu lost heart, and whilst fleeing from Aleppo was treacherously slain. The allegiance of Aleppo was then offered to Il-Ghazi, of Mardin, who, however, hardly found it worth acceptance. It is strange that in a time of such confusion and distrust the Franks did not make themselves masters of the city. Probably, however, they found more profit in promoting dissensions among their foes, than in burdening themselves with so vast a conquest.

In 1119 Il-Ghazi once more took the field, and fortress after fortress fell before him with startling rapidity. Roger of Antioch scorned the sound advice of the patriarch, to wait for King Baldwin, and marched out to an ill-omened spot called the Field of Blood. It was a place deficient both in food and drink. Worse than this, the camp followers carried news of his distress to the enemy. Emboldened by these tidings the Mohammedans routed a small force of Christians near the fortress of Cerep. Thereupon Roger sent forward Mauger of Hauteville with forty knights, and posted others to keep watch at a distant hill-tower.

Next morning the prince and all his army confessed their sins to the archbishop. This solemn work completed, Roger divided his gold among the poor, and then, with something of the true indifference of a Norman baron, went forth for his usual morning ride. His falcons and his hounds accompanied him; his followers took their hunting spears, and the lads were sent ahead to rouse the game. So Roger, "as became a prince," rode over hill and vale to hawk and hunt. But some prescience of disaster prevented him from taking pleasure in the sport. He left his gay companions and turned his steps towards the watchmen on the tower. Even as he rode there galloped up a messenger in headlong haste. "What news?" asked the prince. "With mine own eyes have I seen the enemy swarming over rough places and plain." "Christ," said the prince—"Christ hath granted us to suffer for Him."

Roger hastened back to his tent, but as he donned his armour, and knelt with his host to receive once more the archbishop's blessing, other messengers arrived. Many of the knights had fallen at their post; Mauger was close behind hard pressed by an intolerable host of the enemy. Hardly had the Christians formed their ranks when the standards of the unbelievers began to glimmer between the olive thickets on the hills. Roger bade his little army not to fear the enemy because of their multitude; before-times they had fought valiantly enough for earthly gain or glory, let them now fight as well for God. The Franks were victorious in more than one part of the field; but they were quite outnumbered, and when the Turcoples were seized with a sudden panic, the terror spread to Roger's own band, who likewise dispersed in fear. Then, to crown all, a sudden north wind blew down from the hills and, scudding close to the ground, raised a cloud of heated dust to blind the eyes of the Christians. Roger himself with a few followers fought desperately till, pierced through the brain, he fell dead before the Holy Cross—"his body to the earth, and his soul to heaven" (June 27, 1119).

Had Il-Ghazi marched on Antioch in the first flush of victory the city must have fallen. But his delays enabled the patriarch to restore some measure of confidence, and to keep the city safe till the coming of the king. Baldwin shortly marched out through Rugia to Danit, where he pitched his camp. His heedful wariness foiled an intended night surprise. The battle which ensued was long and doubtful; the Count of Tripoli, who commanded on the right, was driven back on the king's ranks. Evremar, the Archbishop of Caesarea, was struck by an arrow, but to the surprise of all only one drop of blood fell from the wound. This they attributed to the efficacy of the Holy Cross, which Evremar carried in his hands. The archbishop turned the sacred relic towards the foe, and cursed them in its name. The Christians thereon took fresh courage and, renewing the fight, were rewarded with victory (August 14, 1119).

The death of Roger marks a period in the history of the principality of Antioch. Its fortunes in the succeeding years are closely bound up with those of the kingdom of Jerusalem, and will be properly narrated in the following chapter.

A few words will suffice to describe the course of events in Tripoli during these early years. We find there a not dissimilar aspect of Frankish progress in the midst of Mussulman disunion. But the newcomers had a rival in the Egyptian Caliph, whose subordinates contrived during the years of confusion to recover their hold on the Syrian coast. Tyre, Sidon, Tripoli, and Beyrout all passed into their hands, and it was from them that Raymond of St. Gilles and his successors had to win the chief towns of their future county.

Count Raymond, when he found it impossible to protect Laodicea from the greed of Bohemond, had gone to Constantinople to seek the aid of Alexius, and thus shared in the Aquitanian crusade of iioi, though he escaped the worst of the evils that befell his comrades. Afterwards, however, he fell into the hands of Tancred, from whom he had to purchase his release by an undertaking to make no conquests north of Acre. But on Bohemond's restoration Raymond thought himself free to besiege Tripoli. Its emir, Fakr-el-Molk, called in aid from Damascus and Emesa. Raymond had only three hundred warriors in all, yet he contrived to drive back both of the hostile forces in panic, and to shut up the men of Tripoli more closely than before. But as he could not take the city by storm, he established himself on the neighbouring height of Mount Pilgrim, and was still engaged with the siege at his death on February 28, 1105. Raymond appears to have been the noblest of all the early Crusaders; he alone was absolutely faithful in his vow to Alexius, and his conduct is in striking contrast to that of his great colleagues. "Having once begun the fight for Christ," says William of Tyre, "he disdained not to continue his pilgrimage patiently till death. Although with his illustrious patrimony and power he might have lived in abundance in his own land, he chose rather to be an abject in the Lord's service than to abide in the tents of sinners."

On Raymond's death the siege was continued by William Jordan, his nephew. Raymond had, however, left in Mount Pilgrim an infant son, Alfonso. This child was soon sent to France, where a little later his elder brother Bertram resigned to him his father's possessions and started for the East. On his arrival in Palestine Bertram demanded his father's possessions from his cousin William. William denied the claim and appealed to Tancred for aid, while Bertram sailed south to renew the siege of Tripoli on his own account. To secure the aid of the king Bertram offered to do him service. Baldwin feared that the feuds among the Christians would ruin their prospects in the north, and hurrying to Tripoli succeeded in arranging a compromise. William was to hold Arkah and his present possessions; Bertram was to have the remainder of his father's fiefs—if he could obtain them. Tancred, who had a quarrel of his own with Bertram, was pacified by receiving Haifa, Tiberias, Nazareth, and the Templum Domini.

The united forces now laid siege to Tripoli with renewed vigour in March, 1109. Famine was at work within the walls, and the promised succour from Egypt was delayed till contrary winds prevented its coming altogether. The Saracens, in despair, accepted Baldwin's proffer of their lives, but the Genoese supporters of Bertram, eager for plunder, forced their way into the city, slaying all they met.

Before Tripoli had fallen Bertram was left without a rival, for William Jordan had been mysteriously shot with an arrow while riding at night. Bertram now became the king's man, and thus Tripoli was made a fief of the kingdom of Jerusalem.

Bertram died about 1112, and was succeeded by his son Pons, who played a not inconsiderable part till his death in 1137; the successor of Pons was Raymond I., whose son Raymond II. was the foremost figure among the Syrian nobles in the events which preceded the Third Crusade.

X.

THE CONQUEST OF THE LAND—BALDWIN II (1118-1131.)

"O tempora recordationis dignissima."
FULCHER OF CHARTRES.

ON the death of Baldwin I. many of the nobles were in favour of offering the crown to Eustace, the late king's brother. But Joscelin de Courtenay, then lord of Tiberias, gave his support to Baldwin du Bourg, declaring that it was better to accept a good king who was to be had for the asking, than to wait the pleasure of a distant ruler, who might prefer the settled order of his European county to the strain and anxiety of a perilous kingdom. These words carried the greater weight because of the speaker's known enmity for Baldwin, and when the patriarch adopted the same view the nobles elected Baldwin to the vacant throne. Some dissentients, however, sent an invitation to Count Eustace, who received them but coldly. "Not by me," was his noble answer, "shall a stumbling block enter into the Lord's kingdom."

The new king, Baldwin II. was the son of Hugh, Count of Rethel, near Rheims. He had accompanied Godfrey on the First Crusade, but afterwards joined his namesake in his adventurous conquest of Edessa. He, however, rejoined the main army, to share in the sieges of Antioch and Jerusalem. When his cousin became king he obtained the county of Edessa, and the story of his life in the next eighteen years has already been told. He was a man of lofty stature and comely features. His scanty yellow hair was already tinged with white; his beard was thin, though long, and his complexion ruddy for his age. A skilful horseman and an experienced military leader, he never made his advanced years an excuse for inaction. Unlike his predecessor, he was a wary general, careful in organising an expedition, and happy in its results. Above all

112

else he was truly devout in word and deed, a godfearing man, whose hands and knees were hardened with frequent prayer.

The first years of the new reign were devoted to the defence of Antioch and Edessa. Baldwin's victory at Danit has already been described. In the following year (June, 1120), Il-Ghazi returned with a host of Turcomans. These warriors were the moss-troopers of Oriental warfare, to which they came forth, each with his skin of water, sack of meal, and strips of dried meat carried on his steed. They fought for the sake of plunder only, and when Il-Ghazi punished such conduct, they gradually deserted him. Il-Ghazi, abandoned by his army, had to purchase a truce, which was, however, soon broken through the indiscretion of Joscelin de Courtenay, now Count of Edessa.

Matters were further complicated by the revolt of Soliman, son of Il-Ghazi, and ruler of Aleppo, against his father. Soliman appealed for aid to Baldwin, who demanded, as the price of his assistance, the restoration of Athareb. To this Soliman refused his consent, and it was in vain that the king urged how indefensible Athareb was, ringed round with Christian fortresses like a horse with weak legs, who eats a whole granary without gaining strength. These troubles recalled Il-Ghazi, who found himself obliged to purchase a truce by the cession of Zerdana and Athareb (about August, 1121). However, in June, 1122, despite the truce, he crossed the Euphrates, with his nephew Balak the Victorious, and laid siege to Zerdana. Baldwin refused to believe in such treachery. "I have been faithful," said the chivalrous king, "to the treaty, and have defended Il-Ghazi's possessions during his absence, and do not doubt but he will be as loyal on his part." On discovering his mistake, Baldwin called in Joscelin, and advanced to the relief of the beleaguered town. Illness soon forced Il-Ghazi to raise the siege, and on November 3rd he died, while on his way back to Mardin.

Meanwhile a great disaster had befallen the Christians. Balak having laid siege to Edessa, Joscelin came to its relief. Balak's troops were so scattered that he could barely muster four hundred horsemen to meet the count; he must have been defeated had it not been for a recent fall of rain, thanks to which the heavy Frank knights and their horses stuck in the miry soil, and were shot down by the Turkish bowmen. Joscelin and his nephew Waleran were taken prisoners, and when they refused to purchase their freedom by the surrender of Edessa were thrown into prison at Khartpert (September 13, 1122).

Balak's successes called Baldwin to the Euphrates. There, on April 18, 1123, the Christians fell into an ambuscade whilst engaged on a night march for the relief of Kerker. The Franks were massacred piteously, and Baldwin was in his turn also carried off prisoner to Khartpert. Balak then forced his way into Aleppo, and had proceeded to besiege Kafer Tab, when news reached him that Joscelin had escaped from Khartpert.

Joscelin had endeared himself to his Armenian subjects, who determined to make a desperate effort to secure their lord's freedom. Fifty men disguised as merchants, presented themselves one day in August before the gates of Khartpert. One by one with their wares they smuggled their way within the town to the walls of the citadel. There they found the warder of the gates carelessly playing at chess, and kept from all suspicion by his antagonist who was a friend of the conspirators. Throwing off their disguise the Armenians drew their knives and slew the warder; then seizing whatever lances lay at hand they quickly overpowered the Turkish guards. So soon as the king and his comrades were released, they hoisted a Christian flag on the highest battlement. But not daring to risk the journey home, they resolved to hold out in Khartpert till aid should come from Antioch or Jerusalem. Joscelin volunteered to carry the news; with three of his servants, he passed by night through the surrounding enemy, and sent back his ring to Baldwin as a token of his success. After twenty-four hours' wandering they found themselves at the Euphrates; the count could not swim, so his servants extemporised a raft of bladders, and thus they gained the other side. Hungry and thirsty, Joscelin lay down beneath a tree to rest, covering himself under the bushes. His servants meanwhile went to look for food, and shortly came back with an Armenian peasant, of whose simple fare of figs and raisins the count ate gladly. The peasant knew his lord at once and greeted him by name; Joscelin's alarmed denial could not deceive the faithful peasant, and at last, assured of the man's loyalty, the count promised him a piece of gold if he would guide them to a place of safety. "I seek no reward," was the generous answer: "before times you gave me bread to eat, and I am glad to repay you." Then taking Joscelin to his cottage the peasant explained his plan for the count's escape; but first of all wished to kill his pig for breakfast. "Nay," said Joscelin, "thou art not wont to eat a pig at a meal, and that would make thy neighbours suspicious." Then the count was disguised in the dress of the peasant's wife, and set upon the man's ass with his baby in his arms. Thus the strange company set out for Tell-basher; but presently the child began to cry, and so embarrassed the count that he would have left his comrades had he not feared to wound his protector's feelings. At last they reached Tell-basher in safety, and after rewarding the faithful peasant Joscelin set out for Jerusalem and Antioch.

Meanwhile Balak had turned back to Khartpert, and by undermining the rock on which the citadel was built, forced his way inside. The poorer Franks and the Armenians were massacred without pity, whilst Baldwin and Waleran were carried off to Harran. Joscelin was on his way north once more when he heard the news; unable to help his kinsmen he turned his arms against Aleppo. The count's successes in this quarter brought Balak back to the Orontes. Balak reached Aleppo in May, 1124, and soon after marched out against the town of Manbij or Hierapolis. Joscelin, though he could muster but a small army, went out to meet him. The battle at first went favourably for the Christians, but

Joscelin was at length compelled to retreat. Balak was, however, soon afterwards mortally wounded whilst prosecuting the siege of Manbij. Aleppo then passed to Hussan-ed-din, son of Il-Ghazi, from whom Baldwin purchased his release at the price of Athareb, Zerdana, Kafer Tab, some other towns, and twenty-four thousand dinars (August 30, 1124).

Baldwin, however, kept no faith with the infidels, and attacked Aleppo. The inhabitants appealed for help to El-Borsoki, Emir of Mosul, who in February 1125, drove back the Christians and so became Lord of Aleppo; but in June Baldwin in his turn defeated El-Borsoki. The king, however, realised that it was impossible for one ruler to govern both Antioch and Jerusalem; and accordingly he sent for the youthful Bohemond, who came from Italy to Antioch in the autumn of 1126. There the nobles swore fealty to him in Baldwin's presence, and the king gave him his second daughter Alice to wife. Bohemond's rule was short and troubled; he soon found himself at war with Joscelin, and Baldwin had to be called in to appease the quarrel. Some years later Bohemond was surprised and slain at the Meadow of Mantles in Cilicia. He was a youth of great promise, and bade fair to be a valiant warrior. At his death the principality passed to his infant daughter Constance.

Over and above all this warfare in the north, the reign of Baldwin II. was distinguished by many other expeditions. The Egyptians harassed him more than once from Ascalon, and Tughtakin of Damascus was ever ready to further their efforts by inroads from the east. Baldwin retaliated by more than one expedition across the Jordan, as in January, 1126, when he defeated the atabek with great loss near Marj-as-Suffar. But the great event of the reign was the conquest of Tyre during the king's captivity. That city was ruled by an emir in the name of El-Afdal, the Egyptian vizir. Being hard pressed by the Franks, and unaided by their own Caliph, the men of Tyre appealed to Tughtakin, and offered to take him for lord if they might dwell under his protection

Tughtakin sent them aid under an emir Masud, but refused to supplant the Egyptian Caliph. He informed El-Afdal that he was ready to withdraw his garrison directly Tyre was strong enough to do without it. But when a little later El-Afdal was murdered, the Egyptian admiral seized Masud by treachery and carried him off to Egypt. This conduct alienated Tughtakin, and the Franks seized the opportunity for attacking the city.

When Baldwin was taken prisoner by Balak, the Franks had elected, as guardian for the orphan realm, Eustace Grener, lord of Caesarea and Sidon. It happened that in 1123 there came to Jaffa a strong Venetian fleet under the doge Domenicho Michaeli. The doge went up to spend Christmas at Jerusalem, and there agreed with the lords of the land to lend his aid for an attack on one of the cities of the coast. Opinion was divided between Ascalon and Tyre, and it was decided to commit the question to the lot. The names of the two towns were written on two strips of parchment, and these were placed on the altar. Then an "innocent orphan boy" was bidden to take up one of them at random; the lot fell upon Tyre, which city was at once besieged by the combined forces of the Franks and Venetians, under Eustace and the doge. It was to no purpose that Tughtakin came up from Damascus, that a fresh fleet was sent from Egypt, or that the men of Ascalon strove to call off the besieging host by a foray to the very walls of Jerusalem. The last were driven back from the Tower of David; the Venetians defeated the Egyptian fleet; while William de Bures and Pons of Tripoli found the atabek unwilling to abide their onset. All the available forces of the realm seem to have been mustered for the siege, and when it began to flag through lack of military engines, a skilful Armenian engineer was called up from Antioch. At last, broken down by hunger and long privation, the city surrendered; men told in later days that only five measures of wheat were found within the walls. The fall of this city

(July 7, 1124) was a great blow to Islam; "let us hope that God will one day restore it," writes the Arabic historian a century later.

Baldwin II. was an old man, and had no son to succeed him on the throne. Unwilling to marry his eldest daughter Melisend to one of his own nobles, he sought her a bridegroom in Europe. His final choice was Fulk V., Count of Anjou, who reached Acre in the spring of 1129. The marriage was celebrated before Whitsuntide, and the king's son-in-law received Tyre and Acre as his wife's dowry. Two years later Baldwin fell into a fatal sickness; anxious for his soul's health, he quitted the luxury of the royal palace for the patriarch's house hard by the sepulchre of the Lord. There he put on the garb of a monk, and so died August 13, 1131. He was buried with his predecessors before Golgotha, under Mount Calvary.

With Baldwin II. disappeared the last of the great heroes of the First Crusade who had remained in Palestine. His death, too, marks the conclusion of the first stage in the history of the Syrian Franks. Despite the disaster of his eighteen months' captivity Baldwin's reign had been one of prosperity for his kingdom. The ruler of Jerusalem had acquired extended influence in the principality of Antioch, while the great conquest of Tyre had consolidated his own dominion in the south. The period of conquest was now at an end, and after a short period of equilibrium the Christian kingdom entered on a chequered career of loss and gain, which eventually culminated in the conquest of the Holy City by Saladin.

XI.

THE MILITARY ORDERS.

"Triplex funiculus non facile rumpitur."

JAMES DE VITRY.

TO the men of the twelfth century there must have been a marvellous attraction in the tales which every returning palmer or crusader brought back from Syria. Adventure was as the very life-breath of the mediaeval warrior, and in the East if anywhere he could find it to the full, with the added prospect of a sure reward, both spiritual and temporal. Did he perish in the combat, heaven, as St. Bernard told him, would throw open her halls to receive him; was he victor, then the spoils of the vanquished were his. The humblest man-at-arms might acquire wealth through the sack of a Saracen stronghold, or the rout of a Saracen host; the wandering knight might enter the bodyguard of Godfrey or Baldwin, and be recompensed with money or a fief; the greater lord could always hope for conquests on his own account. To the prospect of gain were added two other incentives; the always unsatisfied longing for travel, which then, as now, prompted the noblest spirits of the age to seek ideals far away from home, and the feeling of devotion which urged mediaeval Christians on to pilgrimages, whether near or distant. These impulses together sufficed to keep up a constant stream of visitors to Palestine during many years. Some came, saw, and departed; others however, stayed, and, whether for good or ill, made their home in the East.

Thus in the course of thirty years there had been built up a new kingdom, and, as it were, a new nation. So Fulcher of Chartres could write: "God transforms things according to His will. He has poured the West into the East; we who were westerns are now easterns. We have all forgotten our native soil, it has grown strange unto us." But the most promising feature in this new creation was the rise of military organisations, which might combine and turn to good purpose all those whom restlessness of spirit or devotion of soul drew towards the East.

The credit of the conception of an order of knights sworn to the service of the Cross belongs to Hugh de Payen, the founder of the Templars. But the priority of rank must be yielded to the Hospitallers, who trace their origin to a more ancient institution, established for a different purpose. According to the story preserved by William of Tyre, and in part confirmed from other sources, the merchants of Amalfi having won the favour of the Egyptian Caliph, obtained permission, as it is said, about the year 1023, to found a hospital at Jerusalem for poor and sick Latin pilgrims. The original dedication was to St. John the Almoner, a humble patron who had afterwards to give way to St. John the Baptist. At the time of the First Crusade the master of the hospital was one Gerard, "during many years the devoted servant of the poor." Gerard, who is often regarded as the founder of the hospital, obtained from Pope Paschal II., in 1113, a Bull, which, besides granting him the special protection of the papal see, confirmed to the hospital all the possessions which it then held as well in Syria as in Western Europe. Gerard died in 1118, and was succeeded by Raymond du Puy, a noble from Dauphine, who held his office over forty years, and taking an example from the recently established order of the Temple, gave his own order a military organisation.

The Templars, although they were from the first an order of knights, owed their institution, as did the Hospitallers, to a charitable purpose. In the early days of the kingdom a Burgundian knight, Hugh de Payen by name, made a pilgrimage to Jerusalem. Moved to pity by the sufferings of the Christians through the perpetual attacks of the Saracens, he joined with eight other knights in devoting themselves to the service of protecting the poor pilgrims on the road to Jerusalem. They took the triple vows of chastity, obedience, and poverty, after the

120

manner of regular canons, and obtained from Baldwin II., in the same year that Gerard the Hospitaller died, the gift of a residence near the Temple of Solomon at Jerusalem; originally designated the poor fellow soldiers of Christ, they from this circumstance came to be known as the Knights of the Temple. After nine years at the Council of Troyes, in January, 1128, Hugh obtained from Pope Honorius II., through the influence of Bernard of Clairvaux, a formal Rule, which the famous abbot himself drew up, or at least inspired.

From a religious point of view the Rule of the Templars not unnaturally followed that of the Cistercians, but here it is not necessary to concern ourselves, except with the military organisation of the order. At its head stood the Master, who, though he had great power, was far from absolute, and was obliged even in the field to act by the advice of his council. Second came the Seneschal, and third the Marshal, whose special charge was all that concerned the equipment of the order with arms and steeds. After these came the commanders or preceptors of the provinces, premier of whom was the "Commander of the land and kingdom of Jerusalem," who was also Grand Treasurer, and had charge of the port of Acre, where the knights had their chief maritime establishment. The commander of the city of Jerusalem was Hospitaller of the order, and had to provide for the safe conduct and care of pilgrims. The other provinces were Tripoli and Antioch in the East, and France, England, Poitou, Aragon, Portugal, Apulia, and Hungary in Europe. Last of the great officers was the Drapier, charged with all that concerned the dress of the members. Subordinate officials were the commanders of the houses or commanderies, and the commanders of the knights. The greater officers had all a more or less extensive household, and were allowed four horses each; the ordinary knights had, as a rule, three horses and one squire. Other knights there were *ad terminum*, who had not taken the regular vows, but associated themselves with the order for a time, as Fulk of Anjou is said to have

121

done in the early days before he was king or the order fully constituted. After the knights came the sergeants, or serving-brothers, amongst whom were included some inferior officials, as the under-seneschal and the gonfanonier, whose duty it was to bear the banner Beauseant. Besides the knights and sergeants there was a numerous body of light-armed horsemen called Turcoples, under an officer called the Turcopolier. These formed the fighting force; but there were also chaplains of the order—priests attached to it for religious duties. The "Rule" contains careful regulations as to the admission of new members, which could only be done in a chapter; the aspirant must not be baseborn, a member of any other religious order, or hampered by any worldly ties. In the case of knights he must be of knightly birth, for a sergeant it was enough that he was free-born. The original knights had no regular dress, but wore such motley garb as charity afforded them. Honorius assigned them a white habit, while later on, in the time of Eugenius III., they were granted, as a mark of distinction, a red cross, to be worn on the mantle. The mantles of the knights alone were white, those of the sergeants and squires black or brown, but all alike wore the great red cross.

St. Bernard, shortly after the foundation of the order, draws a somewhat fanciful picture of the knights of Christ. "They live together without separate property, in one house, under one rule, careful to preserve the unity of the spirit in the bond of peace. Never is an idle word, or useless deed, or immoderate laughter, or a murmur, if it be but whispered, allowed to go unpunished. Draughts and dice they detest. Hunting they hold in abomination; and take no pleasure in the frivolous pastime of hawking. Soothsayers, jesters, and story-tellers, ribald songs and stage plays they eschew as insane follies. They cut close their hair, knowing, as the apostle says, that 'it is a shame for a man to have long hair.' They never dress gaily, and wash but seldom. Shaggy by reason of their uncombed hair, they are also begrimed with dust, and swarthy from the weight of their armour and the heat of the sun. They strive earnestly to possess strong and swift horses, but not garnished with ornaments or decked with trappings, thinking of battle and victory, not of pomp and show. Such hath God chosen for His own, who vigilantly and faithfully guard the Holy Sepulchre, all armed with the sword, and most learned in the art of war."

A century later James de Vitry, writing in the light of personal knowledge, says: "When the Templars are summoned to arms, they inquire not of the numbers, but of the position of the foe. They are lions in war, lambs in the house; to the enemies of Christ fierce and implacable, but to Christians kind and gracious. They bear before them to battle a banner half white, half black; this they call Beauseant, because they are fair and favourable to the friends of Christ, to his foes drear and black."

The organisation of the Hospitallers, or the Knights of the Hospital of St. John of Jerusalem, was in its general features similar to that of the Templars, and comprised knights, chaplains, and serving brothers, together with a body of Turcoples. The officers other than the grand master were styled conventual, capitular, or honorary bailiffs. The conventual bailiffs were the heads of the *langues*, or provinces, of which in 1331 there were seven, Provence, Auvergne, France, Italy, Germany, Aragon, and England. The capitular bailiffs or grand priors were the heads of the *langue* in Europe; in the English *langue* there were two grand priors, one for England and one for Ireland. The heads of the houses were called commanders or preceptors. In their religious life the Hospitallers followed the rule of St. Augustine; their mantles were black with an eight-pointed cross of white.

Hugh de Payen and his original eight companions had remained alone for nine years in their primitive poverty, so that, according to a thirteenth-century tradition, two knights rode upon one horse. But after their regular constitution on a military basis both orders grew rapidly in importance, wealth, and numbers. Mention is made of both in different campaigns during the reign of Fulk. Both played a prominent part in the futile siege of Damascus during the Second Crusade, and in the succeeding years the two orders were the mainstay of the kingdom. To their care were entrusted some of the most important of the frontier fortresses; thus the Hospitallers received Gibelin or Beersheba in 1136, and the Templars Gaza in 1149. Templars and Hospitallers fought side by side under their masters Bernard de Tremelay and the aged Raymond du Puy at Ascalon in 1153; the Hospitallers were Amalric's chief support in his Egyptian campaign in 1168, and a few years earlier, in 1163, we find the Templars of Tripoli, under their English preceptor, Gilbert de Lacy, playing a leading part in the contest with Nur-ed-din. In the troublous days that preceded the Third Crusade the masters of the two orders appear as the leaders of the party that favoured active warfare with Saladin. During that Crusade the Templars were foremost among the supporters of Richard, who, according to a thirteenth-century legend, left the Holy Land in the disguise of a knight and on board a vessel belonging to their order. The loss of Jerusalem deprived both Hospitallers and Templars of their original headquarters. After a short interval both were established at Acre, where they remained till the fall of that city a century later marked the end of Frankish rule in Palestine. During this, the last century of Crusading history, the defence of such possessions as yet remained to the Franks in Syria devolved more and more on the military orders. Many nobles, finding themselves unable to defend their fiefs any longer against the foe, sold their estates to the Templars or Hospitallers, and departed westward.

Great as was the power of the knights, their numbers and wealth were not incommensurate. William of Tyre says that in his day the original nine of the Templars had increased to three hundred, which would seem to be a moderate estimate. At the battle of Hattin, in 1187, this order lost two hundred and thirty knights, though only a few weeks

124

previously the marshal and eighty knights had been slain in the fight with El-Afdal. More than three hundred Templars fell before Acre in 1191, and a like number in the battle with the Charismians some fifty years afterwards. As for the Hospitallers, in 1168 they furnished Amalric with five hundred knights and as many Turcoples for his Egyptian campaign. The Templars held eighteen fortresses in Syria, chief of which were Safed, Tortosa, and Athlit, or Castle Pilgrim. The last was a magnificent structure on the coast near Acre, which was commenced in 1218. It comprised a palace for the master and knights, quarters for their subordinates, and a splendid church—the whole adorned with such a wealth of luxury as filled James de Vitry with amazement; even in ruins it forms a majestic memorial of its builders. Of the property of the Temple in Syria we have, owing to the destruction of their records, no exact knowledge, but they had fourteen commanderies besides others in Armenia and Cyprus. The Hospitallers owned 135 casals or villages, beside other property. They had twelve commanderies in Syria, and their fortresses comprised the important castles of Markab, Kerak des Chevaliers, Chastel Rouge, Gibelin, and Belvoir.

Wealth brought in its train the usual abuses. Even in the days of their first master the Hospitallers were engaged in a serious quarrel with the Latin ecclesiastics of the East, due to the grasping pretensions of the knights. The Templars, on their part, earned an early reputation for avarice and arrogance. One story lays the failure of the siege of Damascus at their door, asserting that they took money to raise the siege: an act of cupidity which was miraculously punished by the conversion of the gold into copper in their chests. Their rash assault at Ascalon five years later was put down to a wish to secure the best of the spoil for themselves. So notorious was their arrogance that, when Fulk of Neuilly bade Richard provide for his three daughters, it was an easy jest for the king to bestow "Pride" on the Templars.

Great as was the wealth of the two orders in the East, it was not their main resource. Both had from an early date received large benefactions in Western Europe. Hugh de Payen had visited Henry I. in Normandy in 1128, when "the king received him with much worship, and gave him treasure of gold and silver, and afterwards he sent him to England, where he was well treated by all good men, and all gave him treasures." Alfonso I. of Aragon, Raymond Berengar I. of Provence, and Louis VI. of France were not less forward. In England the Templars settled early in the reign of Stephen at the old Temple outside Holborn bars, whence, in 1185, they removed to the new and more famous Temple on the Thames. The church, which was in this year consecrated by the Patriarch Heraclius, and was completed by 1240, still survives as the finest monument of the order in England. The great William Marshal chose it for his burial-place, and his effigy, with those of two of his sons, still lies in the Round Church. Stephen gave the knights Temple Cressing, in Essex, about 1150, and his queen Matilda Temple Cowley, near Oxford. Many other benefactions followed during the twelfth century, and all our English kings were among their patrons. Henry II. gave them Waterford and Wexford, and John Lundy Island; whilst Henry III. regarded them with such favour that he and his queen at one time chose the Temple Church as their place of burial. Matthew Paris asserts that the Templars possessed no less than seven thousand manors in Christendom.

The Hospitallers, though not nearly so wealthy, had also great possessions. Even in 1113 it is clear that they had considerable property in Western Europe. Indeed, their chief English house at Clerkenwell is said to have been founded by Jordan Briset, who died in 1110. After they became a military order they acquired, in the reign of Stephen, lands at Little Maplestead in Essex, Shandon in Hertfordshire, and Shengay in Cambridgeshire, as also at many other places both then and later.

Wherever their estates were of sufficient importance both orders established houses, or commanderies, which served the double purpose of homes for the aged knights and recruiting stations for young aspirants. Great privileges were bestowed on both orders, and many individual knights rose to positions of importance. One Templar was almoner to Philip IV. of France, and another to Henry III. of England. In Aragon the Templars occupied a position of unique importance, and more than one of its kings was entrusted to their care for training. One result of the peculiar position of the orders in East and West, combined with their great wealth, was to give them exceptional opportunities for the commercial transactions of exchange—a means of increasing their wealth and power of which they were not slow to avail themselves in times of peace.

In addition to the two great orders there grew up about the time of the Third Crusade another order, which, from the nationality of its founders, was known as the Teutonic. In 1128 some German merchants had founded at Jerusalem a hospital, which subsisted till the fall of the city sixty years later. During the siege of Acre in 1190 the charitable work of this hospital (the tending of the sick and wounded) was revived and the active sympathy of many Germans, who had accompanied Frederick Barbarossa, enlisted in its favour. About eight years later the order received a military constitution as a body of knights, to whom were afterwards added, in imitation of its more ancient models, chaplains and serving brothers. In their military organisation the Teutonic knights followed the rule of the Temple, but in their religious life they adopted, like the Hospitallers, the rule of St. Augustine. Their mantle was white with a black cross. Under Herman von Salza, who was Grand Master from 1210 to 1239, the order rose rapidly in wealth and power, and first commenced that work in East Prussia which afterwards made it great and famous. The original seat of the order was at Acre, whence in 1291 they removed to Venice, till a few years later they became entirely German and devoted themselves to the work of maintaining the eastern frontier against the Lithuanians. There they rose to be a famous and important power, which attracted to its ranks many seekers after adventure, amongst whom was reckoned for a time Henry, the first of our Lancastrian kings. The order maintained its independence till Albert of Brandenburg, its last Grand Master, in 1525 converted its lands into a duchy for himself, and so took an important step towards the creation of the modern Prussia.

Another little known and obscure order deserves a passing mention in this place. The Germans were not alone in their charitable work at Acre, and an English priest, William, chaplain to Ralph de Diceto, devoted himself to the work of burying the Christian dead. Afterwards he built himself a chapel and bought ground for a cemetery, which he dedicated to St. Thomas the Martyr. Through the patronage of the sister of Becket a hospital of St. Thomas the Martyr of Canterbury at Acre was built in London on the site of the archbishop's house; and in 1231, when Peter des Roches was in Palestine, he established these knights under the rule of the Templars. These knights of St. Thomas of Acre wore their own mantle with a cross of red and white, and have the distinction of being one of the few peculiarly English orders. They survived in the kingdom of Cyprus till near the close of the fourteenth century.

On the later fortunes of the two greater orders it is impossible to more than briefly touch. That of the Templars was no less disastrous and shameful than that of the Hospitallers was glorious and honourable. After the fall of Acre the Templars transferred their headquarters to Cyprus, whence they made some futile attempts to gain a footing at Alexandria and Tortosa. But their power excited the fear, and their wealth the cupidity of a dangerous foe. Internal dissensions gave Philip IV. of France an opportunity to bring accusations of the most shameful character against the whole order. After nearly sixty knights had been burnt in May, 1310, the royal influence or tyranny prevailed upon Clement V. to decree the suppression of the order in March, 1312; and two years later Jacques du Molay, the Grand Master, after a cruel imprisonment, shared the fate of his subordinates. The proceedings which thus terminated the existence of the Temple in France were a precedent for measures of less severity but like effect in other countries. The falsehood of the graver charges, immorality of the grossest kind, is now generally admitted, yet there seems no doubt that practices of an unseemly nature prevailed at least in the French provinces. Friendly intercourse with the Mohammedans had probably influenced the knights in matters both of belief and conduct, whilst it is more than probable that some taint of heresy had penetrated the order through the admission of Albigensian knights, compelled to choose between the service of the cross and the penalty of death.

Like the Templars the Hospitallers had retired to Cyprus on the fall of Acre; more fortunate they, twenty years later, achieved the conquest of Rhodes, and at the same time, through the downfall of the rival order, acquired a great accession of wealth. At Rhodes the knights of St. John were, during over two centuries, the bulwark of Christendom against the Turks. When at length that island fell before the power of Soliman the Magnificent in 1522, the bounty of Charles the Fifth gave them a new home and a fresh career of glory as the knights of Malta. As a military body the order was long since obsolete, when Ferdinand von Hompesch somewhat tamely surrendered the island to the French in 1798. Recent years have, however, witnessed its honourable revival as a charitable institution, with a special care for the tending of the sick and wounded in war, and after a chequered career the gate of the priory at Clerkenwell has once more become the home of the English *langue*.

No attempt has been made in this chapter to even sketch the full career of the two great orders. But indeed the history of the Latin colonies is the history of the knights of the Hospital and Temple. The orders constituted the most stable element in the Angevin kingdom of Jerusalem; and the later kingdom, subsequent to the Third Crusade, was dependent on them for its very existence. The organisation that was happily devised by Hugh de Payen and Raymond du Puy was the one best suited for the circumstances in which the Syrian Franks found themselves. The climate forbade any hope of success to a regular system of colonisation; the races of Western Europe could not perpetuate their existence in face of the twofold strain of warfare under an Eastern sun. The lessened vigour of the race intensified the evils inherent in the feudal system—the weakness of widows and minors, and the strength of family feud and faction. From these defects the knightly orders were exempt; they could provide more surely that warlike organisation, which the ever-present Saracen and Turk made a necessity; as corporations, whose life-blood came in a fresh and constant stream from the West, they possessed a cohesion and vigour which were no less essential. With them there was no question, as with the Frank nobles of Syria, of private interest or family advantage; they had no interest but to justify their existence by preserving the Holy Land from the Moslem; unhampered by personal or worldly ties they were free and eager to prosecute to the end the sacred enterprise which they had undertaken.

If it be asked how we are to explain the only moderate measure of success which they achieved, the answer is ready to hand. The field was already occupied by another organisation. The co-existence of the feudal and hereditary barons of Syria with these incorporated bodies of new-come adventurers gave rise to perpetual jealousies. Yet, further, there was the weakness natural to the twofold organisation of the orders themselves. In theory there might be no antagonism between them, and the Templar might be ordered in all good faith to rally to the banner of the Hospital, if in the hour of defeat his own failed him. But in practice there could not but be a rivalry between the two, which was fatal to all solidarity of action. Traces of this rivalry are not wanting in the earlier period, as when the Templars refused to support Amalric's Egyptian policy from jealousy at the prime part which the master of the Hospital had taken in inspiring it. In the thirteenth century this feeling of rivalry became more acute, and through the absence of any controlling power more mischievous. The jealousies of the two orders crippled the hands of Richard of Cornwall in 1240-41, and it was with difficulty that the earl could keep the peace between them. In 1243 the Templars broke the truce which Richard, by the advice of the Hospitallers, had made with the Sultan, and openly attacking their rivals, laid siege to them in Acre. Yet, again, after the first Crusade of St. Louis the ill-feeling became so bitter that in 1259 another open war led to a pitched battle, in which the Templars were disastrously defeated. Mutual rivalry of this sort was not less mischievous than the ambition and treachery with which both orders were freely charged by their opponents; such accusations are, however, most noteworthy as evidence of the jealousy with which the knights were regarded by the native nobles. The success of the knights of St. John at Rhodes is sufficient proof of what the two orders might have achieved under happier auspices. Even as things were it was chiefly due to the military orders that the Latin kingdom did in any sense so long survive the conquests of Saladin. Their partial ill-success notwithstanding, the history of the Knights of the Temple, and of the Hospital of St. John at Jerusalem, must always afford some of the most picturesque pages in mediaeval history.

XII.

THE KINGDOM AT ITS ZENITH—FULK OF ANJOU. (1131-1143.)

"Princeps potens et apud suos felicissimus."

WILLIAM OF TYRE.

FULK of Anjou, the new king of Jerusalem, belonged to one of the most powerful families in Western Europe. His ancestors during two centuries had been capable warriors and statesmen, the most prominent of all being that Fulk the Black whose numerous pilgrimages have been alluded to in a previous chapter. Fulk, the King of Jerusalem, was great grandson of Fulk the Black, and son of Fulk IV. by the infamous Bertrada de Montfort, who forsook her lawful husband for Philip I. The young Fulk became Count of Anjou 1109, and had to steer a difficult path through the thick of the Anglo-French complications. But actively engaged, though he was in temporal politics, there was in Fulk a strain of piety, which about 1120 led him to make a pilgrimage to the Holy Land. There he must have been among the very first of the associates *ad terminum* of the Templar knights, to whom on his departure he granted an annual sum of thirty pounds. But even at home his thoughts still turned towards the East, and his secret longings became known to others, so that Louis VI. was led to advocate his marriage with King Baldwin's daughter.

Baldwin's envoys could hardly have made a better choice. Fulk was a warrior, a politician, and something of a saint; more than this he was akin to many of the greatest princes of Western Europe. His two daughters had been married, one to the ill-starred Atheling William who perished in the White Ship, the other, Sibyl, to Theodoric Count of Flanders; whilst his eldest son Geoffrey became, through his marriage to the ex-empress Matilda, the father of our own Henry II.

In personal appearance Fulk was, like David, of a ruddy countenance, but, adds William of Tyre, unlike most people of this complexion, affable, kindly, and compassionate. His chief defect was a weakness of memory so marked that he could not recollect the names of his own servants, and would often offend his familiar friends by asking who they were.

The early years of Fulk's reign were occupied with the affairs of Antioch, where even in her father's lifetime Baldwin's daughter Alice had after her husband's death been intriguing to secure the principality for herself Baldwin had forced her to content herself with Laodicea, but she now resumed her pretensions with the support of Pons of Tripoli and Joscelin II. of Edessa. The nobles of Antioch appealed to Fulk for help; whereupon Pons soon came to terms, and Antioch was placed in charge of Rainald Mansuer. In February, 1133, Fulk was again called north to the assistance of Pons, who was besieged by the Turcomans at Mons Ferrandus. He raised the siege and defeated the marauders near Harenc. The spoils of this victory sufficed to win over those nobles, who still favoured the pretensions of Alice.

It was, however, necessary to find a settled ruler for Antioch, and a husband for its princess, a girl of six or seven. After due consideration Raymond of Poiton, younger son of the Crusading Duke William of Aquitaine, was asked to wed the little heiress, and undertake the defence of her lands. Raymond accepted without hesitation, and set out for Syria forthwith. But he did not dare to travel in his own name, for fear of Roger King of Sicily, who fancied that he himself had claims on Antioch; so he made his way through Italy disguised as a common traveller walking on foot, or riding on pack-horses. He reached Syria about March, 1136, but not even then would his difficulties have been at an end, but for the craft of the Patriarch Ralph, who persuaded Alice that Raymond was destined to be her own husband, and thus secured him a free entry into Antioch.

133

In the following year (1137) Pons of Tripoli was defeated and slain by the Vizir of Damascus. Zangi seized the opportunity, burst across the Orontes, and laid siege to Mons Ferrandus. The young Count Raymond I. appealed for aid to his uncle Fulk. Antioch was at the same time threatened with an attack by the Emperor, John Comnenus. Fulk determined to meet the nearer danger; but his guides misled him, and in a narrow and pathless district of the mountains he was utterly defeated by Zangi (July, 1137). The young Count was taken prisoner, whilst Fulk with a few companions was shut up in Mons Ferrandus. Generously regardless of his own danger the prince of Antioch hurried up at the news; the Count of Edessa followed, and before long the patriarch appeared with the Holy Cross. Zangi therefore offered the king a free exit, if he would surrender the castle, promising on his part to release the count. Fulk accepted these terms, and the allies went back to their own lands.

Meantime John Comnenus had invaded Cilicia with a large army; Tarsus, Adana, Mamistra, and Anazarba had fallen before him, and now he would have captured Antioch also, had not Raymond come to terms and promised to do him fealty. Next spring the Emperor, the Prince of Antioch, and the Count of Edessa took the field together. The united armies laid siege to Caesarea on the Orontes; but as the Latin princes spent their time in playing at dice instead of in fighting, John abandoned the war in disgust and withdrew to Antioch. Entering the city in state he demanded that the citadel should be placed in his hands. Joscelin begged leave to consult the people, and spread the news throughout the city. The angry citizens flew to arms, and in alarm at the uproar the Emperor withdrew his demand, and retired to Cilicia. Four years later in 1142 John was recalled to Syria by the news of Zangi's success: he pitched his camp high among the hills of Amanus, whence he could look down on Antioch, and sent to demand the surrender of the city. Raymond by the advice of his council refused; if the city fell back into Greek hands, it would soon be lost to Christendom as had so often happened before. The approach of winter compelled the Emperor to retire to Cilicia, whence he sent messengers to Fulk announcing his intention to visit the Holy City on a pilgrimage. What might have happened next year is uncertain; but fortunately for the Latins a hunting accident caused John's death in April, 1143, and Manuel his son and successor for the time abandoned his father's projects in Syria.

A few words will suffice to sketch the later fortunes of Raymond. Manuel did not long leave him unmolested, and compelled him somewhat reluctantly to visit Constantinople and renew his oath of allegiance. Afterwards Raymond played a prominent part in the Second Crusade, to the failure of which his folly or vices in some degree contributed. In June, 1149, whilst on an expedition for the relief of Enneb near Hazart, he was induced against his better judgment to pitch his camp in a marshy spot shut in by hills. His fears were justified, for the Turks surrounded the Frankish camp that night and Raymond himself was slain. Of all the princes in the East none left a more illustrious name than he. A Greek legend tells how, when he visited the Temple at Jerusalem in disguise, his mighty stature and warlike bearing revealed him to the priests. Long years after his death an English monk, who had once served in his army told William of Newburgh that the Turks dreaded Raymond as equal to two hundred of their own soldiers. By his death Antioch was left to the rule of his widow Constance and her little son Bohemond III.

Within the strict limits of his own kingdom, the chief trouble of Fulk's reign was a domestic one. Hugh II., Count of Jaffa, had married Emelota, the niece of the Patriarch Arnulf, and widow of Eustace Grener. He thus became one of the greatest nobles of the kingdom, whilst his comely person, high birth, and military vigour left him without a peer in the realm. People whispered that he was paying too

135

much attention to the queen; others in jealousy accused him of harbouring rebellious projects against the king. At length his own step-son, Walter, Lord of Caesarea, accused him of high treason in the royal court. Hugh challenged his accuser to single combat, but before the day came fled for refuge to Jaffa. This conduct was taken as a proof of guilt, and the court condemned him in his absence. Hugh in indignation took ship for Ascalon, and demanded help from the Egyptians against his lord. Heartened by such an alliance the men of Ascalon renewed their predatory raids, whilst Fulk prepared to besiege Jaffa, and many of Hugh's vassals, Balian of Ibelin among them, threw off their allegiance to the count. However the Patriarch William soon made peace; Hugh was to submit to three years' exile, but before he could leave the kingdom he was stabbed whilst playing dice outside an inn in Jerusalem (1132 A.D.). Rumour at once declared that his assailant had been suborned by the king. Fulk to clear himself had the unhappy wretch ruthlessly tortured but to no purpose. Hugh recovered, and going over-sea died in Apulia. This was not the only scandal in which the queen was concerned; but Fulk was at length reconciled to her, and lived on such friendly terms with her as to be accused of luxuriousness.

The course of events on his eastern border increased Fulk's power by making him a patron instead of an enemy of Damascus. The famous Ismailian Bahram had so won the favour of Tughtakin, that the atabek entrusted him with the strong fortress of Banias or Caesarea Philippi. There he was succeeded by his adherent Ismail, whilst on Tughtakin's death an Ismailian vizir became all-powerful at Damascus under his (Tughtakin's) son Buri. The heretical vizir, hating his fellow countrymen, offered to betray Damascus to the Franks; but the plot was discovered, the traitor beheaded, and six thousand of his supporters massacred in Damascus alone (September, 1129). Ismail in wrath or terror surrendered Banias to the Franks and took refuge in Jerusalem. Three years later, when Fulk was in the thick of his contest with Hugh of Jaffa, Shams-el-Muluk, son of Buri, and atabek of Damascus, recovered the fortress. But the atabek was a weak and effeminate ruler, who offended his subjects by offering to surrender the city to Zangi. The prince's mother then had her son murdered, and when Zangi appeared before Damascus he was repulsed by one of Tughtakin's Mamluks called Anar. Anar became vizir for another of Buri's sons, and when in 1139 Zangi again pressed Damascus hard, he turned in despair to the Franks, promising in return for their aid to help them to recover Banias. The bribe took, and Zangi, fearing to meet the double attack, withdrew. Anar then joined the Franks in besieging Banias in May, 1140. Timber was brought from Damascus, and before long a huge siege castle was erected, so lofty that in the chronicler's quaint words "the folk of Banias seemed to fight with angels rather than with men." The siege was not, however, ended till Anar's envoys found their way within the walls, and induced the emir to surrender by the promise of a pension at Damascus. Banias was restored to its old lord, Renier Brus, and was made the see of a Latin bishop.

Fulk died on November 13, 1143. He had spent the autumn at Acre, where one day as he rode in the country his followers started a hare. The king joined in the sport, seized a lance, and rushed in pursuit. His horse stumbled, and as Fulk lay on the ground the heavy saddle struck him on the head. He was carried back to Acre, where he lingered for three days and then died. Fulk was buried in the Church of the Holy Sepulchre at Jerusalem, on the right hand near the entrance. His death caused great mourning—the more so perhaps since his two sons were but children—Baldwin, aged thirteen, and Amalric, aged seven.

XIII.

ZANGI AND THE FALL OF EDESSA.
(1130-1149.)

"A cry that shivered to the tingling stars."

TENNYSON.

FULK had been a successful ruler of his little kingdom, and had well maintained if he had not indeed extended its power. Yet his reign had witnessed a slow though momentous change that was pregnant with disaster for the Franks. One by one the Mohammedan lords on the Orontes and Euphrates had acknowledged the supremacy of the Viceroy at Mosul, and abandoned their mutual discords. This unification of the power of the Mussulmans, which was the first step towards stemming the tide of Latin conquest, was mainly the work of one man, Zangi, the atabek of Mosul.

Imad-ed-din Zangi was the son of a favourite counsellor of Malek Shah, who became lord of Aleppo, and fell fighting for his master's son. Zangi was but ten years old at his father's death, and fought his first campaigns against the Franks in the service of Maudud, with whom he was present at the great battle near Tiberias, when he rode up to the very gate of the city and struck it with his lance. Afterwards he entered the service of Mahmud, who made him his agent at Bagdad and Irak, and on the death of El-Borsoki promoted him to be governor of Mosul (1127 A.D.).

At this time the Mohammedans were in the very depths of despair. "The Franks," says an Arabic writer, "were spread far and wide; their troops were numerous and their hands extended as if to seize all Islam. Day after day their raids followed one another; through these they did the Mussulmans much mischief, smiting them with desolation and ruin. Thus was the happy star of the Mussulmans darkened, the sky of their puissance cloven in twain, and the sun of their prosperity dimmed." . . . "The Frankish possessions stretched from Mardin and Chabakhtân to El-Arish on the Egyptian frontier, with hardly a break, except for a few strong cities, such as Aleppo, Emesa, Hamah, and Damascus. Their incursions were pushed as far as Diar-bekr, and the district round Amida; they spared neither those who believed in the unity of God nor those who denied it. From Upper Mesopotamia to Nisibis and Ras Ain they robbed the folk of money and of goods; at Harran they weighed down the inhabitants with scorn and oppression. In their misery men longed for death. Commerce was interrupted, and the roads to Damascus save that which passed by Rakka and the desert left deserted. Even those towns not actually conquered had to pay tribute in return for their freedom. Frankish agents visited Damascus itself, passed the slave markets in review, and set free all Christian captives from Asia Minor, Armenia, and elsewhere." It was Zangi's destiny to change all this; to inspire his people with courage; to lead them to their first successes, and thus to pave the way for his son's conquest of Egypt, and for his third successor's conquest of Jerusalem. To Mohammedans of a later generation it seemed as though Zangi were God's special servant chosen by Him to accomplish the protection of His people.

Zangi's first conquests were against his Mohammedan rivals; for he could not attack the Franks till he had vindicated the authority of Mosul over the lands east of the Euphrates. After establishing himself firmly in Mosul he captured first Jezirat-ibn-Omar, and then Nisibis and Sinjar. After this he determined to secure his position on the Orontes, and turned his attention towards Aleppo.

At this time Aleppo was so weak that its inhabitants paid half their revenue to the Franks down to a mill hardly twenty paces from the town. Zangi entered on possession of Aleppo in June, 1128, next year he took Hamah, and in 1130 began his warfare with the Franks by the conquest of Athareb, a frontier fortress which, says Ibn El-Athir, "held the Mohammedans as it were by the throat." According to the later legend when King Baldwin heard of the siege he called his council together. Some thoughtless warriors made light of the new danger. One, however, took a different view. "Was not this the young warrior who had ridden up to the gate of Tiberias? Had we not better scatter his forces before they grow great?" These words decided Baldwin to relieve Athareb. Zangi advanced to meet his enemy. The issue was never doubtful. "The swords of God," in Ibn El-Athir's expressive words, "* found their scabbards in the necks of His foes." Zangi waded through a sea of blood, trampling down the Franks; this victory was followed by the capture of Athareb.

Zangi's successes were not, however, achieved except in the face of great disadvantages. In 1129 he had to contend against a rival Dubais, who sought to become Emir of Mosul. Two years later the disputed succession to the sultanate involved him in a series of conflicts which occupied most of his time for twelve years to come. In 1133 he was besieged for three months in Mosul, and it was not till 1143 that he finally made his peace with Mahmud's brother Masud.

By that time Zangi was the most powerful chief in Islam. After many failures he had made himself supreme on the Tigris, whilst as lord of the Orontes, he was ready to take the field against the Franks. The course of events soon gave him a favourable opportunity for the great work which he had so long contemplated—the recovery of Edessa.

Zangi's greatest opponent had been Joscelin de Courtenay, Count of Edessa, a kinsman of Baldwin du Bourg, who had endowed him with the rich fief of Tell -basher. Afterwards, for some offence, he was deprived of his lordship, but in 1118 Baldwin gave him back his old fief, and made him Count of Edessa also. From this moment his life was one of restless activity, his ravages extended southwards to Aleppo and Manbij; and eastwards as far as Nisibis, Amida, and Rakka. His name became a terror in Mohammedan lands, so that an Arabic writer calls him, "A Satan among the infidels." After a life of war and turmoil he lost his life as a warrior should in warfare. As he lay on his sick-bed he learnt that the Sultan of Iconium was besieging Cresson. His son was too cowardly or too sluggish to venture out against so vast a host, and Joscelin, angered at such pusillanimity, had himself carried to the war on a litter. The Sultan retreated at the rumour of his coming; the dying count returned thanks to heaven for having made him a terror to the infidel even in the gates of death. This was about 1131; the count was succeeded by his son, Joscelin II., a warrior of whom even Christian writers have but little good to say. Joscelin II. had something of his father's valour, but was given to wantonness and luxury, and though capable of vigorous action at times, preferred a life of ease to one of war. So he abandoned the hardships of Edessa for the comfort and pleasure of Tell-basher. The other Latin warriors followed his example, and Edessa was left to the unwarlike Armenians, and a few Latin merchants. The town was strongly fortified, but for security its peaceful inhabitants trusted to ill-paid mercenaries. "Thus," says William of Tyre, "Joscelin lost the whole region his father had ruled so well."

The defenceless state of Edessa gave Zangi his opportunity. After a siege of twenty-eight days, the town was captured on December 14, 1144. A promiscuous slaughter ensued, which raged till Zangi gave orders to sheath the sword. But even then he spared the Armenians only; all the Frank prisoners were butchered before Zangi's eyes, and their wives and children carried into captivity. The citadel held out for a few days, till want of water forced it to surrender. A garrison was placed in the conquered town, and Zangi passed on to capture the other Frankish towns of Upper Mesopotamia.

Zangi did not live to reap the fruits of his great conquest. For two years later, in September, 1146, as he was besieging Jaber, some of his own Mamluks stabbed him while he lay asleep in his tent. One who was there told the father of Ibn El-Athir how he entered the tent and found

141

his lord still alive. "On catching sight of me he fancied I was come to give the last blow, and lifted his forefinger as if to beg for mercy. As for me I stopped short, crying out, 'Oh, my master, who has done this?' He had no strength to answer, and at that very moment he breathed his last." Of Zangi's three sons, Nur-ed-din succeeded him at Aleppo, and Sayf-ed-din at Mosul.

Zangi's conquests paved the way for the future successes of Nur-ed-din and Saladin. He was the first Mussulman chief to win any permanent success against the Franks; and under his rule the Orontes valley became united against the invader. The contrast between the country as he found it, and as he left it, cannot be better stated than in the words of one who himself remembered the misery of the days before his coming. Ibn El-Athir's father had seen Mosul in ruins so that a traveller might stand in the centre of the town without seeing a single occupied house; under Zangi it became one of the most prosperous of Mohammedan towns. Zangi had reduced the Ortokid princes to his rule, established order at Aleppo, and made his authority paramount at Hamah, Emesa, and even at Damascus. He had taken many Frankish strongholds; last of all he had made the conquest of conquests when he wrested Edessa, "the eye of Upper Mesopotamia," from the invader. The Franks, who, at his accession, took tribute from Aleppo, and ravaged as far as Mardin and Nisibis, were driven back, and forced to act on the defensive, while prosperity once more began to smile upon the Mohammedans.

There were many noble features in Zangi's character; he was a valiant soldier, an able general, and a wise statesman; his worst fault was a tendency to trickery and falsehood. As a ruler his subjects marvelled at his care for all matters, great or small, and the untiring activity, which seemed to make him know things almost before they happened. To his subordinates he was a severe disciplinarian: "There must be but one tyrant in my lands," he used to say. He was indeed feared with a mortal terror: once he found a boatman sleeping at his post, the man awoke from his slumbers to meet the gaze of the atabek, and the sight so overcame him that he fell down dead.

The immediate result of Zangi's great conquest was to rouse the princes of the West to undertake the Second Crusade. The story of that enterprise will be told in another place, but the later fortunes of Count Joscelin and of Edessa form the fitting sequel to the events just described.

In November, 1146, at the invitation of the Armenians of Edessa, Count Joscelin made a night attack whilst the. Turkish garrison slept. The city was taken with little difficulty, but the citadel held out till Nur-ed-din came to their assistance. Joscelin then determined on retreat, and the citizens, rather than face the vengeance of Nur-ed-din, resolved to share his fortunes. As they filed through the gates the Turks from the citadel fell upon them in the rear, whilst Nur-ed-din's army barred all progress in front. The slaughter was terrible; only those Armenians escaped whose bodily vigour or swift steeds enabled them to keep up with the Frankish host. Among the slain was Baldwin of Marash, one of the few Frankish chiefs, who had won the love of their Armenian subjects; Joscelin himself escaped to Samosata.

Somewhat later, probably towards the end of 1149, during a fresh attempt on Edessa, Joscelin fell into the hands of Nur-ed-din's viceroy at Aleppo. Nur-ed-din had a deadly grudge against the count, who had sent the armour of Nur-ed-din's squire to Masud of Iconium, hinting that this gift should soon be followed by that of the atabek himself. By Nur-ed-din's orders Joscelin was blinded, and left to languish in a dungeon at Aleppo, till his death nine years later.

Joscelin's captivity was speedily followed by the loss of all that remained of his once prosperous county. In the expressive words of William of Tyre, Edessa was ground between the upper and nether millstone. Masud of Iconium had taken Marash in September, 1149,

143

and made further conquests during the next few years. By a bargain more nominal than real, the Franks handed over their last possessions in Edessa to the Greeks, Joscelin's wife and children taking refuge at Antioch. It was not long before the Greeks lost these acquisitions to Nur-ed-din, and in 1154 that prince put the crown to his father's work by the capture of Damascus. Henceforth Aleppo and Damascus were subject to one lord, and the first effectual step towards the conquest of the Latin kingdom was accomplished.

XIV.

THE SECOND CRUSADE.
(1146-1149.)

"Poi seguitai lo 'mperador Currado,
Ed ei mi cinse della sua milizia
Tanto per bene oprar gli vienni a grado."

DANTE, *Paradiso*, xv.

("Then I followed the Emperor Conrad, and he belted me of his soldiery, so high
in his favour did I come by good works.")

THE fall of Edessa was a keen reproach to the princes of the West,
who, as Otto of Freisingen complains,, were wasting their strength in
internecine slaughter whilst the very existence of the Holy Land was
threatened by the pagans. The evil tidings were brought by some
Armenian bishops to Pope Eugenius at Viterbo; but though, his letters
to Louis VII. and the nobles of France, and his renewal of the old
privileges granted to Crusaders by Urban II. had their due effect, the
eloquence of the great St. Bernard of Clairvaux was by far the most
potent agent in bringing about the Second Crusade.

Bernard was now in the very height of his fame, being about fifty-
four years old. He had long taken a special interest in the Latin
kingdom of Jerusalem, and had corresponded with Queen Melisend. His
uncle was a Knight Templar, and eventually Grand Master of that
order, for which Bernard himself drew up a code of rules. The third son
of a Burgundian noble, he had devoted himself from boyhood to holy
living and study, stedfastly resisting all the efforts of his elder brothers
to divert his mind to secular pursuits. More than this, he induced his
haughty brothers one after another to forsake the world, so that at last
the youngest, Nivard, was left alone in his father's house. His eldest

brother, Guido, saw the lad playing with his comrades, and thinking sadly of an almost extinct house, bade him remember that he was now sole heir of their father's lands. "Heaven for you, and earth for me," cried Nivard, "that is not a fair division;" and a little later he too followed his brothers' example. At twenty-three Bernard became a monk at Citeaux under Stephen Harding, who presently made him abbot of the newly founded monastery of Clairvaux. His fame for sanctity and learning so increased that when Innocent and Anacletus were contending for the Papacy it was Bernard's influence that decided the French prelates in favour of the former claimant. Nor was he less eminent in the intellectual than in the practical world; he refuted the heresies of Abelard and of Gilbert de la Porrée, and reformed the still more dangerous Henrician apostacy in Southern France. With his marvellous eloquence, strong practical turn of mind, and religious enthusiasm he was the very man to be the apostle of a new Crusade.

The weight of Bernard's influence enrolled in the service of the Cross two princes of the first rank—Louis VII. of France and Conrad III. of Germany. Louis was now about twenty-five years old. With his father, Louis the Fat, the house of Capet had begun to show some signs of real kingly power, and by his own recent marriage with Eleanor of Aquitaine the young Louis had brought that important duchy under the direct rule of the French king. Louis VII., like his great grandson Louis IX., was a man of pious disposition. Two considerations of religion quickened him to undertake the Crusade: first, his brotherly anxiety to perform the pilgrimage vowed by his dead brother Philip; secondly, his remorse for his sacrilege at Vitry, where, during the war with Theobald of Champagne, he had set fire—to the church and so caused the death of thirteen hundred unoffending people.

Conrad III. was the grandson of Henry IV. and nephew of Henry V. He was in Palestine when his uncle died in 1125, and on his return found the throne occupied by Lothair, Duke of Saxony. With his brother

Frederic, Duke of Swabia, he rebelled against the new king; but after a time a reconciliation was effected by Bernard of Clairvaux. In 1138 he succeeded to the throne of Germany; but his reign was much troubled by a feud between Leopold of Austria and Welf of Bavaria; and at the very moment when he promised to join in the Second Crusade he was surrounded by difficulties in Bavaria, Poland, Hungary, and Lorraine.

In the spring of 1146 a great council was held at Vézelay, where Louis took the cross from Bernard's hands, and as there was no room within the fortress showed himself to the people, with the cross upon his breast, from a wooden tower erected in the plain outside. Bernard, by his oratory, so moved his hearers, that he had to tear up his own robes in order to satisfy their demand for crosses. From Vézelay Bernard passed into Germany, preaching as he went; miracles dogged his steps; for the blind saw, the deaf heard, and the lame walked when Bernard signed them with the Holy Cross. At Christmas he came to Spires where the king was holding his midwinter council. Conrad had declared that he had no mind for the Holy War; but in a sermon on Christmas-day Bernard boldly renewed his call. In another sermon two days later he pictured the great king standing before the judgment-seat of Christ, Who asked: "Oh, man, how have *I* failed in ought of my duty towards *thee*?" Then as Bernard dwelt on Conrad's riches and power, the king at last burst into tears and declared himself ready to do the Lord's service wherever the Lord should call him. Hardly had Conrad spoken when the whole concourse took up the cry of "Praise to God." Bernard was not the man to lose his opportunity. He signed the king upon the spot, and taking down a banner from above the altar, entrusted it to Conrad to carry in the army of God.

Louis meantime had made great preparations, and after some negotiations with Roger of Sicily, had decided to journey by land, much to that prince's disgust. At Whitsuntide, 1147, the Pope gave the pious king his pilgrim scrip, and placed in his hands the famous banner of St.

147

Denys, "under whose protection the kings of France were always victorious." The French mustered at Metz, where they were joined by the English and Normans under Bishop Arnulf of Lisieux. Louis made an elaborate code for the governance of his host, as to which Odo of Deuil remarks, "I will not set it down on paper since it was not kept."

Conrad, with whom went his nephew Frederick, the future emperor, had started from Ratisbon without waiting for Louis, at the end of April, 1147. His vast army kept little or no military order, and after entering the Eastern Empire its progress was hardly more than a drunken rout. Provisions were seized without payment, and since Conrad could give no redress the Greeks retaliated by cutting off the drunken stragglers. Whilst Conrad lay encamped between Adrianople and the Byzantine capital, a sudden flood in the river Melas swept away his tents and drowned thousands of his men. Manuel offered his sympathy, and anxious to be rid of his unwelcome guests urged them to cross the Bosphorus without delay. But Conrad was bent on seeing the wonders of Constantinople, and urged on for the capital; there he encamped in the suburbs, but though the national jealousy broke into open war he did not dare to attack so strong a city. After much bickering the Crusading host at length crossed the Bosphorus, and Conrad then humbled himself so far as to beg guides of the Byzantine emperor.

The journey through Asia Minor was one long disaster. Greek and French writers alike charge Manuel with treachery; Nicetas says that he had ordered chalk to be mingled with the flour supplied to the Crusaders, and cheated them by the use of base coin; now he also stirred up the Turks against them, whilst his guides first misled and then abandoned them. The Crusaders found themselves with no alternative between famine and death, or retreat: Slowly and painfully they retraced their steps, whilst the Turkish hordes pressed close upon their rear. Odo, as he calls to mind how the swarms of unarmed pilgrims clogged the progress of the host, laments that the Pope, when he forbade them to take dogs or falcons with them, had not ordered the weak to stay at home, and the hale to exchange their staves for bows. Conrad was himself wounded twice by arrows; and perhaps barely one tenth of his followers found their way back to Nicaea.

Meanwhile Louis had been following close in Conrad's footsteps. Odo of Deuil, who was in Louis' company, complains that "the Germans who preceded us had disturbed everything, and on this account the Greeks fled from our army." Everywhere there were tokens of Greek distrust; the city gates were closed, and provisions let down from the walls by ropes, with baskets into which the purchasers had to place their price.

Louis, like Conrad, would tarry in Europe to see Constantinople. Had he been of an adventurous; disposition he might have anticipated the Fourth Crusade. For Roger of Sicily was at war with Manuel, and there were not wanting French nobles to counsel immediate war with the Emperor, who was said to have concluded a twelve years' peace with the Turks. "The walls of the city," urged the Bishop of Langres, "are very weak; the people are a feeble folk; the Emperor has never scrupled to make war upon the Christian princes of Antioch; were Constantinople once fallen there would be little need for further activity." Louis, however, refused such treacherous advice and made friends with Manuel. The two princes, says Odo, "became as brothers," and Manuel acted as Louis' guide when he visited the churches of Constantinople.

But when at last the Bosphorus was crossed, difficulties arose. Manuel would furnish no guides till Louis and his barons did him homage; the French king conceded the point, and then started for Nicaea. Here he heard of Conrad's disaster, and, grieving for his misfortune as though it were his own, went out to meet the Emperor. The combined armies agreed to bear one another company along the coast; after a toilsome march they reached Ephesus, where messengers from Manuel overtook them with the news that the Turks were gathering to oppose their progress.

This news determined Conrad to return and winter at Constantinople. Louis, however, continued his march, and, after spending Christmas in the valley of Decervion, pushed on over the snow-covered hills, and across the swollen stream towards Laodicea. The passage of the Maeander was triumphantly forced, and the French marched through Laodicea in high spirits. But only two days beyond that town the Crusaders met with their greatest disaster. A precipitous range of hills, "whose summit appeared to touch the heavens, whilst the torrent at its base seemed to descend to hell," barred their way. By a fatal error the van, under Geoffrey de Rancogne and Amadeus of Savoy, the king's uncle, instead of halting on the ridge, descended to pitch their tents on the southern slope. The Turks, and even Greeks, who thronged the heights above, sent down a hail of arrows, which swept the sumpter-horses into the abyss below. The pass was choked by an unarmed crowd, which, cut off in front and in the rear, was mercilessly massacred. Louis, with a noble disregard for his own life, strove to come to their assistance; but not having proposed to cross the pass till next day, he had only a few nobles with him, and was hopelessly outnumbered. "I," says Odo, "who, being a monk, could do nothing but call upon the Lord, and urge others to fight, was sent to carry this news to the camp." Geoffrey in vain endeavoured to return, whilst Louis, hampered with the crowd of panic-stricken pilgrims, could do nothing in the rocky way, where the heavy horses and long lances of his knights were of no avail. From the safe security of the hills the Turks still poured down the deadly storm of stones and trunks of trees. Louis himself only saved his life by seizing on to the roots of a tree, and so scaling the summit of a rock. There he kept his assailants at bay, until, not knowing who he was, they drew off at dusk to seek an easier prey.

Next morning a doleful spectacle appeared. It seemed the death-blow of the whole Crusade: "The flower of France had withered away before it could ripen into fruit at Damascus." The loss of baggage reduced many of the rich men to poverty, and the clamour against Geoffrey de Rancogne rose to such a height that he would have been hanged had not the king's uncle shared his fault. Louis did what he could to reorganise his army, and, resuming the march, reached Attaleia on February 2nd.

From Attaleia Louis made his way to Antioch by sea; before starting he agreed with the Greek governor for the safe conduct of the mass of the pilgrims by land to Tarsus, Needless to say, the Greeks betrayed their trust. The very Turks proved kinder, for, taking pity on the sufferings of the Crusaders, they gave them bread to eat. "Many of the Christians forsook their religion and went over to the Turks. Oh! kindness, more cruel than Greek treachery, for giving bread they stole the true faith." . . . "God," continues Odo, "may pardon the German Emperor, through whose counsel we encountered such misfortune, but how shall He spare the Greeks, whose cruel craft slew so many in either army?"

It was early in March, 1148, that Louis reached Antioch, where Raymond, his wife's uncle, welcomed him kindly, hoping that the French Crusaders would help him to conquer Aleppo and Caesarea. Louis was, however, anxious to reach Jerusalem, and refused the proposal, which was practicable enough, as well as one of similar tenour from his own cousin, the other Raymond of Tripoli.

Conrad meantime had reached Acre by sea, and after a great council had been held it was decided to march against Damascus. From the place of muster at Tiberias the host, with the Holy Cross at its head, marched across Jordan; first went the barons of the land under King Baldwin, next the French, and last the Germans. The mud wall that surrounded the famous gardens of Damascus offered no bar to the advance of such an army. But the thick orchards with their narrow footpaths, and their growth of fruit and herbage, formed a far better protection to the city. Everywhere through the length and breadth of this vast stretch of green and trees the ambushed Saracens opposed the invaders' progress; or penned up in lofty buildings, which here and there rose up like stone islands out of a sea of green, shot down their arrows from above. At last, after long fighting, the woods were cleared, and the Christians, wearied out with heat and thirst, made for the river, only to find a fresh army drawn up against them. "Why do we not advance," cried Conrad from the rear, and learning the cause, burst through the French battalions to the van. There, in true Teutonic fashion, he and his knights leapt off their war-horses, and, closing up behind their shield-wall, soon swept back the enemy within the city. "The siege now began in earnest, and would have been brought to a successful issue," says William of Tyre, "had it not been for the greed of the great princes, who commenced negotiations with the citizens." At the advice of traitors the camp was shifted to the south-west, where, so ran the rumour, the wall was too weak to withstand the feeblest onset. But here the Crusaders found a more deadly enemy than strong fortifications; for in their new position they were cut off from the river, and deprived of the orchard fruits; and through lack of food and leadership despair fell upon the host, until men began to talk of retreat. There was jealousy, likewise, between the Syrian Franks and their Western allies, and out of this too fertile source of evil Anar, the Vizir of Damascus, was not slow to reap profit for himself He pointed out to the former the folly of helping their brethren to seize Damascus, the capture of which would be but the prelude to the seizing of Jerusalem also. His arguments, supported as they doubtless were with bribes, brought about the abandonment of the siege. A proposal to besiege Ascalon was also defeated by the jealousy of the Syrian Franks, and after a while Conrad sailed home in disgust.

Louis stayed in Palestine till Easter, 1149, and then he too went home by sea. Despite his own -misfortunes he never lost his interest in his Eastern brethren. Time after time the later kings of Jerusalem appealed to him for aid. In his latter years he sent Geoffrey Fulcher, the Templar,' to visit the Holy Places on his behalf; with one letter Geoffrey sends home the royal ring with which he had in the king's name touched each sacred shrine. In 1151, after news reached France of the death of Raymond of Antioch, Louis' great minister, Suger, though he had urgently opposed the king's own Crusade, would have organised another on his own account had not death cut him off in the midst of his plans. Next year Louis divorced his wife Eleanor, at too long an interval for us to suppose that his action was in reality, as alleged, for her misconduct on the Crusade. Yet Eleanor was beyond all doubt in some degree concerned in the intrigues which led to the final failure of the expedition. Scandal connected her name with that of her uncle, Raymond of Antioch, and though that prince may have only sought to find through her influence some means for diverting the Crusading host to his own aggrandisement, his conduct certainly excited the jealousy of Louis. Raymond's disappointment, whether in love or in war, and Louis' suspicion, were not unimportant factors in the ruin of the expedition. Other tales of a more fabulous character make Eleanor ride, like another Penthesilea, at the head of a band of Amazon ladies, and represent her as the heroine of amours with Saladin, then a mere boy of thirteen.

The miserable termination of the Second Crusade excited in Western Europe a feeling of humiliation and wrath, which vented itself on Bernard as the prime mover in the enterprise. To Bernard himself the disaster came as the bitterest of blows. "We have fallen on evil days," he writes, "in which the Lord, provoked by our sins, has judged the world, with justice indeed, but not with His wonted mercy. . . . The sons of the Church have been overthrown in the desert, slain with the sword, or destroyed by famine. We promised good things, and behold disorder! The judgments of the Lord are righteous, but this one is an abyss so deep that I must call him blessed who is not scandalised therein."

Disastrous as the Second Crusade was for the fortunes and fame of those who had taken the chief part in its inception and performance, it was of little more service to the Latin kingdom of Jerusalem. It did not materially weaken the Mohammedans, nor substantially strengthen the Syrian Franks, whilst the seeds of mutual distrust that were now sown between the latter and their Western brethren were to continue to bear bitter fruit. One episode alone serves to brighten this dark page of history. A North European fleet, chiefly composed of English, conquered Lisbon from the Moors, and thus rendered a lasting service to Christianity. It is with pardonable pride that our English chroniclers dwell on the contrast between this achievement of a humble band of pilgrims, and the disaster which attended the great and splendid host, that had gone forth under the leadership of emperor and king to be swept away like a spider's web.

XV.

LOSS AND GAIN.
(1143-1169.)

"O thou sword of the Lord, how long will it be ere thou be quiet? Put up thyself into thy scabbard, rest, and be still. How can it be quiet, seeing the Lord hath given it a charge against Ashkelon, and against the sea shore?"—Jeremiah xlvii. 6, 7.

§ 1. *Baldwin III. and Ascalon.*

ON Christmas Day, 1143, six weeks after his father's death, the youthful Baldwin III. was crowned and anointed by the Patriarch of Jerusalem. For some years the land was ruled by his mother Melisend—a woman "well-skilled in all secular matters, and so far above her sex as to be able to put her hand to great deeds."

But young as he was Baldwin soon showed signs of the warlike stock from which he had sprung, and in the second year of his reign undertook a somewhat rash and hazardous expedition across the Jordan. Anar, the Vizir of Damascus, had a quarrel with the Governor of Bostra in the Hauran, who offered to surrender the city to Baldwin. The temptation was too great for Latin honesty to resist, and the forces of the kingdom were mustered at Tiberias. It was in vain that Anar offered to buy the invaders off, Baldwin declared that his honour was at stake, and led out his army to the plain of Medan. Here the Franks were surrounded at night by the enemy; retreat was impossible, and with the knights at their head the army slowly made its way to Adhirah or Adratum, the city of Baldwin d'Etampes. Three days later they sighted Bostra from afar, but that very night came the news that Nur-ed-din's troops had been admitted to the city. There seemed to be no course but to retreat with what speed they could. Some advised that the

155

king at least should secure his own safety, and that of the Holy Cross, by riding off on John Goman's horse, the fleetest and strongest in the host, but this Baldwin refused as unworthy of a king.

Morning broke and showed Nur-ed-din issuing from the city at the head of a huge army, to join the Turks, who hung on the Christian rear. The retreat began, but without any fear or precipitancy in the "iron people" of the Franks. The sick and even the dead with arms in their nerveless hands were set upon camels and packhorses to give the appearance of strength where none existed. At first the Franks held their own, but when the smoke from the adjoining thickets that had been fired by the Saracens was blown in their faces by the wind, their sufferings became unendurable. "Pray for us," cried the soldiers, as they raised their blackened faces to the Holy Cross, which was borne by Robert, Archbishop of Nazareth. Robert turned the sacred relic towards the flames, and as he did so the wind seemed to shift and carry the smoke back upon the foe. Thus the Franks obtained a respite, but they had no guide, and the way by which they were returning was unfamiliar. From this fresh strait they were again miraculously delivered; for there went before them on a white steed an unknown knight with a red banner in his hands; like an angel of the Lord he led them by easy stages to unsuspected waters, and in three days conducted them across the waste from the Cave of Roab to Gadara.

At first Baldwin and his mother ruled conjointly without any jealousy. But when the young king was grown to manhood, busy flatterers persuaded him that such dependence was unworthy. Melisend had appointed as constable of the kingdom Manasses de Herges, her father's sister's son. Manasses' haughty bearing angered the great nobles and the young king, who accordingly resolved to deprive his mother of all authority. So at Easter, 1152, Baldwin refused to let his mother share in the ceremony of his coronation at Jerusalem, and demanded one half of the kingdom for himself. After much discussion the king was assigned Tyre and Acre with the coast, his mother Jerusalem and Nablûs. But this did not content Baldwin, who soon afterwards expelled Manasses from the kingdom, seized Nablûs, and besieged his mother in Jerusalem. The citizens opened the gates to the king, and Melisend, after a few days' resistance in the Tower of David, was forced to capitulate. Nablûs was restored to her, but from this time she led a retired life till her death on the north.

For fifty years Ascalon had been as an open sore in the side of the Franks. Now that Baldwin was master of his kingdom, he determined on a great effort for its reduction. Four years previously he had rebuilt Gaza, and put it in the hands of the Templars; this fortress, with the previous ones at Gibelin, Ibelin, and Blanchegarde, ringed Ascalon in upon the south, the east, and the north.

For so great an enterprise all the forces of the land were called up, and on the 25th of January, 1153, the siege was began. Gerard of Sidon was stationed off the harbour with a fleet to prevent all succour from Egypt. For six months the town was besieged without effect, the defenders keeping careful guard, and by night hanging glazed lamps along the walls that gave light as in the day, and prevented any attack under cover of the dark. When Easter brought its usual complement of pilgrims, Baldwin, by an arbitrary exercise of his kingly power, called up all, pilgrims and sailors alike, from the ports, and forbade any vessels to sail for Europe. The ships themselves he bought, and of their timbers constructed wooden castles and the various warlike engines of mediaeval warfare.

After a time a fleet was sent from Egypt to the succour of the town. Gerard of Sidon fled in terror from his post, whilst the townsfolk gathered fresh courage, and would have burnt the wooden castle near the eastern gate, had not a sudden wind driven the flames back upon the city wall. Then was their device turned to their own destruction, for the fire secured such a hold that it could not be subdued. At daybreak

157

the sound of a mighty crash roused the sleeping host to discover that a great part of the wall had fallen. The Templars, headed by their master, Bernard de Tremelay, eager to secure the city for themselves, rushed recklessly into the breach. There refusing all other help, they were cut off from retreat, and the master with forty of his knights fell victims to their greed or to their valour. The citizens then repaired the breach by a temporary defence, whilst the Christians turned back to their tents almost ready to abandon the siege. Baldwin himself was in favour of retreat, but at last the other party, led by the patriarch and Raymond, Master of the Hospitallers, prevailed. Once more the trumpets sounded to arms, and after a terrible fight that lasted all day the Christians were victorious. The men of Ascalon now sued for terms, and on the 12th of August were suffered to depart for Egypt with their wives, their children, and their goods. The Christians, with the Holy Cross at their head, then entered Ascalon, which was bestowed on the king's brother, Amalric, who from this time appears in charters as the Count of Ascalon.

Four years later, in 1157, the arrival of the veteran Crusader, Theodoric of Flanders, with his wife Sibylla, the king's half-sister, encouraged Baldwin to an enterprise in the north. The moment was propitious, for Nur-ed-din lay sick, as it seemed, unto death, but the usual jealousies among the leaders destroyed the opportunity. Siege was laid to Caesarea on the Orontes, a fortress which Nur-ed-din had lately captured from its lord a cousin of the famous Saracen warrior and poet, Ossama, whose autobiography has been recently and strangely recovered. The Crusaders soon forced their way into the town, and might easily have mastered the citadel had not quarrels broken out in their ranks. Baldwin, supported by the great lords, designed the city for Theodoric of Flanders; but Reginald of Châtillon, a French adventurer, whom Constance of Antioch had taken for her second husband, claimed it as part of his principality and declared that whoever possessed it must do homage to him. This was more than the proud spirit of the Flemish count could bear: he had never done homage save to kings. At last, unable to agree among themselves, they broke up the siege and returned to Antioch. Early next year the Crusaders took Harenc, which was entrusted to Reginald of St. Valery. Theodoric and Baldwin then went south, and after some further achievements Theodoric returned home, reaching Arras in August, 1159.

In the previous year Baldwin, desirous to secure a closer alliance with Constantinople, had sent envoys to beg a member of the Imperial family for his bride. Manuel consented, and despatched his niece Theodora, a girl of thirteen, with a splendid dowry of one hundred thousand besants, not to speak of bridal gifts worth forty thousand more. Theodora reached Tyre in September, 1159, and a few days later was crowned at Jerusalem. Shortly afterwards Manuel returned the compliment by asking for a French bride. His envoys rejected Melisend, the sister of Raymond of Tripoli, in favour of the superior beauty of Maria of Antioch. The rejection of his sister so enraged Raymond that he turned the twelve galleys, which he had prepared for his sister's escort, into pirate barks, and laid waste the mainland and islands of the Empire, sparing neither age nor sex.

In the summer of 1159 Manuel appeared with a vast army in Cilicia. He came so suddenly that Thoros, the Armenian prince, could barely escape from Tarsus to the mountains. Reginald, who had been scheming with Thoros against the Greeks, presented himself humbly at Mamistra. Barefooted and bare-armed, with a rope round his neck, he fell prostrate before his offended lord, and so "turned the glory of the Latins into shame." Manuel was pleased to be reconciled, and proceeded towards Syria. Near Antioch he met Baldwin, who also showed due humility, sitting on a lowly seat beside the Imperial throne. Manuel then entered Antioch in triumph, Reginald holding his horse's bridle, and Baldwin, stripped of all regal ornaments, riding at his side.

The presence of so enormous an army alarmed Nured-din, who promised to release all his Christian captives. "On these conditions," says the Greek historian, "the Emperor stayed his hand;" but the forbearance was more probably dictated by the news of a conspiracy at Constantinople.

After Manuel's departure, Nur-ed-din took Marash and Cresson from Kilij Arslan. Baldwin seized the opportunity to ravage the territory of Damascus, but Saladin's father, Ayub, who was governor of the city, bought him off by a bribe of four thousand besants. About the same time (November 23, 1161), Reginald of Antioch fell into an ambuscade near Cresson, and was carried prisoner to Aleppo. Nur-ed-din then extended his ravages to Tripoli and Harenc, and was only checked from going further by the approach of Baldwin.

Baldwin came to Antioch in the autumn of 1162. According to the custom of the time, he took some pills from Barek, the Count of Tripoli's doctor, to fortify his constitution against the winter. A feverish dysentery ensued, and getting no better, he proceeded first to Tripoli, and then to Beyrout, where he died, February 10, 1163, in the thirty-third year of his age. His body was carried to Jerusalem and buried in the Church of the Holy Sepulchre with his ancestors. Wherever the corpse was brought, says William of Tyre, there was mourning such as was never shown for any prince in history. The very dwellers in the hills came down to share in the funeral procession as it slowly wound on its eight days' march from Beyrout to Jerusalem. Even the Saracens sympathised, and Nur-ed-din, when advised to seize the opportunity for an inroad, refused with noble scorn: "We ought to pity this people's .righteous sorrow, for they have lost a prince whose like is not now left in the world."

Baldwin was, tall of stature and largely built, comely featured and of a florid complexion, with prominent eyes, yellowish hair, and a somewhat full beard. William of Tyre praises him for his attention to the church services, but admits that before his marriage he had been licentious. He had many of the qualities most useful for a ruler. He was affable to all men, and would jest with his friends in public; more than this, he could bear a joke at his own expense. He was kind-hearted and generous, but somewhat careless as to how he supplied his pecuniary needs. He had a quick intellect and a good memory. His knowledge of the customary law of his realm astonished his own nobles, who came to him for advice on legal difficulties. Above all else he was commode litteratus, by which we may infer that he knew Latin. What time he could spare from public business he used to devote to reading. History was his favourite study; he delighted to read about the deeds of ancient kings, and loved to converse with learned clerks and wise laymen. Both nobles and people loved him; for he was patient in hardships, and a wary leader in war, who never lost his presence of mind even in the most adverse circumstances.

§ 2. *The Struggle for Egypt.*

The history of Egypt during the twelfth century is nothing but a record of waning power and bloodshed. The Caliph was overshadowed by the vizir, whose authority was tempered by assassination or rebellion. In 1154, Abbas, the vizir, and his son, Nasr-ed din, at the instigation of the poet-statesman Ossama, murdered their master, and made his infant son Caliph; but a speedy retribution came upon them at the hands of Es-Saleh [Talaï], Governor of Upper Egypt, and Abbas and his son were driven into the Syrian desert, where the Templars took Nasr-ed-din prisoner. The captive prince was on the point of declaring himself a Christian, when his captors, by a double act of treachery and greed, sold him to his enemy, Es-Saleh. The new vizir after a short reign of six years was stabbed by his emirs in 1161; and his son was quickly overthrown by another competitor, Shawir, the Governor of

Said. Shawir found a dangerous rival in the Arab Dirgham, and was forced to take refuge with Nur-ed-din. There had thus been three vizirs in one year.

The relations of the Franks with Egypt at this time are very obscure; but there are reasons for thinking that the Caliph of Cairo paid annual tribute to Baldwin III. In September, 1163, Amalric made Dirgham's refusal to continue this payment a pretext for declaring war. Dirgham, beaten in battle, saved his land from conquest by letting in the Nile; and Amalric, unable to contend with nature, drew back into Palestine. Next year Shawir obtained from Nur-ed-din an army under Shirkuh the Kurd. Dirgham hastened to make terms with Amalric, but before the Franks could come to his aid, Shirkuh was at Cairo and his opponent dead.

The presence of Shirkuh soon proved burdensome to Shawir, who in his turn appealed to Amalric. The Frankish king readily accepted the invitation, and besieged Shirkuh at Pelusium in July. After a three months' siege, the news of Nur-ed-din's invasion of Northern Syria made Amalric offer favourable terms, which Shirkuh, ignorant of what was taking place, accepted.

But Shirkuh, though defeated for the moment, was too enamoured with the wealth of Egypt to entirely abandon his designs; he bided his time till, in 1167, his preparations were ready, and he once more started for the Nile. But Amalric was before him, and had already compelled Shawir to renew his submission and increase the tribute, in return for the promise of protection against his dangerous foe. To make his position more sure, the king required that this bargain should be confirmed by the Caliph, for which purpose he despatched Hugh of Caesarea and Geoffrey Fulcher, the Templar, as his ambassadors. Under the guidance of Shawir the two envoys were introduced to the palace of the Caliph. As they passed between marble columns, under golden ceilings, and over floors of rich mosaic, the rude Frank soldiers

162

marvelled at a display such as neither Europe nor their own country could produce. Their astonished eyes gazed on marble fishponds with pellucid water, birds of strange songs and marvellous plumage, beasts that seemed to belong rather to the world of art and dreams than that of waking life. At length, in the presence chamber, a pearl-embroidered curtain rose, and revealed the Caliph seated on a golden throne. El-Adid promised all that the envoys asked, but when desired to pledge his honour with his hand, hesitated for a moment before he proffered his gloved hand to Hugh. The rude knight blurted out: "Truth has no covering; princes when they pledge themselves should have no secret thoughts." The Caliph, with a forced smile, accepted the challenge and drew off his glove.

After some desultory operations and the arrival of reinforcements from Palestine, Amalric achieved a partial success, which compelled Shirkuh to retreat. The Franks overtook the Turks at Babein. Some of the emirs were for declining battle, but one turned the scale by a few stinging words, in which he bade the cowards stay at home with the women; Nur-ed-din had sent them to fight, and fight they must. The battle which ensued was indecisive; though Amalric was victorious in his part of the field, Shirkuh withdrew in safety towards Alexandria.

Amalric then determined to lay siege to this important city, the defence of which had been entrusted by Shirkuh to his nephew Saladin. Hard pressed by the Franks without, and in fear of the unfriendly citizens within, Saladin soon found it necessary to appeal to his uncle. Shirkuh himself had meantime been endeavouring, without success, to capture Cairo, which was held by Hugh of Ibelin. He was therefore ready to come to terms, and an arrangement was made for the surrender of Alexandria, and the complete evacuation of Egypt by the invading Saracens (Aug. 4, 1167). After this success, Amalric returned to Palestine; his triumph indeed seemed complete, for a Frankish guard and agent were established at Cairo, and Shawir had to pay a yearly tribute of one hundred thousand dinars.

Soon after his return, Amalric married on the 29th of August, 1167, as his second wife, Maria, a grand niece of the Emperor Manuel. The Emperor, by pointing out to his ally the weakness of Egypt, and its consequent danger from Nur-ed-din, roused him to fresh thoughts of conquest. Amalric's own greed and poverty made him lend a ready ear to the temptation, and before his envoy, William of Tyre, could return from Constantinople, he had determined on a fresh invasion. Contemporary rumour alleged that Gerbert Assallit, master of the Hospital, advised this breach of the peace, in the hope of benefit to his debt-stricken order, and despite the opposition of the Templars.

The campaign began in October, 1168; Pelusium was stormed and sacked on 3rd of November, and ten days later Amalric appeared before Cairo; the Frankish fleet was brought up the Nile, and the city would have surrendered had not Amalric loitered on the march so long. Shawir had, meanwhile, appealed to Nur-ed-din, and now by false promises of money to be paid, deluded the avaricious king, until the approach of Shirkuh in December. Amalric marched back to meet his new enemy in the desert, but Shirkuh slipped by unnoticed, leaving the Franks to return home from their bootless campaign.

The withdrawal of Amalric sealed the fate of Egypt; Shawir found his Turkish ally more dangerous than his Frank foe; a futile conspiracy by the vizir gave Shirkuh a plausible excuse for beheading the man whom he had come to aid, and establishing himself in his place. Shirkuh held the position he had coveted so long for less than three months, and dying on March 23, 1169, was succeeded by his nephew the famous Saladin.

Meanwhile Manuel and Amalric had concerted a joint campaign for the following autumn; a Greek fleet was to join with a Latin army in besieging Damietta. Had the design been accomplished the city must have fallen; but the ships were becalmed, and the consequent delay gave Saladin time to regarrison Damietta. The siege was however commenced, and prosecuted with vigour if with little success; the Greek fleet could not force the boom which blocked the river from the sea, whilst above the town the water gave easy access to reinforcements; thus the numbers inside increased, till the besiegers were in greater peril than the besieged. "There crept a murmur through the people, and almost all were of one mind, that our toil was wasted, and that it would be safer to return home than to die by hunger or the sword." So orders were given to raise the siege, and the one formidable armament undertaken by the Greeks and Latins in conjunction came to a disastrous end.

William of Tyre, who was absent that year from Palestine, says that the king and nobles attributed their failure to Greek fraud. Whatever the truth of their complaints, it is certainly clear that mutual distrust prevented the allies from taking full advantage of their opportunities.

The conquest of Egypt by the lieutenant of Nured-din was important for Islam, inasmuch as it led two years later to the suppression of the Fatimite caliphate, an event which was soon followed by the death of the hapless prince El-Adid. Yet more important was the fact that the wealth of the Nile was now at the disposal of the lord of Aleppo and Damascus, who from his ports of Damietta and Alexandria could attack the yearly pilgrim fleets, and thus as it were sever the main artery of the Christian kingdom. The full effects of the conquest were not, however, to be felt as yet, for Saladin was but an unruly vassal. Still the time was only deferred when the valleys of the Orontes and Nile would own but one master in fact and in name. When that day arrived no human power could well have saved the kingdom of Jerusalem from its fate.

XVI.

THE RIVAL KINGS—NUR-ED-DIN AND AMALRIC.
(1163-1174.)

"The fierce joy that warriors feel
In foemen worthy of their steel."

SCOTT.

ZANGI'S death had secured a respite for the kingdom of Jerusalem, through the division of his dominions, and the not unnatural jealousy of his sons. Nur-ed-din at Aleppo regarded his elder brother with a feeling of suspicion, which Sayf-eddin's generous conduct with some difficulty dispelled. On Sayf-ed-din's death in 1149, there was again some danger of open war between Aleppo and Mosul. But by the mediation of Jamal-ed-din the Vizir, who pointed out that whichever was victorious, the real advantage would rest with the Franks, a compromise was arranged under which Mosul was left to a third brother Kutb-ed-din till his death in 1170.

Nur-ed-din's character was marked by craft and greed, yet he was one of the greatest princes that ever ruled in Syria. The Christians themselves acknowledged his valour and success; to the Mohammedans of this century and the next he was a model of every virtue. "Though so great a persecutor of Christians," writes William of Tyre, "he was a just ruler, wise, and religious, so far as the traditions of his race permitted." It was for his justice above all that his subjects loved him; he would take no unjust tax from his vast dominions, but like any private man lived of his own; when his wife complained of her poverty, and slighted a gift of three shops in Emesa as insignificant, "I have nought else, for all I have I hold only as treasurer for the faithful," was his reply. He once left his game of ball to appear before the cadi at the suit of a private person, and when the decision was given in his favour, resigned

166

his claim in favour of his opponent. His justice enticed strangers to his dominions, one of whom, after his death, having appealed to Saladin in vain, went in tears to the tomb of Nur-ed-din. The popular sympathy forced Saladin at last to make recompense; the man then wept again, and when Saladin asked his reason, replied that he wept for a ruler who could do justice even in the grave.

Though himself a skilful warrior, and like his father careful of his soldiers' rights Nur-ed-din would permit no plundering. Yet his followers loved him, and stood firm in battle, for they knew that if they perished their master would be true to their children. When some of his soldiers grumbled at his bounty to the dervishes, he rebuked them saying, "These men have a right to live at the public expense; I am grateful to them for being content with only a part of what they might justly claim. So, too, when an emir slandered a learned doctor from Khorassan, Nur-ed-din replied, "If you speak ill of him, I shall punish you severely, even though you tell the truth. His good qualities are enough to cover his faults, whereas you and your like have vices many times greater than your virtues."

Nur-ed-din was a great builder, and provided for the re-fortification of the chief cities of Syria, especially after the earthquake of 1169. He raised mosques everywhere, and founded hospitals in various towns. Many years after, Ibn El-Athir, disgusted with his paid physician sought advice from the hospital at Damascus; he would have paid for the service done him, but his gift was refused, with the remark, "Doubtless you are rich enough to pay, but here no one is too proud to accept the gifts of Nur-ed-din."

The Mohammedan law as regards food, drink, and dress was carefully observed by Nur-ed-din, who unlike previous rulers enforced the same obedience on his subjects. His court was marked by a strictness of etiquette, which did not suffer any one to sit in his presence, except Ayub, the father of Saladin. Very different was that of

167

Saladin, where a visitor found himself unable to make the Sultan hear through the babble of so many voices all talking at once; "At Nur-ed-din's court," he exclaimed, "Nur-ed-din's sight alone made us as motionless as if we had a bird perched on our heads; in silence we listened when he spoke, and he in turn lent attention to our speech."

One amusement alone did Nur-ed-din permit himself—namely, the game of "ball on horseback," a pastime which appealed to him as a rider of unusual skill. When reproached for this, he replied: "I do not play to amuse myself, but for needful recreation, since a soldier cannot always be fighting. Moreover, while playing at this game, we have our horses ready against a sudden attack by the foe. Before God this is my only reason for playing." "Rarely," says Ibn El-Athir, "has a prince made of his very amusements an act of high devotion."

There was much of high religious feeling in Nured-din's character, and this feeling permeated his whole life of active warfare against the Christian intruder. When told how his brother had lost an eye in fighting for the Holy Cause, Nur-ed-din refused to offer his condolence, "for could my brother but see what Allah hath in store for him in Paradise, he would willingly lose his other eye in such a cause." Nor was Nur-ed-din any more regardful of his own safety. One day a friend rebuked him for his carelessness, bidding him consider what would become of Islam should its chief defender fall. "Who," was Nur-ed-din's noble reply, "who is Mahmud (i.e., himself) that you should speak thus of him. Our country and religion have a defender better than me, and that defender is God."

In his earlier years Nur-ed-din could venture only on foraging raids. But gradually his power grew, and in 1154, as we have already seen, he captured Damascus. Good fortune attended him, for Joscelin of Edessa had already become his prisoner, and a few years later in 1161 Reginald de Châtillon, prince of Antioch, whilst engaged in a plundering expedition to the west of the Euphrates, fell into an ambuscade and was taken prisoner to Aleppo. The young Bohemond then assumed the rule of his principality. Nured-din conceived that the occasion was favourable for an attack, and in 1163 invaded the county of Tripoli. A force of Aquitanian pilgrims recently arrived under Geoffrey Martel, together with the Templars under Gilbert de Lacy, and a body of Welshmen under Robert Mansel, opposed the Turks with such success that Nur-ed-din himself barely escaped with his life. In .the following year Nur-ed-din's turn came; whilst many Franks were absent in Egypt he laid siege to Harenc; Bohemond of Antioch and Raymond of Tripoli forced him to raise the siege, but in the subsequent engagement were defeated and carried prisoners to Aleppo. It was the news of this disaster that compelled Amalric to concede such favourable terms to Shirkuh.

There is no need to trace the progress of Nur-ed-din's power during the next few years. But in 1170 the death of Kutb-ed-din of Mosul gave Nur-ed-din an opportunity to interfere in that quarter to the advantage of his own power. Saladin was, however, already threatening to prove a dangerous rival, and would lend his nominal lord no aid against the Franks, lest their subjection should be but the prelude to his own. The danger at last forced Nur-ed-din to contemplate an invasion of Egypt. In this strait Saladin's father recommended his son to adopt a policy of submission, pointing out in private that humility would avert the intended invasion, and that destiny meanwhile would run its course. This policy had its due effect, and Nur-ed-din found sufficient employment in warfare with the Franks and the Sultan of Iconium until his death on May 15, 1174.

The death of Nur-ed-din was followed speedily by dissensions in Syria. His son and successor, El-Malek Es-Saleh, was a boy of eleven, whose weakness led his cousin of Mosul to conquer at his expense. In these troubles Saladin saw his opportunity; on November 28, 1174, he entered Damascus, and a month later, having captured Emesa and

Hamah on his way, laid siege to Aleppo, from which a threatened invasion by the Franks soon forced him to withdraw. The intervention of Sayf-ed-din of Mosul led only to his own defeat, and almost to the final displacement of Es-Saleh, who, however, continued to rule over a diminished, territory till his death at the end of 1181.

We must now return to consider the last years of the reign of Amalric. Throughout his reign that prince had felt that his chief hope of support lay in a close alliance with Constantinople, and his return from his last Egyptian expedition was shortly followed by a visit to the Byzantine capital. Manuel received him nobly, "as was due to the king of Jerusalem and the advocate and defender of the venerable scenes of our Lord's passion and resurrection." Etiquette forbade even a king to sit in the Emperor's presence when he received in state, but after Amalric had entered the royal chamber, curtains fell suddenly and excluded the greater number of the courtiers. Manuel then rose from his golden throne, embraced his guest, and set him on a lowly seat hard by. But though the Emperor lent a ready ear to his visitor's projects for the easy conquest of Egypt, and distributed gifts with splendid magnificence, he went no further, and Amalric returned home a disappointed, if a richer, man.

The events of the previous year had probably moved Amalric to thus seek the aid of the Emperor. In June, 1170, a great earthquake had well-nigh ruined many cities of Northern Syria. Antioch, Tripoli, and Tyre, as well as the Mohammedan cities of Hamah, Emesa, and Aleppo, all shared in the disaster. The earthquakes continued during three or four months, and imposed upon the warring races a short period of peace, for "each man was occupied by his private misfortune, and while harassed by his own grief, forbore to set troubles for another." In the following December Saladin took advantage of the prevalent weakness to attack Darum, a fortress which was held by the Templars. Amalric hurried up in time to save the citadel, but not the town. Saladin,

170

however, managed to slip past him to Gaza, and there, too, succeeded in sacking the town and mercilessly slaying the defenceless citizens and country folk who had congregated for safety. The citadel was kept safely by its warden, Milo de Planci, who wickedly refused its shelter to the Christian fugitives. With this measure of success Saladin was content to go back to Egypt, whilst Amalric busied himself with the restoration of his fortresses.

The last days of Amalric were embittered by the ambition of the Templars. The castles of that order hemmed in the mountainous territory of the Assassins, from whom the knights exacted a yearly tribute. In the hope of escaping this impost the chief of the Assassins offered to turn Christian; Amalric readily acceded, and promised to recompense the knights out of his own purse. The Templars, however, distrusted his goodwill or his power, and at the instigation of Walter de Maisnil, "an evil man with one eye," slew the envoys of the Assassins on the borders of Tripoli. Such a crime enraged the whole kingdom, but Odo de St. Amand, the Master of the Temple, claimed the right to punish his knights as he choose, and protected the murderers. Amalric could not brook such defiance; with the assent of his council, he seized the offenders by force and sent them in chains to Tyre; probably he would have pursued the matter further had it not been for his own sudden death.

When Nur-ed-din died in May, 1174, Amalric, unlike his great and generous rival, had no compunction about invading a kingless realm; he accordingly laid siege to Banias, but allowed himself to be bought off by Nur-ed-din's widow, and withdrew to Tiberias. There he was seized with a dysentery, but would not take to his bed or suffer himself to be carried in a litter; on horseback he rode through Nazareth and Nablûs to Jerusalem. His illness increasing he desired the Greek and Syrian physicians, who were in attendance, to give him a purging draught, and when they refused had resort to the more compliant but less skilful

Latin doctors. For a time he seemed to improve, but the disease returned with fresh violence, and on July 11, 1174, Amalric died in the thirty-eighth year of his age.

Amalric was of middle height, and somewhat corpulent, but of comely features and a presence which proclaimed his rank. He had bright eyes and an aquiline nose, with golden hair and a full beard. In manner he lacked the gracious affability which had endeared his brother to all classes of his subjects, and would rarely enter into familiar conversation. Neither was he so well educated as Baldwin had been, but his understanding was quick, and his tenacious memory made good use of his scanty leisure. History was his favourite study, and his liberality supplied William of Tyre with manuscripts for the compilation of his great work on Arabic history, now unfortunately lost. His serious disposition gave him no taste for plays or dice, though he was passionately fond of hawking. Though regular in religious observances he seems to have been something of a sceptic, and perhaps a disbeliever in the immortality of the soul. In his private life he was very licentious and in his public much given to avarice; this latter failing he excused on the plea that if a prince saved he was less likely to rob his subjects, and better equipped against a sudden emergency; certainly, when his realm was in peril, he spared neither his purse nor person, and even in private matters was often liberal, as when he subscribed largely to ransom his cousin Raymond of Tripoli.

With all his faults Amalric had many of the qualities of a great ruler, and his death at this moment was a serious blow to the kingdom of Jerusalem. So valorous and so politic a king would doubtless have been able to reap some advantage from the weakness of the heir of Nur-ed-din, and the ambitious rivalry of Saladin. Would but the princes of the West have forgotten their private feuds, and supported the great but futile expedition that William of Sicily sent against Alexandria this self-same year; would but the Eastern Franks and the Greeks have cordially united for once, there is no telling what successes might have resulted. But there was now no hand that could unite for one purpose the scattered forces of Christendom. Armies that might have shattered the realm so slowly and laboriously built up by Zangi and Nur-ed-din, were dissipated in predatory raids and desultory enterprises. The Sicilian fleet sailed back from Alexandria after a purposeless siege of a week; Manuel turned his arms against the Sultan of Rûm and met with signal disaster; the forces contributed by Western Europe were not the chivalry of two kingdoms, but the scanty following of an English earl and a Flemish count. The opportunity was lost and never returned. The death of Amalric was the knell of his kingdom.

XVII.

THE RISE OF SALADIN.
(1174-1185.)

"Solo in parfe vidi 'l Saladiho."
DANTE, *Inferno*, iv. 129.
("Alone and apart I beheld Saladin.")

THE successor of Amalric was his son Baldwin, a boy of barely thirteen, who through his mother, Agnes of Edessa, inherited the blood of the house of Courtenay as well as of that of Anjou. His father had taken the greatest care for his education, and entrusted him, when only nine years old, to William of Tyre, as one of a little group of noble youths to whom the great historian imparted some of that Western lore with which his own mind was so copiously stored. Baldwin did not fail to do his tutor credit; he had a quick apprehension and a retentive memory, and like both his father and uncle was an eager lover of history. He was of comely form, much resembling his father both in manner and appearance, and even in his youth gave promise of rare abilities should he reach maturer age. But despite the good qualities, which have made him one of the true hero kings of history, his friend and tutor could not look on him without sympathy and tears, for Baldwin was a leper.

He was still a child when the first symptoms of the fell disease appeared. When playing with his comrades the lads would test one another's endurance by running their nails into each other's arms. Baldwin alone would give no sign of pain; this indifference, which was at first taken as a sign of strength of will, proved to be due to the absence of any power of feeling in his right hand and arm. Later on he became a hopeless leper; and though he was for a time carried even on warlike expeditions in a litter, he was at length compelled to renounce

174

his royal duties and appoint a regent. After a short but heroic life harassed with continual misfortune he died when only twenty-three, leaving his kingdom on the verge of ruin.

The influence which Milo de Planci had possessed under Amalric pointed to him as the guardian of the young king. But the great barons could not brook the rule of a stranger from Champagne, and turned to Raymond II. of Tripoli as their head. Raymond was the most powerful and wealthy noble in the realm, and claimed the guardianship of the king as his next of kin, and as a debt of gratitude that he owed to Amalric. The dispute was still unsettled, when the murder of Milo at Acre in the autumn of 1174 removed the chief obstacle to Raymond's ambition.

Raymond, who was now about thirty years old, was descended not only from the hero of the First Crusade, but also, through his mother, from Baldwin II. His character must be judged by the subsequent events of his life; but this much may be remarked, that he had won the esteem of William of Tyre, who may almost be said to write as a partisan whenever the Count of Tripoli is in question. In person Raymond was slightly built, with sharp visage and flashing eyes; in character he was prudent and cautious, though he could be vigorous in an emergency. To his own hereditary county he had added by his marriage with Eschiva, widow of Walter of Galilee, the possession of the great stronghold of Tiberias.

The weakly health of the young king made the choice of a husband for his elder sister Sibylla one of the first necessities of the time. The choice fell on William of Montferrat, a kinsman of Philip Augustus and Frederick Barbarossa, who was married to his bride in the autumn of 1176, and received with her the cities of Jaffa and Ascalon. The marriage was of short duration, for in the following June William fell ill and died, leaving his wife with child.

Just after this misfortune the young king's cousin Phillip of Flanders arrived at Acre in August, 1177. With a great show of humility and disinterestedness he refused the proffer of the guardianship of the realm. He had come to the Holy Land not to seek power, but to do the Lord's will. He would obey any duly constituted regent, as if he were his own liege lord, or lend his ready aid for an expedition to Egypt. The value of these professions was too soon apparent. When Reginald de Châtillon, who after a long captivity had been released from his Saracen gaol, was nominated as the king's proctor and general, Philip testily declared that there was no need of such an officer, and that a man should be chosen who could bear all the authority for the proposed expedition, and would be fit to rule Egypt as its king if successful. When so obviously selfish a suggestion was rejected, Philip, shifting his ground, urged that a new husband should be found for Sibylla. This untimely proposal proved to spring from one of Philip's followers, the Advocate of Bethun, who had offered to surrender all his patrimony to the count, if he could secure Baldwin's two sisters for the wives of his own sons. Such an offer was rejected by the council off-hand as dishonouring to themselves and the king. But Philip soon found" a fresh subject for the display of his ill-humours. Manuel had sent an embassy to urge the immediate despatch of the Egyptian expedition; when Philip's opinion was sought, he pleaded his ignorance as a stranger, but urged that the time of year was unsuitable. The council regarded these as but bald excuses, and offered to supply a sufficiency of all that was needed for the journey. Then Philip refused point blank: he would not run the risk of perishing with hunger in Egypt, he had been accustomed to make war in fertile lands: let them choose some less dangerous quarter, and he would gladly join them to strike a blow for Christ

There may have been something of prudence in these arguments, but it was generally felt that the count's utterance of them lacked sincerity. To the council it appeared hard to abandon the expedition when a

Greek fleet actually lay at Acre, but they felt that there was no choice in the matter. Scarcely had they made this resolution when Philip declared his willingness to go to Egypt, or wherever the council wished. The Greeks were still willing to proceed, if the count would only take an oath to act honourably and openly. This natural stipulation did not, however, commend itself to Philip, and the Greek envoys, feeling further negotiation to be useless, departed homewards. Thus through the obstinacy or timidity—William of Tyre does not scruple to say the bad faith—of the Flemish count, the Eastern Christians lost their last opportunity of striking what might have been a fatal blow at the power of Saladin.

Men suspected that Philip's conduct had been influenced by Bohemond of Antioch in the hope of aggrandisement to his own power. But if so, the prince's hope was vain, for though Philip went north in October, 1177, his aid was no more valuable in that quarter than elsewhere. The time was opportune enough, and the Frankish army laid siege to Harenc with good prospects of success. But the allurements of gambling and the luxurious pleasures of Antioch, that lay so close, proved fatal to military discipline, and the siege was raised with no more to show than an uncertain bribe. After this inglorious campaign Philip of Flanders sailed home from Laodicea at Easter, 1178, "leaving behind him a memory that was in no wise blessed."

Meantime the withdrawal of so many of its defenders to the north had left the kingdom open to the attacks of Saladin on the south. His troops scoured the country at their will; Ramleh and Lydda were sacked and burnt, and for the first time for five-and-twenty years the Holy City itself was threatened. The more experienced warriors advised Baldwin not to risk a battle, but with a few followers he hurried up to Ascalon. There he was joined by the Templars from Gaza, but even then he had only 370 knights to meet a host of six-and-twenty thousand, which included a thousand Mamluks in yellow tunics, the special guard of

Saladin's person. Nevertheless, the Franks went out bravely on November 25th to meet their foe. According to Saladin's own account the Christians charged just as he was executing a strategic movement; another contemporary Arabic account says that the Mohammedan host was surprised whilst watering; but all writers admit that Baldwin achieved a glorious victory. The Turks were utterly routed, and Saladin himself barely escaped upon a swift camel with scarcely one hundred horsemen.

In the following autumn Baldwin erected a fortress on the Upper Jordan, which was named Castle Jacob, from a tradition that its site was the scene of the patriarch's meeting with Esau. In April, 1179, after entrusting his new castle to the Templars, the king led an expedition into Saracen territory. The army scattered in all directions in search of plunder, till Baldwin was left alone with only a few followers in a rocky gorge. Here he was surprised by the Saracens, and though Henfrid of Toron brought his young lord safe out of danger, it was at the cost of his own life; for a few days later his wounds proved fatal to the gallant constable, whom even Mohammedans admired for his courage and warlike skill. In June Saladin retaliated by an invasion of the kingdom. The Franks mustered to meet him in force, but the rashness of the Templars under Odo de St. Amand converted a promising opportunity into a disastrous defeat. Odo himself and many nobles were taken prisoners, and two months later Saladin's victory was crowned by the capture of Castle Jacob. The double disaster was aggravated by the long-continued drought, which during five years had impoverished the territory of the Franks. The king's sickness, which grew worse yearly, added to the troubles of the time, and to guard against future mishaps a fresh husband was now found for Sibylla in the person of Guy de Lusignan. In the face of such dangers Baldwin felt it prudent to beg for a truce; Saladin welcomed the proposition, and in 1180 peace both by land and sea was established for two years. Such an agreement was a

178

heavy blow to Christian pride; for the first time since the Franks set foot in Palestine was a treaty drawn up on equal terms without any special advantage being secured for the Christians.

There was now peace for a period of two years. The Franks were, however, troubled by internal dissensions. Raymond of Tripoli, though nominally protector, never entered their land, and Baldwin fell more and more under the influence of the count's enemies, and, above all, of his mother and uncle, Joscelin the Seneschal. An open breach with Raymond was only prevented through the intervention of those wiser nobles who saw in the count the most trusty defender of the kingdom.

Meantime the course of events favoured Saladin. After a brief raid into Tripoli, which was not included in the truce, he had withdrawn to Egypt, and prepared to meet the threatened attack from Sicily. About this time Sayf-ed-din of Mosul and Es-Saleh of Aleppo both died, and left their dominions to Masud, a brother of the former. Masud's counsellors urged him to take advantage of the defenceless state of Damascus during Saladin's detention in Egypt. Their advice was rejected by the prince, who would not break his treaty with Saladin; but a little later Masud gave Aleppo to his brother Imad-ed-din in exchange for Sinjar, a bargain which excited the alarm of the lord of Egypt.

Other circumstances besides the peril of Damascus determined Saladin to return to Syria. The danger to Egypt had passed away with the diversion of the Sicilian fleet to the Balearic Islands and its subsequent destruction. The truce, moreover, was nearly at an end, and there were not a few causes of dispute between Baldwin and Saladin. Reginald of Châtillon had captured some Arab merchants, for which the Sultan retaliated by the detention of one thousand five hundred pilgrims, who had been wrecked near Damietta. Baldwin, despite the warnings of Count Raymond, made an ill-managed and futile attempt to intercept Saladin on his way across the desert. Meanwhile, as Raymond had foreseen, the Syrian emirs took the opportunity to invade Galilee,

179

and, as they returned home with their spoil, inflicted a yet more disastrous blow on the Christians. In the region of Soad (or "Black Country") beyond Jordan the Franks had converted some caves in the face of a precipitous rock into an almost impregnable fortress. This stronghold, through the carelessness of its lord, had been left in charge of unwarlike Syrians. Either by force or by fraud the Saracens captured its lower stages, and thus compelled the other portion to surrender. According to the Arabic historian, this victory broke the arm and power of the Franks.

Saladin now led an army across the Jordan, and, after attacking Beth-Shan without success, went on towards Belvoir. The Franks had mustered at Tiberias, and, on advancing to Forbelet, suddenly found themselves surrounded by the enemy. Old men declared that they had never seen such a host of infidels since the Latins first came into Syria.

The Saracens were twenty thousand men ready for battle, the Christians had only seven hundred horsemen. "Saladin and his chiefs," writes William of Tyre, "had but one mind, namely, to hem us in, so that none could escape. Yet by the mercy of God did our men, bearing themselves bravely, issue the better from the conflict; and that though many, whose names for very shame we will not write, withdrew themselves from the toils of war." Only a few Christian knights were slain, but the Saracens were so disheartened by their losses that they at once recrossed the Jordan. The Franks then went back to the fountain of Sepphoris.

In August, 1182, on the arrival of his fleet from Egypt, Saladin crossed the Lebanon and laid siege to Beyrout. The news of this fresh attack came to the Franks at Sepphoris, and at the same time they received intelligence that Saladin's brother, El-Adel Sayf-ed-din—known to Crusading chroniclers as Saphadin—had appeared before Darum. Baldwin had not sufficient forces to meet the double attack. After taking counsel with his nobles, he decided to grapple with "the more dangerous disease." No time was lost, and within seven days thirty well-appointed galleys were ready at Tyre and Acre. The fleet reached Beyrout to find the harbour already clear; for Saladin, after commencing the assault with vigour, had suddenly changed his mind and ordered a retreat. An invitation from the Governor of Harran had afforded him the opportunity for more important conquests further east.

For the next few months Saladin was conquering beyond the Euphrates. He passed the great river and called the Mohammedan princes to his side; Edessa and Nisibis were taken and given to his friends, while Masud fell back before him on Mosul. News came that the Franks had been plundering in the neighbourhood of Damascus. But Saladin would not turn back: "If the Christians destroy our villages, we will take their towns." So he rode on to Mosul. "As he looked upon the city," writes the Arabic historian, "his heart was filled with fear; for he saw how walls and parapets were crowded, so that there was not one part that had not its warrior." The Caliph had sent envoys to mediate between the combatants. Saladin offered to surrender his late conquests in return for Aleppo; but Aleppo was not Masud's to give. However, Saladin found Mosul too strong for capture, and after taking Sinjar he turned west to besiege Aleppo. Imad-ed-din had no means of defence, and soon consented to resign Aleppo in return for Sinjar, Nisibis, and some other places. "Thus," says the Arabic writer, "he sold Aleppo for the vilest price, and gave away a stronghold of the greatest importance in exchange for some little towns and cultivated fields." The people of Aleppo cried shame upon him, declaring he was only fit to be a washer of clothes. This conquest (June 12, 1183) marks the consolidation of Saladin's power; he was now beyond all dispute the head power in the Mohammedan world, and might bend his undivided energies towards the great work of his life—the expulsion of the Franks from the Holy City.

181

Saladin's absence had given Baldwin an opportunity of attacking Damascus and its neighbourhood. In the autumn of 1182 one plundering expedition penetrated to the very suburbs of the city, and on its return recaptured the mountain fortress in Soad. In December a great council was held at Caesarea, where it was decided to make a fifteen days' expedition towards Bostra. The Franks under the command of Count Raymond crossed the Jordan at the ford of Jacob, and plundered the Saracen territory to within a few miles from Damascus.

And now the news of Saladin's successes began to make men fear the ruin of the Latin realm. "For," says William of Tyre, "his departure had given us grave matter for thought; we were right anxious lest he should return yet stronger than before." In February, 1183, there was a great council at Jerusalem; king and nobles were alike so poor that they could not perform their proper duties; a scheme was therefore devised for the general taxation of all classes; the money so obtained was not to be used for the common needs of the realm, but, to be stored at Jerusalem and Acre as a provision against some great emergency. With the news of the fall of Aleppo, the alarm grew yet wilder; the Christians, realising their weakness, began, to strengthen their fortifications especially round Beyrout. Bohemond of Antioch also came to the king at Acre with an appeal for aid; he was granted three hundred horsemen, but soon afterwards made a truce with Saladin; about the same time he sold Tarsus to Rupin of Armenia, as that city was too distant and costly for defence.

After the conquest of Aleppo, Saladin once more crossed the Jordan to Beth-Shan (September 29, 1183). Baldwin had mustered his forces at Sepphoris, but, being too ill to lead them in person, entrusted the command to his brother-in-law, Guy de Lusignan. Saracen freebooters ravaged the whole region round; they forced their way—for the first time—to the Greek monastery on Mount Tabor, destroyed Forbelet, and from the hills above Nazareth looked down upon the city of our Lord's childhood. When the Italian merchants on the coast heard of the invasion they put off their intended voyage, and hurried up to join the king's army. Never, so old men said, had Palestine seen so vast an array of Crusaders; there were one thousand three hundred knights and over fifteen thousand well-armed foot; among them were great nobles from Europe: Henry, Duke of Louvain and Ralf de Maleine from Aquitaine, together with the lords of the land, Guy de Lusignan, Reginald de Châtillon, Baldwin and Balian of Ibelin, Reginald of Sidon, Walter of Caesarea, and Joscelin de Courtenay. But this splendid opportunity for crushing Saladin was lost through internal jealousy; the lords of Palestine refused to obey Guy de Lusignan, whom they despised as a man "unknown and of little skill in military matters;" they trumped up excuses for inaction, and after eight days the Saracens went back home. A month later Saladin laid siege to Reginald of Châtillon's strong castle of Kerak. Reginald had just married his stepson, Henfrid IV. of Toron, to the king's younger sister, and the castle was crowded with jesters, minstrels, and others come to help in the wedding festivities. The place was, however, too strong to be taken even by the combined forces of Saladin and his brother El-Adel, who joined him from Egypt; so when the Franks advanced to raise the siege, Saladin withdrew to Damascus. Next year he made another unsuccessful expedition against Kerak; on his way back he burnt Nablûs, and set free the Mohammedan prisoners in Sebaste. This was his last engagement for some years in Palestine. In the summer of 1185 he was warring against Mosul; in the end, after some negotiations conducted by Baha-ed-din the historian, Masud of Mosul came to terms with his rival.

Saladin was now lord supreme of all the Mohammedan princes. He might reckon on being followed to war by the various princes of the house of Zangi, who ruled at Sinjar, Mosul, and Mardin; perhaps also by Kilij Arslan of Rum; certainly by all the Ayubite princes whom he had established in the valleys of the Orontes and Nile. Saladin's policy had led him to keep all the great cities of Egypt and Syria in the hands of his own family. Thus his kinsmen, Taki-ed-din, Izz ed-din, and Nasr-ed-din held Edessa, Baalbec, and Emesa; his sons, Ez-Zahir and El-Afdal, were lords of Aleppo and Damascus, and his brother, El-Adel, ruler of Egypt. All along the frontier there lay a line of strong generals or princes ready at any moment for a foray into Christian lands. The Mohammedans only waited to exchange their tactics of defence or desultory raids for one of active warfare, till the lord of Syria and Egypt, the overlord of Mosul and Rum, should give the word for a general coalition to drive the Christian invaders out of Syria.

XVIII.

THE FALL OF JERUSALEM.
(1183-1187.)

"Vae terris ubi rex est puer."
Ecclesiasticus.

THE position of the Christian kingdom was now one of extreme peril. The king was sick unto death, and there was no hope for the land save in aid from abroad, which aid was slow to come. Louis VII. of France, so long the hope of the Latin East, had been dead three years, and Philip Augustus, his son, was hardly of the stuff from which Crusading heroes were made. Henry of England had more than enough to occupy him in his home troubles; yet for many years past he had sent annually large sums of money to the great orders at Jerusalem, there to be stored against his own intended coming. The kings of France and England had more than once talked of a Crusade; and Frederick the Emperor, after the conclusion of his papal and Italian disputes in 1179, had also meditated an expedition to the East. But all these things were mere projects; internal dissensions, mutual distrust, and perhaps unsteadiness of religious zeal kept the great European lords at home.

Meanwhile the kingdom of Jerusalem was in a state of rapid decay. The young king had appointed his brother-in-law, Guy de Lusignan, his proctor in the year 1183, retaining for his own use only the city of Jerusalem, and an income of ten thousand besants. Popular rumour, as represented by William of Tyre, declared that Guy was totally unequal to his high office. Certainly the nobles, jealous of an alien's power, did the new ruler homage with reluctance, and the majority of them, whether honestly or not, urged the superior claims of Raymond of Tripoli. Matters came to a climax when the great muster of the Christians, under Guy's leadership, effected nothing, and when Guy refused, very illiberally, to entertain Baldwin's desire to exchange Jerusalem for Tyre. As a consequence it was decided in a great council held at Jerusalem that Baldwin's little nephew, his sister Sibylla's son by her first husband, William of Montferrat, should be solemnly anointed king. The story cannot be better told than in the quaint words of one who may himself have been present at the ceremony. "When the matter was thus settled, the king bade crown the child. So they led him to the Sepulchre and crowned him. And because the child was small, they put him into the arms of a knight to be carried into the Temple of the Lord, to the end that he might not appear to be of less Stature than the rest. This knight was a stalwart man and tall, having to name Balian d'Ibelin, one of the barons of the land." The ceremony took place on the 1st of November, 1183.

The revolution which thus transferred the crown to the infant Baldwin V. seems to have been the work of the hereditary nobles of the land, and was chiefly brought about by Baldwin of Ramleh and his brother Balian of Ibelin. The regency was offered to Raymond of Tripoli, who accepted the office on condition that he should hold it for ten years. To guard against suspicion the strongholds were placed in the charge of the two great orders, while the care of the young king's person was entrusted to his great uncle, Joscelin de Courtenay. On the other hand, Raymond received Beyrout, to indemnify him for any expenses that he might incur.

Meanwhile Guy de Lusignan held sullenly aloof. The king further proposed to dissolve his sister's marriage, and with this intention summoned Guy to Jerusalem at the beginning of 1184. The count, however, withdrew to his own city of Ascalon, and, together with his wife, refused to obey the royal summons. Baldwin then came to enforce his orders in person; but the gates were barred before him, and the walls crowded with the citizens, who looked calmly on whilst the king in vain demanded entrance. Baldwin had to withdraw to Jaffa, and shortly afterwards summoned a great council at Acre; there the internal dissensions of the kingdom became plain. The masters of the Temple and the Hospital fell on their knees before the king and begged him to pardon his brother-in-law; when their petition was refused they left the court and city in anger. Guy, on his part, made the breach wider by plundering some Arabs who were under the royal protection. From all that follows it would seem that there were two parties in the state; on the one side the native nobles, on the other the aliens; at the head of the former was Raymond of Tripoli, chief of the latter was Guy de Lusignan or Reginald of Châtillon. Raymond and his party seem to have believed in the impossibility of active resistance to the Saracens. It may be that they were only abiding their time till the coming of a new Crusade should justify them in taking the offensive once more; but so far as the evidence of contemporary writers, both Christian and Arabic goes, they were actually in communication with Saladin, and anxious for a truce which might ensure them their own in safety. Prominent in this party were Bohemond of Antioch, Reginald of Sidon, and possibly the two brothers, Baldwin and Balian of Ibelin.

The party of the aliens was possibly moved by a more genuine religious enthusiasm. Guy de Lusignan may perhaps have been influenced by merely selfish aims; but selfishness can hardly be predicated of the masters of the Temple and Hospital, and possibly not of Heraclius the Patriarch; family affection may, however, account for the part played by Joscelin de Courtenay. The members of the two great orders had not entered on their Eastern life in search for ease or luxury; their vows bound them before all else to fight the pagan, and to extend the boundaries of the Lord's kingdom; the very thought of passing long years without striking a blow for Christ was to them insupportable; thus their constant clamour was for war, and in this they were well supported by Reginald de Châtillon. The long years of his captivity in a Saracen prison had made that noble the bitterest of foes, and he never lost a chance of striking a blow at Saracen trader or soldier; his reluctance to hold his hand whether in peace or war was to lead a few years later to the ruin of the kingdom.

At that same council of Acre, where the quarrel of these two parties had been made so manifest, it was determined to appeal to the sovereigns of Europe for help. Heraclius the Patriarch and the two Grand Masters were entrusted with the mission to the West. Pope Lucius III. gave them letters to assist their plea, and they bore the keys of the Holy Sepulchre together with the royal banner of the kingdom to Henry II. at Reading. In the spring of 1185 almost all the barons and knights of Henry's dominions from the Cheviots to the Pyrenees took the cross, and the kings of England and France likewise promised their support. Yet, nevertheless, the patriarch went home a disappointed man with only barren promises where he had looked for material aid.

The character of Heraclius is a curious problem. He is said to have been a native of Auvergne, and became Archbishop of Caesarea about 1175; on the death of the Patriarch Amalric in 1180 his was one of the two names submitted to Baldwin IV. by the canons of the Holy Sepulchre. His competitor was none other than the great historian of the Latin kingdom in the East, William of Tyre. It was rumoured at the time that William, on hearing of the canons' choice, offered to relinquish his own claims, if by so doing he might exclude his rival; he had read in ancient chronicles, so he was reported to have said, that as one Heraclius had been the saviour of the Holy City, so another one would be its ruin, the Archbishop of Caesarea, he continued, was the man to whom this ancient prophecy pointed. The king, however, under the influence of his sister's prayers appointed Heraclius. William then appealed to Rome, whither he went to prosecute his cause in person; success was already crowning his efforts, when he died, as it was whispered, of poison administered by his rival's envoys. This was not the only scandal that attached to Heraclius' name; he lived in open

188

immorality, and kept his mistress at Jerusalem in such state that strangers deemed she was at least a baron's wife. Much of this is probably legend, though legend of only a slightly later date; yet it seems to show in what sort of esteem the patriarch was popularly held.

Baldwin IV. died in 1185, whilst Heraclius was still in the West. Raymond secured an immediate popularity as regent by concluding a four years' truce with Saladin. There is no telling how long he might have preserved the kingdom had it not been that as in the days when the Greek princes were sieging Troy there was strife among the chiefs. There is something of an epic ring in the history of the ruin of the Latin kingdom of the East as we read it in the pages of the Continuator of William of Tyre.

Gerard de Rideford, a French knight, came to Palestine to make his fortune. Doubtless he looked to win such a prize as that of Reginald of Châtillon, who gained the hand of the widowed princess of Antioch, or of Fulk of Anjou, who received a kingdom with his wife. At last his opportunity came and he asked for the hand of the heiress of Botron, a lordship in the county of Tripoli. But Raymond rejected his petition, and married his ward to a rich burgher from Pisa, who was said to have bought his bride for her weight in gold, Gerard, who had all a French knight's scorn for an Italian usurer, quitted Tripoli in wrath. He joined the Templars, and by 1185 had become Grand Master of the order. But he still sought an opportunity to avenge the wrong which rankled in his breast. At last his chance came. In September, 1186, the child king died at Acre, and was carried by the Templars to Jerusalem for burial. Gerard formed a plot with Count Joscelin, and they took Heraclius and Reginald of Châtillon as their partners; Sibylla was hastily summoned to Jerusalem, the city gates were shut, the walls were manned with troops, and no one was suffered to come in or go out.

Raymond, suspicious that something was wrong, had sent a man-at-arms in disguise to discover what was happening. In the Church of the

189

Holy Sepulchre the spy heard Reginald bid the assembled people take Sibylla for their queen, and the multitude with one voice declare they would have no other ruler than the daughter of Amalric and the sister of Baldwin. Two crowns had been brought from the royal treasure house. One was now placed by the patriarch on the head of the new queen with these words: "Lady, you are but a woman, wherefore it behoves that you have a man to stay you in your rule; take the crown you see before you, and give it to him who can best help you to govern your realm." On this Sibylla called her husband, and as Guy knelt before her set the crown on his head, saying, "Sire, take this crown, for I know not where I could bestow it better." It was rumoured that as the Grand Master of the Temple took the new king by the hand he was heard to say: "This crown is well worth the marriage of Botron."

If Raymond of Tripoli had harboured any designs on the crown it was now too late. The utmost he and the barons assembled with him at Nablûs could do was to set up a king of their own in the person of Henfrid of Toron, the husband of King Amalric's second daughter, Isabella or Melisend. Henfrid, however, fearing the greatness thrust thus suddenly upon him stole away the same night to Jerusalem. There he presented himself before Sibylla, who, in anger at his absence from her coronation, would not return his greeting. He stood before her, says the quaint old chronicler, scratching his head like a shamefaced child, and muttering something about their wanting to make him king by force. The queen caught up his words, and understanding their drift, granted him her pardon, and despatched him to do his homage to the king.

Most of the Frank lords now recognised Guy's coronation as an accomplished fact, and did homage. Two alone remained implacable: Baldwin of Ramleh, who, renouncing his fiefs, fled in defiance to Antioch; and Raymond of Tripoli, who remained on his lands, sullenly nursing his discontent, and if rumour may be trusted intriguing with

Saladin. It was apparently about this time that Reginald of Châtillon, notwithstanding the truce, swooped down on a Saracen caravan on its way through his lordship of Kerak. It boots not to inquire whether Saladin's sister was one of his captives; for Saracen writers fully bear out the words of the Frank chronicler: "The taking of this caravan was the ruin of Jerusalem;" Saladin forthwith sounded the tocsin for the Holy War.

By the advice of the Master of the Temple, Guy now summoned his host to Nazareth, with the intention of besieging Raymond in Tiberias. The count on his part seems to have called upon Saladin for aid, which, if we may trust Ernoul, Saladin was prepared to give. Civil war was, however, averted by the prudence of Balian of Ibelin, who pointed out the danger of forcing Raymond into an alliance with Saladin, and volunteered his aid to effect a reconciliation. But Raymond demanded with firmness the repayment of his expenses as regent, and so the winter passed away with nothing done.

Easter had come and gone, and Saladin was mustering his forces. The royal council advised peace with Raymond; "for Guy had already lost the wisest knight in the land, Baldwin of Ramleh; if he lost Count Raymond too, he was indeed undone." Balian was accordingly sent to Tiberias with the two Grand Masters. On reaching Nablûs, Balian stayed there to transact some business, whilst his companions rode on to Faba, or La Féve. At evening Balian left Nablûs, and rode as far as Sabat, where he turned aside, and tarried at the bishop's house till the warder's horn proclaimed the day. In the morning after hearing mass, he proceeded on his journey. This slight delay prevented his being present at the battle of Nazareth, and perhaps caused the downfall of the kingdom. On reaching Faba Balian found the castle and the tents before its walls alike deserted, whilst the castle gate stood open; in amazement he bade his servant Ernoul, to whom we owe our knowledge of these eventful years, dismount and enter. Ernoul went shouting up and down without reply, till at last he found two sick men in a room; they told him that the Grand Masters had arrived the previous day, but had departed at once on hearing how a body of Saracens had crossed the Jordan.

According to the romantic story of the Frank chronicler, El-Afdal had begged Count Raymond to grant him a day's excursion across the Jordan. Raymond's position was too delicate for him to venture on a refusal. He bargained only that El-Afdal should harm neither town nor house, and return the same evening. So on the morning of May 1st, El-Afdal crossed the Jordan to plunder and to slay. The watchmen from the towers of Nazareth saw the valleys filled with the Saracen host, and roused the city to arms. The news reached the two Grand Masters at Faba; with their followers, and forty royal knights from Nazareth, they rode out to meet the foes, seven hundred against seven thousand. The issue was disastrous: the Master of the Hospital and sixty of his knights were slain, whilst of the Templars only two besides Gerard de Rideford escaped.

This was the further news which Balian shortly heard. He rode in haste to Nazareth, and summoned all the knights at Nablûs to come to its defence; next day with the Master of the Temple he went on to Tiberias. In the presence of such a catastrophe all private hate was hushed; Raymond agreed to a reconciliation and to a meeting with Guy. As soon as the king saw his late rival approaching he sprang from his horse to greet him, and when Raymond bent his knee before him, raised him up and embraced him warmly. A general muster was then ordered to take place at the fountain of Sepphoris, midway between Acre and the Sea of Galilee. In view of the emergency, the Master of the Temple put at Guy's disposal the treasure which the King of England had sent him year by year, and with this money soldiers were hired who bore King Henry's arms upon their shield.

In July, when the host was gathered, the Countess of Tripoli sent word that Saladin was besieging her in Tiberias, and that she could hold out no longer. A council was summoned, and Raymond addressing the king said: "Sire, I would fain give you good advice, if you only trust me; but I know full well that none will believe." When bidden to speak freely, he recommended that Tiberias should be left to its fate. There was no water on the road, and to attempt its relief would be to court certain destruction. "If I lose wife, retainers, and city, so be it; I will get them back when I can; but I had rather see my city overthrown than the land lost." This noble speech carried conviction with it, and at midnight the council broke up. Then Gerard de Rideford once more found his opportunity, and coming to the king's tent urged him to reject the counsel of the "traitor count." "The king durst not refuse him, for that he had made him king, and delivered to him the great treasure of the King of England." The fatal order to march at dawn proved too well the truth of Raymond's forecast; some three miles from Tiberias, in a rocky and waterless spot, the Christians were hemmed in by the Saracens; unable either to advance or to retreat, they were forced to pitch their camp. Next day (it was Saturday, July 4, 1187) found them disheartened and disorganised; faint with the heat and with thirst they could offer no effectual resistance; by evening their army was routed, their king a prisoner, and the Holy Cross the spoil of the infidel.

The principal captives were led to the tent of Saladin. Among them were Guy, his brother Geoffrey, and Reginald of Châtillon. By the Sultan's orders a cooling draught was handed to the king, who drank and passed the cup to Reginald. "Know," said Saladin, through an interpreter, "that it is you and not I who have given him to drink." Then the Sultan called for a sword, and with his own hand cut off Reginald's head; thus he fulfilled his oath, and revenged the plunder of his caravan.

The great battle of Hattin was the death-blow to the kingdom of Jerusalem as it had existed in the days of Baldwin III. and Amalric. At one stroke it had lost the chief of its leaders and the majority of its defenders; Raymond, it was true, escaped from the battle, but only to die of despair fifteen days later at Tyre; of the other great lords Balian alone was alive and free. In such a strait the Christians seemed powerless to resist their victorious foe; within little over two months Saladin had secured almost every stronghold of importance from Beyrout to Ascalon. A few scattered fortresses, such as Safed and Kerak by the Dead Sea, held out till next year; but when Ascalon had fallen on the 5th of September only two of the great cities still remained in Christian hands—Tyre in the north and Jerusalem in the south. The safety of the former was due to Conrad of Montferrat, the defence of the Holy City was the work of Balian of Ibelin and the Patriarch Heraclius.

Balian had escaped from Hattin to Tyre. Thence he sent to Saladin, begging leave to conduct his wife and children to Jerusalem; if that leave was given he would only stay a single night in the city. Saladin courteously granted the desired permission. The citizens, however, would not let Balian depart; Heraclius also declared that it would be a greater sin to keep such a promise than to break it,—" It will be great shame to you and your heirs after you if you leave the city of Jerusalem in her perilous strait.' "Then did Balian promise to stay, and all that were in the city did him homage, and took him to lord." The peril of the city was in truth extreme; only two knights were to be found within the walls, and they were fugitives from the great battle. In his emergency Balian knighted sixty of the burgesses, and stripped the silver roofing of the Holy Sepulchre to provide himself with money. From all the district round the people came flocking into the city, till they had filled every house, and many were encamped in the open streets.

At last, on September 20, 1187, Saladin appeared before the walls. The history of this eventful siege cannot here be told in detail. Its hero

194

was Balian, though the French chronicler gives to Heraclius a meritorious part; it was the patriarch who, according to this account, persuaded the warriors to take thought of the defenceless women and children when they proposed to hazard all on one desperate onset on the foe; it was Balian, however, whose skill kept the walls whilst he could, and who at last persuaded Saladin to accept a ransom of ten dinars for every man, five for every woman, and one for every child under seven years of age. It is impossible to reconcile the French account of the collection of the ransom of the poor with the reproaches hurled on the selfish citizens by the author of the Latin treatise, "De Expugnatione Terrae Sanctae"—an author who was actually wounded during the siege. Much legend has no doubt found its way into the accounts of the fall of the Holy City even as they have been preserved for us by contemporary writers; but there is one story too characteristic to be altogether omitted. After every effort had been made to purchase the relief of the poorer Christians, after a tax had been levied in every street, and the King of England's treasures at the Hospital thrown into the common fund, there yet remained a large number for whom no ransom could be paid, and who were thus doomed to perpetual slavery or death. In pity for their sad condition, Saladin's gallant brother El-Adel or Saphadin went to the Sultan, and, reminding him how the city had been conquered by his help, begged to have a thousand slaves for his portion of the spoil. Saladin inquired for what purpose he desired them. "To do with them as I will," was the reply. They were accordingly handed over to El-Adel, who promptly set them free. Then came the patriarch making a like request, and received seven hundred. After him Balian of Ibelin was granted five hundred more. Then said Saladin: "My brother has made his alms; the patriarch and Balian have made theirs. Now would I make mine also." Accordingly at his bidding all the aged folk in the city were liberated: "This was the alms that Saladin made of poor folk without number."

195

So on October 2, 1187, Jerusalem was once more in the hands of the Moslem, and the greatest aim of Saladin's life was accomplished. It was for this, as he himself said, that when called to the government of Egypt at the age of thirty he had relinquished the use of wine, and all the pleasures of his youthful life. Forty-three years previously Zangi had turned the tide of Christian success by capturing Edessa. After Zangi's death, so ran the story in the East while Saladin was yet alive, a Mohammedan devotee beheld the great atabek living at his ease in the very fairest part of Paradise, and asked him how he came to occupy so honourable a place. "God," was the reply, "has pardoned all my sins for the conquest of Edessa." If this was the reward of Zangi, what recompense might not the liberator of the Holy City look forward to at the hands of Allah "Jerusalem," Saladin once sent word to Richard I., "is as much to us Mohammedans as it can be to you Christians, and more. It is the place whence our prophet made his night ascent to heaven, and it will be the gathering place of our nation at the Great Judgment." No wonder, then, that there was joy in Islam when the Temple was again in Mohammedan hands, and when, on the following Friday, after the golden cross that shone above the sacred dome had been taken down, the prayers of the Faithful once more went up to Allah from Mount Moriah. "Thus," says the Arabic historian, Saladin's bosom friend and confidant, "thus did God suffer the Mussulmans to retake the town for the anniversary of the nightly journey of their prophet; a certain sign that this people is the only one whose doctrine is agreeable to Him."

XIX.

THE LIFE OF THE PEOPLE.

"For manners are not idle, but the fruit
Of loyal nature and of noble mind."

TENNYSON, *Guinevere.*

THE political and social life of the Latin kingdom of Jerusalem was almost the counterpart of the political and social life of the great kingdoms of Western Europe. In particular it resembles the great monarchy which the same French race built up at almost the same time in our own land, and there is a curious parallelism between the charters of the Norman and Angevin kings of England, and those of the French and Angevin kings of Jerusalem. With the political organisation of the land we have already dealt, and here we shall concern ourselves with the social life and habits of the Latin settlers and their subjects.

To begin at the top of the scale, the life of the Frankish nobles in Syria no doubt closely resembled that of their Western cousins. Of the life of the mediaeval knight we can by the combined aid of history and romance form a fairly adequate idea. His childish years would be spent in his father's castle, hunting and hawking with his parents, till when about twelve years old, he would be sent from home to be trained in knightly accomplishments at the court of some great knight or king. Letters, too, were not neglected, for some tincture of Latin and French was a necessity; and so we find that William of Tyre had a sort of school for the instruction of the king's son, the future Baldwin IV. and his young companions.

The attainment of manhood was marked by the conferring of knighthood, for which the ordinary age seems to have been from twenty to five-and-twenty, though Geoffrey of Anjou and his son, Henry Fitz-Empress, were knighted at fifteen and sixteen respectively. To this ceremony there was at an early date attached a religious significance. In a curious romance of the thirteenth century Hue de Tabarie is made to set forth to Saladin all the mysterious qualities of the rite. The order of knighthood, Hugh tells his captor, is open to no unbeliever; to confer it on such a one were like trying to stifle the stench of a dunghill with a silken mantle. Still Saladin perseveres in his desire to receive the honour, submits to the bath, and is clothed in the white garments of chastity; over them is cast a red cloak, typical of the blood to be shed in defence of Holy Church. Then the Sultan is shod by his instructor with black shoes, symbolical of the earth from which he sprang and to which he must return; the white belt round the loins, the gold spurs on the heels, and the sword at the side, have each their appropriate significance of chastity, obedience, and justice.

Romance and history also help us to a picture of the knight's accomplishments. Like Richard of Normandy he could fence, manage his falcon, chase the deer, and slay the boar. Like Huon of Bordeaux he could serve at dinner, break a horse, wield a lance, and at chess and tables fear no antagonist. Other graces, too, should he possess; so Doon of Mayence was bidden by his father to be courteous in bearing, attentive to religion, liberal to the poor; to be modest in the display of his accomplishments, and not to pretend to a skill or knowledge which he did not possess.

For his amusement outdoors, the knight had hunting, hawking, and tournaments; indoors he had chess, tables, and the *jeu des dames*, but above all else the minstrel's song. With the Crusaders the favourite themes of minstrelsy were the "Song of Antioch," and the achievements of Godfrey. The minstrel was dependent on the liberality of his hearers, which sometimes provided but a poor reward; so the jougleur in "Huon of Bordeaux" sings:—

"Silence for the song I tell,

> For, by God, 'tis chanted well;
> Fair the tale and nobly set,
> Still I get no guerdon yet,
> Better largesse, good my friends,
> Or full soon my story ends,"

and when this appeal fails to produce a due effect, the minstrel playfully invokes the curses of the fairy king—Oberon—the semi-hero of his poem:—

> "By deity of Oberon the great,
> I here declare you excommunicate.
> Yea! every man of you who will not join
> Loosing his purse to give my wife a coin."

On the other hand, if the minstrel roused the enthusiasm of his hearers he reaped a rich reward. In the same romance the old minstrel bids Huon "Take service with me, and thou shalt see folk give me mantles so many that it will go hard with thee to carry them all." Even the noblest warriors were not above practising the art, and Richard I. could bandy verses with the Duke of Burgundy and the Dauphin of Vienne. The greatest of the troubadours, like Bertrand de Born and Pierre Vidal, were friends of princes like Richard of England and Alfonso of Aragon.

Of other indoor recreations tables corresponds to backgammon, and the *jeu des dames* to draughts. But the chief was chess, which figures in grave historical pages as well as in almost every mediaeval romance. We find the Crusaders amusing themselves with this game during the long siege of Antioch in 1098, and in the "Chanson de Roland" Charlemagne and his paladins are depicted as whiling away their leisure beneath the walls of Cordova with chess and tables. The game itself is of Eastern and perhaps Indian origin, but may have been known in the West as early as the ninth century, for tradition speaks of a set of chessmen—preserved at Paris till the last century—as one of the gifts of Harunel-Rashid to Charles the Great. Historically, however, it does not appear till two centuries later, when it was so popular that Peter Damiani lamented its prevalence among the clergy; fifty years later still it was one of the amusements forbidden to the Templars. A little treatise on chess problems dates from the beginning of the fourteenth century, but mediaeval interest in the game was not purely scientific, for the players had commonly some stake, thus Charlemagne plays for his kingdom, and Huon of Bordeaux for his own life and the hand of the Sultan's daughter.

A more distinctly gambling, and therefore perhaps more popular, game was tables, which was a favourite amusement with Baldwin III., and our own King John, the record of whose losses at tables to his favourite, Roger de Lacy, is preserved. Gaming was a great vice during the whole period and had to be specially forbidden by Louis IX., who when on his voyage from Egypt to Acre, caught his brother, the Count of Anjou, playing tables, and threw the board into the sea; however, the count played openly at Acre, and got much credit for generosity by the bestowal of his gains on the needy A strange story is that of the exiled Englishman who in his passion for play lost all to his very shirt at Acre; unable to show his face among Christians, he wandered into the far east and at last took service with the Tartars as an interpreter, and was sent by them to negotiate with the princes of Europe.

The peculiar amusement of the mediaeval knight was the tournament. Tournaments do not become prominent in our English chronicles till the reign of Henry III., but on the Continent date back much earlier, and since they were forbidden to the Templars in their original statutes, must have been common about 1130; at the end of the century they were the favourite occupation of the young King Henry, son of Henry II. Tournaments were also popular in the East, and the great jousts held in Cyprus in 1231, to celebrate the knighting of Balian of Ibelin, led to the war of that year. It was no doubt by the Crusaders that this sport was introduced to the Byzantine Greeks, and won the fancy of the chivalrous Manuel Comnenus, who at Antioch unhorsed two Latin warriors with his own hand. A more primitive amusement was the quintain, which consisted of a hauberk and shield hung on a post, at which the players tilted, the proof of skill being to pierce both shield and armour or even overthrow the post. On the fondness of the Frankish nobles for the chase somewhat is said elsewhere. Above all other sport they delighted in hawking, and a whole chapter of the Assize of Jerusalem deals with the law relating to falcons.

Turning to the more serious business of life we find one of the first difficulties of the Crusaders was due to the necessary intercourse with a people of strange manners and stranger speech. Yet even in the earliest days of Crusading history we meet with instances of familiarity with the Arabic tongue. It was one of the many accomplishments of Tancred, and the Christian interpreter who was sent to Corbogha was a knight called Herluin, perhaps a Norman, who, like Tancred, had learnt the language in Southern Italy. A generation later the office of dragoman seems to have been held as a kind of feudal fief, and under Fulk and Baldwin III., we read of a William Dragomannus, who owned a house at Jerusalem. Later still it was customary for Saracen children to be brought up among Christians, and Christian children among Saracens. Doubtless this custom softened the asperity natural to rival creeds and races, and so the great Christian nobles of Palestine became friendly with their Saracen neighbours. Of this familiarity we find abundant examples; Henfrid of Toron once owed his safety when on a plundering raid to the friendship of a Saracen emir; Hugh of Caesarea could treat with the Caliph of Cairo in his own tongue. One great lord, possibly Reginald of Sidon, had so keen an interest in Saracen literature, that he had a special clerk to interpret it to him. Reginald of Châtillon again is stated expressly to have spoken the Saracen tongue, a faculty that he probably acquired in the long years of his captivity. But with all the intercourse between the two races there seems to have been little close acquaintanceship on either side with the literature or learning of the other. Among the Christians, however, one name is pre-eminent for knowledge of all languages, namely, that of William of Tyre, who wrote his Mohammedan history—now unfortunately lost—entirely from Arabic sources as a counterfoil to his history of his own land, which was compiled from Christian authorities.

It must not, however, be supposed that the Frankish nobility of Syria was lacking in luxury and culture; more probably for their age they were in advance of their Western cousins. The Latin conquest was followed by the erection of numerous castles, churches, and monasteries, many of which, by their solidity and magnificence, bear witness to the skill of their builders, and the facility with which they had learnt from their Byzantine and Saracen contemporaries. The necessities of the climate and the example of the natives led to much luxury and splendour. In the towns where military defence was not of the first importance, the residences of the nobles and even of the wealthy citizens were built round open court-yards, cooled by fountains playing in marble basins, and decorated by the skill of Greek and Arab artists. In their dress also, the Franks, when not engaged in warfare, imitated the luxury of their enemies, and often adopted the flowing robes of the East. So when in 1192 Saladin made Henry of Champagne a present of a tunic and turban, the Christian prince replied: "You know that we are far from despising the tunic and turban; I shall certainly make use of your presents."

The great nobles of Syria must have depended for their wealth, very much as did their Western cousins, on their rural possessions. The country as distinguished from the towns was divided into *casals* or villages, inhabited by "Syrians," "Bedouins," or, as they are otherwise styled, *rustici*, who paid a quarter or a third of the net produce of their harvests to their lord, with perhaps extra payments of fowls, eggs, cheese and the like, at the great festivals. As in England the land was roughly measured into "plough-lands" (*carrucae*), or as much as a single man would plough in a year. The cultivation of the land was subject to strict rules: the land tilled for corn one year was used for beans or some similar crop the next; in some cases the amount of seed to be used for each plough land was definitely fixed. The population of the casals was not very numerous, and was perhaps stationary or even declining; there seem to have been rarely more than twenty men (heads of families) in a single casal, with a holding of from one to two and a half plough-lands a-piece. The *rustici* were attached to the land, and were sold along with the estate. They were regarded with a certain amount of scorn and suspicion by their Frankish lords, who, whilst admitting that they were "needful for the land," found them useless for military service except in small numbers as light-armed archers. Perhaps they were rightly charged with being but lukewarm in their attachment to the Franks, and ready to sell information to the Saracens. There is very little evidence as to the monetary value of the casals; but we know that when Hugh of Ibelin had to raise his ransom money in 1160, he received seven thousand besants for several large casals, and when Julian of Sidon sold some forty casals to the Teutonic knights about a century later, he received from twenty-three thousand to twenty-four thousand besants.

Passing away from the great lords and their country dependents we come to the town population, the foreign merchants, the Syrian Franks or *Pullani*, and the foreign settlers. The foreign trade was mostly in the hands of the great Italian cities, and, above all, of Venice, Genoa, and Pisa. The Genoese made their appearance at the Port of St. Simeon during the siege of Antioch in 1098, and by maintaining communications with Cyprus and the Greek Empire, furnished the Crusaders with supplies on their march to Jerusalem. Baldwin I. promised them one-third of all the money they helped to earn, and a quarter in every town they helped to acquire. Bohemond gave them a footing in Antioch, but they were specially powerful in the county of Tripoli, where Bertram gave them one-third of his capital itself. Much, however, of their first acquisitions were afterwards lost; but at a later time they had a quarter at Acre and were very powerful in Armenia, where they had their own viscount and court of justice. The Pisans like the Genoese appear during the progress of the First Crusade, and enjoyed the patronage of their compatriot, Dagobert, who afterwards became Patriarch of Jerusalem. They were established at Antioch in 1109; in 1156 the Pisans in Syria were under a viscount, but we find a Pisan consul at Antioch in 1170; they had also a quarter at Acre, and establishments at Jaffa, Tyre, Tripoli, and Laodicea.

By far the most important of the trading communities was that of the Venetians, who, however, were later on the scene than their rivals of Genoa and Pisa. A Venetian fleet appeared at Jaffa in 1100, and many privileges were granted by Geoffrey and Baldwin I. But the great triumph of Venice was the taking of Tyre in 1124, when they assisted in the capture of the city with a fleet of one hundred and thirty vessels under the doge, Domenicho Michaeli. This achievement was the occasion of their obtaining special privileges, which gave them the pre-eminence in the kingdom of Jerusalem itself; they were promised a yearly pension of three hundred besants, a payment which later kings, from Fulk onwards, found it convenient to disallow; they were also to have a church, street, bath, and oven, in each of the king's towns, and in those of his nobles, with the right to use their own measures, not only in their private transactions, but even in sales to other people; in purchases they were bound to use the royal measures. In the principality of Antioch and county of Tripoli the Venetians obtained but little footing. In 1183 we find the Venetian communities under the rule of viscounts, but in the next century there appears an official styled the

"Bailiff of Syria," who resided at Acre or Tyre. In other towns there were consuls, who were responsible for the good order of the community.

Amongst other Italian cities the first place belongs to Amalfi, which had traded with Syria from the early years of the eleventh century. Of non-Italian cities Marseilles was alone conspicuous.

There was much commercial rivalry between the merchants of the various cities, and especially between those of the three great cities. From the Third Crusade onwards the dissensions of the Venetians, Pisans, and Genoese, were the cause of much open bloodshed, and were no slight factor in determining the final downfall of the kingdom.

Probably at the head of all the Syrian Franks in social position stood those who could pride themselves on their pure Western blood, and they are perhaps the "Franci" whom the author of the "Itinerary of Richard" distinguishes from the Syrians. But numerically they must have been far less important than the half-castes, or *Pullani*. These latter represent, if we may trust Suger, those who were born of a Syrian father or mother; James de Vitry, on the other hand, defines them as the offspring of the early conquerors by the Apulian wives, for whom they sent over in the first days of the kingdom; practically, however, the word means simply the Eastern Franks. Gradually they gave themselves up to all the corruptions of the climate, and became lazy frequenters of the baths, luxurious, wanton, quarrelsome, and litigious; they took up Eastern habits and adopted an effeminate dress. Their womenkind were subjected to an harem-like isolation, and hardly allowed to venture out to church, so that private altars were erected in their chambers, at which wretched and ignorant chaplains officiated; but though only allowed to visit church once a year, these ladies contrived to go to the public baths three times a week, and in their seclusion gave themselves up to all the superstitious practices of the East.

Lastly come the foreign settlers, who were only too often the offscouring of the West, evil-livers, who were glad to escape the consequences of their crimes by pretended pilgrimages to the East. In Syria they soon fell back into their old ways, and became brothel keepers, tavern haunters, and gamblers, "monstrous men," says James de Vitry, "who fled from the West to the Holy Land, changing indeed their sky, but not their mind." Such was the natural fruit of papal dispensations, and an unbounded belief in the efficacy of pilgrimages. But as a contrast to these worthless folk were the industrious and frugal Italian traders, sober of life, but lavish of words, who maintained their own freedom and laws under their own leaders: "a folk very necessary to the Holy Land," especially in naval affairs, who endured an Eastern climate better than others because of their moderation in food and drink. Side by side with them were the wilder Germans, Bretons, Frenchmen, Englishmen—extravagant, sensuous, gluttonous, wine-bibbers, but, for all that, devout in their religion, and much given to alms and arms.

Thus there was in Syria a strange conglomeration of races and creeds: "from every quarter of the world, of every tribe and tongue, from every nation under heaven, did devout pilgrims flock to the Holy Land." Jerusalem itself was exempted from all food taxes by the generosity of Baldwin I., so that the poorest pilgrims might find abundant provision there. Jerusalem gloried in the two places of special devotion, the Church of the Holy Sepulchre on Mount Zion and the Templum Domini, or Temple of the Lord, on Mount Moriah. But there was no lack of other places of devotion. At Hebron was the tomb of the patriarchs, hardly more than fifteen years before the fall of Jerusalem there was living at Bethlehem an old knight, who told Ali of Herat that fifty years before as a boy he had himself penetrated to the chamber in the rock and seen the bodies of the great father of the Hebrew race and his earliest descendants. Nazareth boasted of the House of our Lord; Tortosa of the famous Church of our Lady, the first altar according to Eastern tradition that was ever reared in her name—to which the pious Joinville made a pilgrimage; Tyre of the tomb of Origen; Bethlehem of the stall where Christ had lain, and the cave of St. Jerome; Antioch of the Cathedral of St. Peter; Edessa of the tombs of St. Thomas and St. Thaddeus, and of the renowned sepulchre of the holy king Abgar.

Nor was religion the only attraction in Palestine; the merchants were no less important than the pilgrims. The harbours from Ascalon to St. Simeon were thronged with the vessels of every nation of Europe; pre-eminent above them all was Acre. Other towns were the seats of special industries; Antioch was famous for its silken cloths; Tripoli for its cotton and silk factories; Beyrout for its iron works; Tyre for its glass and pottery, and for its dye works; Tiberias for its carpets; Nablûs for its oil and soap. The land itself produced fruits of all kinds, which were exported to Italy if not further west; so that John of Salisbury relates how at a banquet in Italy he was regaled with the delicacies of all lands, from Constantinople and Cairo to Barbary and Tripoli. Chief among these fruits were the lemon, the bitter orange, and the citron, and, above all, the sugar-cane, which the early Crusaders found so refreshing on their weary march to Jerusalem; less strange were the figs and cucumbers and melons. But many of the delicacies which James de Vitry enumerates must have been brought by caravan from more distant lands.

From time immemorial the ginger and musk of China and Thibet had come by way of India and Ceylon to the ports of the Persian Gulf, thence to be carried by caravans over Western Asia. From Bagdad the caravans made their way by the Tigris and Euphrates to Rakka, Edessa, and Harran, and thence to the great Mohammedan cities of Hamah, Aleppo, and Damascus, and so to the Christian ports on the coast. The caravans from Damascus to Egypt passed through the lordship of Montreal, and the tolls were so rich a source of revenue that

Baldwin III. specially reserved them when he granted the lordship to Philip of Nablûs. It was the exactions of Reginald of Châtillon on these caravans that caused his feud with Saladin, and so led to the ruin of the kingdom. Of the trade on the coast Acre was the centre, and it is astonishing to read the long list of merchandise that here paid toll to the kings of Jerusalem; in it we find pepper, citron, cloves, lemons, aloes, sugar, cardamon, the wines of Nazareth and Sepphoris, and all the manufactured products of Christian Syria itself.

It must, however, be remembered that the trade route of the Euphrates and Syria was subordinate to that of the Red Sea and Egypt, in so far as concerns the commerce between India and China and the nations of Europe. Still the Venetian Marino Sanuto, writing soon after the fall of Acre, states that, whilst the heavier goods came by way of Egypt, the lighter and more costly wares were brought by caravan to Acre, Antioch, and elsewhere. It would seem that the land-borne spices were reckoned to have a rarer relish than those that had suffered from the long journey by sea, and the rough handling incidental to frequent transhipments.

It was into the midst of this feudal and military realm, into the midst of this busy mart of agriculture, manufacture, and trade; into this land which was the focus of the devotion, the curiosity, the ambition, and the greed of every nation from Ireland to India, and from Norway to North Africa, that in 1187 Saladin burst with such appalling velocity and such fatal effect. Like a castle of cards or a fortress on the sands the whole kingdom of Jerusalem shuddered, collapsed, and fell; three months sufficed to work its ruin from the confines of Armenia to the borders of Egypt, and from the Jordan to the Mediterranean; in the spring it seemed full of life and vigour, in the autumn it lay prostrate in utter destruction. The causes of this sudden fall may here fitly detain us.

William of Tyre, regarding the events of his own day with the eyes of a priestly if philosophic historian, would have us attribute the misfortunes of his land primarily to the sins of its people. The Latins of the East had forsaken God; God in His turn was now forsaking them; the old fervour was gone, no longer were the princes of the West ready to make their whole life a pilgrimage, as had done Godfrey of Bouillon or Theodoric of Flanders. More weight is to be laid on the historian's second cause: the degeneracy of the Frankish race under an Eastern sun in the midst of Eastern luxury; even Arabic writers noted this and tell us that in the latter half of the twelfth century, the individual Saracen was far more nearly a match for the individual Christian than he had been fifty years earlier. Most important of all is the fact that during this century the valley of the Orontes passed from the divided rule of a score of petty lords under the supremacy of one Sultan. When the Sultan further became lord of Egypt and carried his conquering arms to the Euphrates and the Tigris, it was evident that the star of Islam was once more in the ascendant. The Mohammedans took fresh courage under their victorious leader, and in their turn embarked on a holy war against the enemies of their faith.

But there was another cause at work to which historians have perhaps paid too little attention.

Long and repeated minorities of the kings gave the opportunity for internecine strife to arise among the nobles. Even in the narrative of William of Tyre we can trace signs of two factions, the one of the nobles, and the other, so to say, of the king's friends; it was the same struggle that led in England many years later to the Barons' War. The old-established nobility of Syria were careless of fresh conquests; their ancestors had won vast estates, pleasant lands, and boundless wealth through the expenditure of blood and toil; they themselves were of a weaklier brood, and asked only to be allowed to pluck the grapes that ripened in the vineyards that their fathers had planted and tilled and dressed. Hence under such a leader as Raymond of Tripoli, sick of warfare, sick of toil, longing for ease and delighting perhaps in the

209

nobler graces of civilisation—in art and literature and science—the Syrian nobles were eager only for a peace that would let them live their pleasant life as seemed good to them—free from care, free from danger, free from war. Perhaps Raymond thought also that under the altered condition of things—now that Islam was one, and gradually closing in upon the doomed kingdom—this was the wisest course to pursue; better so to speak by the payment of tribute to preserve what they had, than by open war to risk the loss of all.

Over against this peace party may be set the party of the foreigners and the great military orders who, under the leadership of Reginald of Châtillon, looked at matters from a very different point of view. Perhaps they were eager to carve out new principalities for themselves; perhaps they longed merely for the excitement and distinction of war with the infidel; or, as is more likely still, they had a truer insight into the drift of affairs. They saw that for a little kingdom situated as theirs was—hemmed in by hostile powers to the north and south and east, and with all capacity for expansion cut off by the sea on the west—there was only one sound policy. The sword must keep what the sword had won; not to advance was to recede, not to conquer to be conquered. Hence their rivalry with Raymond; hence Raymond's friendship with Saladin; hence Saladin's enmity with Reginald. This feud between the new men and the old, the strangers and the foreigners, is but faintly reflected in the pages of William of Tyre; for his is as purely a court history as is that of his contemporary Robert de Monte, who, dedicating his work to Henry II., barely mentions the quarrels between the king and Becket. But on turning from William to his continuator Ernoul, we see the truth at once; we feel that we are no longer reading sober history but a party pamphlet. Glancing back in this light at the pages of William of Tyre, we become dimly conscious that the greatest of all historians that the world had seen since Tacitus, who was as great in action as he was great in thought, is himself but the spokesman of a political party; an historian whose presentation of facts, as distinct from the facts themselves, is little more to be trusted than would have been a history of North's ministry from the hands of Burke, or a life of Pitt from the pen of Fox.

XX.

THE THIRD CRUSADE—THE GATHERING OF THE HOST.
(1188-1191.)

"Say, Muse, their names, then known, who first, who last,
At their great emperor's call as next in worth.
Came singly."   MILTON, *Paradise Lost*, i.

THE news of the fall of Jerusalem reached Europe about the end of
October, 1187. It is hard at this distance of time to realise the measure
of the disaster in the eyes of the Western world. It was not merely that
the Holy City had fallen; that all the scenes of that Bible history which
constituted emphatically the literature of mediaeval Christendom, had
passed into the hand of the infidel. It was all this and something more;
the little kingdom of Jerusalem was the one outpost of the Latin Church
and Latin culture in the East; it was the creation of those heroes of the
First Crusade whose exploits had already become the theme of more
than one romance; it lay on the verge of that mysterious East with all
its wealth of gold and precious stones and merchandise, towards which
the sword of the twelfth-century knight turned as instinctively as the
prow of the English or Spanish adventurer four centuries later turned
towards the West. If the sword had won much, much yet remained for it
to win; Aleppo the chief town of Northern Syria, Damascus the garden
of the world, Alexandria the storehouse of the East—all these and other
prizes fired from time to time the ambitions of those who aspired to
rival the successes of the two Baldwins, of Raymond and Reginald, or of
Fulk and Guy; while for those who fell in battle and lost the prize of
temporal power, there was secured an eternity of happiness in heaven.
Thus Palestine inspired alike the imagination, the enterprise, and faith
of Western Christendom.

No wonder that both religious enthusiast and knightly adventurer were stirred to the very utmost at the tidings of Saladin's victory. Pope Urban III. was alleged to have died of grief for the loss of the Holy City. Unfounded though that report was, we know with what profound emotion the news was received in the papal court, where the cardinals laid aside their luxury, and pledged themselves to take the cross and beg, if need be, their way to Palestine. Nor was the feeling less profound in the lands beyond the Alps; it was not, we may be sure, any peculiar grief which made Abbot Samson of Bury St. Edmund's (familiar to all readers of Carlyle's "Past and Present") wear sackcloth next his skin, and leave off animal food from the time when he heard that the Holy City was in the hands of the infidel.

One of the first acts of the new Pope, Gregory VIII., was to bid the princes of Europe lay aside their private quarrels and unite for the service of Christ in a new Crusade. First to take the Cross in November, 1187, was our own Richard, then Count of Poitou; two months later, on January 21, 1188, the kings of France and England were reconciled by the Archbishop of Tyre, and both received the cross at his hands; their example was quickly followed by the Count of Flanders. The three princes agreed that white, red, and green crosses should be the badges of their respective followers.

Nor was the enthusiasm confined to words; the famous Saladin-tax in England, and perhaps in France also, bound every man, on pain of excommunication, to contribute a tithe of his means for the contemplated expedition; to all who would pledge themselves to personal service, special privileges were offered. In England the Crusade was preached by Baldwin of Canterbury himself; in his journey through Wales the archbishop was accompanied by the famous Giraldus Cambrensis, who made this the occasion of his "Itinerary." The foremost preacher in France was Berter of Orleans, the echo of whose eloquence has come down to us in the song which bears his name. Many nobles in both countries followed the example of their kings, but before long the feud between Henry and Philip broke out again. Time after time the expedition was postponed, and it was nearly three years after the fall of Jerusalem, when Henry himself was dead, that the chivalry of France and England were led over sea by their feudal lords to share in the siege of Acre.

The kings of the Spanish peninsula were too busy with the infidel at their own gates to go and fight for the Faith at the other extremity of the Mediterranean. In Italy, however, William of Sicily was first of the great princes to act; when the Archbishop of Tyre, in his black-sailed galley, brought the news of Hattin, William had forthwith diverted to the relief of the Holy Land the fleet which he had collected for an attack on Constantinople. This armament, under its great admiral, Margaritus, saved Antioch from Saladin, helped to preserve Tripoli, strengthened Conrad at Tyre, and recovered Jaffa. William was preparing for a fresh expedition when his death, and the troubles which ensued put an end to the design.

A yet more potent sovereign had already pledged himself for the second time to the service of the cross. Forty years had passed since Frederick Barbarossa had borne his part in the Second Crusade, and now as a man of nearly seventy he renewed the promise of his youth. The troubles of the great Emperor's reign had come to an end, and it had seemed that he might now close his life in peace; but all thoughts of rest were banished by the news of the fall of Jerusalem, and Frederick, though last to take the cross, was first to take the field. Whilst Richard and Philip were banded together in treason to their father and fellow-Crusader, the aged Emperor was already toiling through Hungary and Bulgaria on his way to the East. In the previous year his envoys had obtained from Isaac Comnenus the promise of ample provisions, but the promise of the Greek proved as worthless as ever. Not, indeed, but what Isaac may well have looked on this new enterprise with alarm. Bright,

214

though perhaps misty, visions of a Latin Empire in the East long floated before the eyes of Western Europe. William of Sicily had actually been preparing for such an attempt, and later legend tells how Richard of England hoped to crown the glory of his life by the conquest of so rich a prize. In 1188 the world was full with whispers of a coming change; strange prophecies were told to ready ears, and many hoped that in Frederick they might find the yellow-haired king of the West before whom the golden gate of Constantinople was to open; might he not also be destined to fulfil that other prophecy, and drive back the last remnant of the unconverted Turks beyond the withered tree.

On May 11, 1189, Frederick's great army started from Ratisbon. In Hungary he was received hospitably, but on entering Bulgaria in July he began to experience the nature of Greek promises. Markets were ill provided, and the natives dogged the line of march to cut off stragglers or in the hope of plunder. At Philippopolis on the 24th of August there came the news that Isaac had made a league with Saladin, and contrary to all right and custom thrust the German ambassadors into prison. Isaac's promises were clearly valueless, and Frederick accordingly sent word to his son Henry at home to hire all the ships he could in Italy, and send them to Constantinople in readiness for its siege in the following March.

Isaac presently took alarm, released the envoys and came to terms. The German army then went into winter quarters at Adrianople; in February, 1190, they started once more, and soon after Easter, which fell this year on the 25th of March, crossed the Bosphorus and entered Asia. At Laodicea they reached the dominions of Kilij Arslan, who, by his envoys had promised Frederick good guidance and stores of food. It was, however, soon evident that Kilij Arslan was no more to be trusted than Isaac; no food was brought for sale, and as the army toiled along the rocky ways that led to Iconium their steps were dogged by the hostile Turks. When at length, on the 18th of May, the Crusaders appeared before his city, Kilij Arslan, declaring that it was not he but his son who was to blame for the past, came to terms and opened to the Crusaders an abundant market.

From Iconium Frederick passed on towards Cilicia. Leo, the Prince of Armenia, sent him envoys with promises of all support and goodwill. But on the 10th of June while the army was struggling over the rocky hills that separated Cilicia from Lycaonia they were startled by the news of the Emperor's death. Desirous to avoid the labours of the recognised path which wound up the rocks above the river Saleph, Frederick had determined to make a short cut; with his attendants he came down to the river side; the day was hot, and willing to shorten his journey, and at the same time cool his heated limbs the Emperor attempted to swim the rapid stream; the swirl of the waters sucked him down, and so "he, who had oftentimes escaped from greater dangers, came to a pitiful end." His followers sadly carried his body to Tarsus, where they buried the intestines with great reverence; his bones were taken to Antioch and interred in the Church of St. Peter.

Thus perished the noblest type of German kingship—the Kaiser Redbeard, of whom history and legend have so much to tell. Tradition was soon busy with his death. Men could not believe that he was gone away for ever from his own land: like Arthur, he was but in hiding for a time, and would return in some hour of supreme necessity to save the empire which he had ruled. The spot which witnessed his destruction was fabled to have been marked out by fate from remote antiquity, and a rock near the river's fount was alleged to bear the ominous words— "HIC HOMINUM MAXIMUS PERIBIT" ("Here shall perish the greatest of men").

After Frederick's death the German host divided into two. One body went to Tripoli; the rest, under the Duke of Swabia, made their way to Antioch, where they stayed for some time, recruiting themselves after their labours, and assisting the prince of that city in his warfare.

It was not till June, 1190, that Richard and Philip Augustus were ready to commence their journey. The two kings met at Vézelay, and proceeded in company to Marseilles, whence Philip sailed in a Genoese fleet for Sicily, and landed at Messina on the 16th of September. Richard had ordered his fleet to meet him at Marseilles, but the English Crusaders, mindful of the exploit of their forefathers nearly half a century before, stopped on the way to help Sancho, of Portugal, in his warfare with the Moors. It was the 14th of September before they reached Marseilles.

Meanwhile Richard, impatient of delay, had started in a single galley. Slowly he sailed from port to port along the western shores of Italy, varying his journey from time to time by a ride on shore. At last, on the 23rd of September, he joined his main fleet, and entered Messina in state and pomp amidst the blare of trumpets, whilst the Frenchmen and Sicilians on the beach marvelled at the splendour of his coming.

The two kings stayed on in Sicily for six months. The winter was passed in unseemly wrangling; Tancred, the new ruler of the island, was an illegitimate grandson of Roger I.; he had seized the person and property of his predecessor's widow, Joanna, and she, as Richard's sister, naturally turned to her brother for protection. An ill-advised quarrel soon gave Richard a pretext for an attack on Messina; "Quicker than priest could chant matins," says the old chronicler, "did King Richard take the city." Such prompt action brought Tancred to his senses and though Richard did not get the golden table and chair, which he claimed as part of his sister's dower, he received what was perhaps more useful, namely, forty thousand ounces of gold.

If the taking of Messina proved Richard's military prowess, his castle of Matte Griffin, or Check Greek, showed him as the skilful engineer; and the great Christmas feast, when he gave his guests the golden goblets which they used, displayed his generosity. Now also, though late, he recognised his sin against his father, and showed the sincerity of his sorrow by submitting to public penance. In the presence of all his prelates he confessed his sin, and "from that hour once more became a God-fearing man."

On the 30th of March, 1191, Richard's mother, Eleanor, brought to Messina her son's destined bride, Berengaria of Navarre. That same day Philip had sailed for Palestine, but Richard did not start till eleven days later. The English fleet, which numbered more than one hundred and eighty vessels, was scattered by a great storm two days after it set sail. Richard himself put in at Crete; but some of his ships were wrecked on the coast of Cyprus, and the crews thrown into prison by order of Isaac Comnenus, the ruler of the island. A little later the ship which carried Berengaria and her future sister-in-law, Joanna, reached Limasol. Somewhat doubtfully they accepted Isaac's invitation to land next day, Monday, the 6th of May; but that same afternoon the sails of the main fleet appeared on the horizon, and on the following morning the king himself arrived. Richard was not the man to suffer tamely the wrongs which had been done to his followers; when Isaac refused redress, the English king determined to use force; a short campaign of three weeks sufficed for the conquest of Cyprus, and Isaac was imprisoned in chains of silver.

At Cyprus Richard married Berengaria, and after a month's stay in the island sailed, on the 5th of June, for Palestine, in the company of Guy de Lusignan, who had come to meet him with many of the great Syrian nobles. On his way Richard encountered and sank a great Saracen vessel laden with provisions for Acre, and after two days entered the harbour of that city in triumph. "For joy at his coming," says Baha-ed-din, "the Franks broke forth into public rejoicing, and lit mighty fires in their camps all night long. And seeing that the King of England was old in war and wise in council, the hearts of the Mussulmans were filled with fear and dread."

XXI.

THE THIRD CRUSADE—THE SIEGE OF ACRE.
(1189-1191.)

"Corpses across the threshold; heroes tall
Dislodging pinnacle and parapet
Upon the tortoise creeping to the wall;
Lances in ambush set."

TENNYSON, *"A Dream of Fair Women."*

WE must now turn back to record the fortunes of the Christians in Palestine during the interval between the fall of Jerusalem and the arrival of the main host of the Crusaders under the kings of France and England.

Guy de Lusignan had been set free towards the beginning of July, 1188, but not until he had promised to abandon his claim on the kingdom. From this engagement he was soon released by the clergy, who assured him that there was no binding force in such an oath. Near Tortosa he met his wife, and with her proceeded to Antioch at the invitation of Bohemond. The year passed in anxious expectation of succour from Europe. But by the following spring Guy had assembled a little army, and feeling sufficiently strong to take the initiative, marched southwards to Tyre. Conrad refused him admission to the city, declaring that God had entrusted it to his care, and he would keep it; if the king sought a resting-place let him find it elsewhere. After four months' vain delay near Tyre, Guy marched on to Acre with an army which now numbered seven hundred knights and nine thousand foot, gathered from every nation in Christendom. With this little force he set down to besiege that great and strong city on the 28th of August, 1189.

Acre lies on an inlet of the Mediterranean which bears its name; a tongue of land running southwards into the sea serves as a partial

219

protection for the harbour; at its extremity rose the famous "Tower of Flies," which, together with a chain, helped to guard the harbour; to the east the city overlooked a fertile plain. The harbour of Acre was the best in the kingdom properly so called, if not along the whole coast of Syria, and the town itself was the chief emporium of Frankish trade. In recent years it had been gradually supplanting Jerusalem as the royal residence, and had become the recognised landing-place for pilgrims from the West. "Acre," says an Arab writer, who visited it some five years before this time, "is the column on which the Frankish towns in Syria rest. Thither put in the tall ships which float like mountains over the sea. It is the meeting-place of crafts and caravans: the place whither Mussulman and Christian merchants muster from all sides."

At a little distance from the walls a small hill rises above the level of the plain; here Guy pitched his tent, whence he could look forward over the city for the sails of his expected friends. But to the east a less pleasant sight soon met his gaze, as one after another the Saracen contingents hastened up to hem in the Christian army between the river Kishon and the sea; before long the Christians were themselves besieged, and their numbers were so few that they could not prevent the Saracens from passing almost at their will to and from the town.

The siege had hardly commenced when the first ships of the autumn passage began to arrive. First came the Frisians, closely followed by a contingent from Flanders and England. Then came the hero of the siege, James of Avesnes, a warrior proud and turbulent in his own land, but in the eyes of his fellow Crusaders the model of all chivalric virtues—in counsel as Nestor, in arms as Achilles, in faith as Regulus. Other arrivals were Robert of Dreux, grandson of Louis VI., and his brother Philip of Beauvais, the warrior prelate of the expedition; the Counts of Brienne and Bar, and the Landgrave, Louis of Thuringia, whose influence induced Conrad of Montferrat to lend his aid to an enterprise, from which he had as yet held sullenly aloof. By mid-

September the Christians perhaps numbered nine thousand horse and thirty thousand foot, and were able to establish an effectual blockade. Saladin therefore determined on an attempt to break through their lines, and in the early dawn of September 14th, a sudden onset from both the city and the camp proved successful; despite their valour, the Christians could not prevent the passage of the loaded camels into Acre, nor the escape of one of Saladin's sons from the beleaguered town.

Three weeks later Guy retaliated by an attack on the Sultan's camp; the Saracens gave way before the charge of the Franks, who were already plundering Saladin's tent, when a sally from the town cut off the Christians in the rear, and called Geoffrey de Lusignan to his brother's aid, from the camp which he had undertaken to guard. In vain did the Templars offer a stout resistance to the new attack; twenty of their knights were slain, and among them Gerard de Rideford, the Grand Master. Gerard died a hero's death; his comrades urged him to seek safety in retreat; "God forbid," was his reply, "that men should say of me to the shame of our order, that to save my own life I fled away leaving my fellows dead behind me." Nor was Gerard alone in his gallantry; Guy himself, in the true spirit of chivalry, rescued his enemy Conrad from, the imminent danger of death, whilst James d'Avesnes owed his safety to the self-sacrifice of one of his knights. In the end the Christians lost the day, but they gained, nevertheless, a substantial advantage, for the Saracens were so exhausted, that Saladin gave orders to fall back on El Kharruba, about twelve miles southeast of Acre.

The Christians turned this respite to the best use; in order at once to secure their own position, and to complete the blockade, they dug a deep trench outside their camp from sea to sea, and strengthened it with a wall of earth. Night and day they toiled at the task till all was finished. Young and old, men and women, all joined in the labour, and the Christian historian records with enthusiasm, how when one woman was mortally wounded in the midst of her labour, she adjured her husband to let her dead body be flung into the mound, that thus she might further in death the work for which she had sacrificed her life.

The winter passed away without any important result, though the Egyptian fleet succeeded in revictualling the town on October 31st, and two months later drove the Christian vessels to seek shelter at Tyre. Saladin occupied himself with preparations for mustering a large army; Baha-ed-din was sent on an embassy to summon the lords beyond the Euphrates, and to beg aid of the Caliph; both missions proved successful, and in April, 1190, the various contingents began to arrive. Meantime Conrad had brought back the fleet from Tyre, and, in return for a compact, by which he was to have Tyre, Sidon, and Beyrout, lent his hearty aid. But though the Christians could now confine the Saracen fleet at Acre, they still could not prevent the entry of provisions from time to time. The siege was nevertheless prosecuted with vigour from the land side; three great towers of wood were constructed, and fitted with engines; when manned by five hundred men a-piece, they were brought to bear on the walls. Perhaps the town would have fallen save for the energy of a young charcoal-burner of Damascus; but by his direction certain ingredients were mixed together in pots, which on being hurled against the towers set them ablaze; thus they were all destroyed, and the confusion of the Christians was increased by an attack from the Saracen camp, which was maintained during eight days.

After this many of Saladin's best troops were called away to oppose the Germans near Antioch. This circumstances perhaps encouraged the Christian common folk, contrary to the will of their leaders, to sally out on July 25th against the foes surrounding them. The wrath of the chiefs was powerless against the lust for spoil, which stirred the crowd to madness; for a moment the suddenness of the attack made it successful, and the rude host was soon rifling the tents of El-Adel. But the Saracen soldiery quickly mustered to arms, and the Franks, who had no thought except for the plunder, woke up to find their retreat entirely cut off. Hardly one would have escaped but for the valour and self-devotion of an English clerk, Ralph of Hautrey, Archdeacon of Colchester. The Christians themselves admitted a loss of over five thousand men, and Baha-ed-din, who rode over the plain after the battle, declares that he had to cross "waves of blood," and that he could not count the number of the dead.

The next few months were passed in comparative quiet, but were marked by the coming of the first large contingents of the French and English hosts; the former under Henry of Champagne and Theobald of Blois, the latter under Ranulf Glanville, Archbishop Baldwin of Canterbury, and his destined successor, Hubert Walter, then Bishop of Salisbury. About the same time the Germans arrived from Tripoli, under Frederick of Swabia; but of the vast host which started from Ratisbon, scarcely five thousand were now left.

Count Henry brought with him ten thousand men, and he was at once appointed to command the army in place of James d'Avesnes and the Landgrave, who had so far held the office by turns. The attack from the land side still met with but indifferent success, but at sea the blockade was so strictly maintained, that famine began to press hard on the besieged. Saladin, however, maintained his communications with the town, through the agency of a messenger named Eissa. This man would creep down to the shore at dark, carrying in his belt letters and money for the payment of the troops; thence plunging into the waters he would strike out for the harbour, often diving beneath the very keels of the Crusaders' ships. At last one of his journeys proved fatal, and a few days later the citizens of Acre found his dead body on the sand with his belt still untouched. "Never before," says the Arab historian, quaintly, "had we seen a man pay a debt after his death."

Provisions grew scarce within the town, but the state of the Christian camp was scarcely less doleful. Archbishop Baldwin, writing home, says: "The Lord is not in the camp; there is none that doeth good. The leaders strive one with another, while the lesser folk starve, and have none to help. The Turks are persistent in attack, while our knights skulk within their tents. The strength of Saladin increases daily, but daily does our army wither away."

Saladin, however, on October 20th, went into winter quarters at Shefr 'Amr close to El Kharruba; for the unhealthiness of the place was proving fatal to himself and to his troops. His troops began to murmur at the long campaign, and one by one many of his chief followers withdrew, till in March, 1191, the Sultan was left with only a small force. On the other hand, the stress of winter had prevented the Franks from watching the harbour with the usual closeness, and Saladin had contrived to throw, a fresh garrison into the town (Feb. 13th). Moreover famine was rife in the Christian camp, and during the enforced idleness of winter the soldiery gave way to dicing, drinking, and even worse. Baldwin took the evil that he saw around him so much to heart, that he fell sick, and after a short illness died, thankful for his speedy delivery from his sojourn in so godless an army. Conrad had withdrawn to Tyre, and promised to send provisions thence; but he either could not or would not fulfil his engagement, and at length the famine grew so severe that the knights slew their chargers to save themselves from death. When it was known that an animal had been slaughtered, men flocked together from all parts of the camp to beg or steal a portion for themselves. Men of noble birth might be seen going out into the plain and eating grass like cattle, others ran about the camp like dogs on the scent for old bones. At last, one Saturday early in March, a ship arrived with a cargo of grain, and by the following day the price of a measure of corn had fallen from a hundred pieces of gold to four. After this there was an end of the famine, and only those grieved who, like a certain

Pisan, had hoarded their grain in the hope of an even higher price; "But his wickedness did God show by a plain token; for it chanced that his house suddenly took fire and was consumed with all that was in it."

About the end of March, 1191, Saladin renewed his leaguer of the Christian camp; but the besieged within the city were now hard pressed, and the Sultan could do no more to help them than to order an attack on the Christian camp whenever the Christians made a special effort against the town. Philip Augustus arrived on April 20th, and Richard on June 8th; it seemed for the moment that Acre must fall at once. The machines which the King of England had constructed in Sicily, including the huge wooden tower Matte Griffin, were brought to bear on the walls. But before anything had been effected, the old feuds broke out afresh; Guy and Conrad renewed their quarrel, and the latter departed coming of fresh forces. Philip soon recovered, and on July 3rd a great effort to carry the town was made; though the assault fell short of complete success, the defenders were reduced to despair. Richard, though still unwell, was eager to emulate the deeds of his rival; so a few days later he had himself carried to a shed whence he could direct the efforts of his engineers; in his ardour he himself aimed the shots from the balista, while his miners worked with such vigour that at length a piece of the wall fell down with a crash. At last—so the story was told, a little later in England—on July 8th, as the Christians were keeping watch, there shone round them a sudden light, "for fear of which the guards became as dead men;" in the midst of the light appeared the Virgin, bidding those to whom she spoke bear her message to the kings; let them abandon their efforts against the walls, the city should be theirs on the fourth day.

Next morning the rulers of the city begged for a truce, and promised to capitulate if Saladin did not send immediate help. The Sultan was forced somewhat unwillingly to consent to terms; Acre was to be given up together with two hundred knights and fifteen hundred other

Christian captives; the Holy Cross was to be restored, and the sum of two hundred thousand besants paid to the Crusaders. So after a siege of nearly two years, on Friday, July 12, 1191, the Christians once more obtained possession of Acre. The city and the captives were divided between the two kings; Richard took possession of the royal palace, whilst Philip hung his banner over the house of the Templars. But even in the hour of victory the princes quarrelled one with another as to their respective shares therein. Leopold of Austria—so the story goes—had set up his banner side by side with that of the King of England as though arrogating to himself an equal share in the triumph; with Richard's connivance, if not by his command, the duke's banner was torn down and cast into the ditch. Leopold, feeling himself unable to revenge this indignity, departed for his own land, bearing in his breast the seeds of a direful hatred for the English king.

XXII.

THE THIRD CRUSADE—THE CAMPAIGNS OF RICHARD.
(1191-1192.)

"Yet in this heathen war the fire of God
Fills him: I never saw his like; there lives
No greater leader."

TENNYSON.

HARDLY was Acre taken; hardly had the two kings established themselves in their quarters in the city; hardly had the papal legate, the Cardinal Adelard of Verona, and his brother bishops, reconsecrated the churches which for four years had been polluted with Mohammedan rites; hardly had the Pisan merchants begun to exercise their former privileges and renew their former trade, when the slumbering jealousy of the two kings once more brought peril on the common enterprise.

Philip Augustus owed no ordinary gratitude to the late King of England and his sons; it was the young Henry who had stood by Philip's side at his coronation and helped to raise the crown that bore too heavily on the boy-king's head; it was the elder Henry who by his wise statesmanship had preserved the first years of Philip's reign from rebellion and civil war; later, when Richard was at feud with his father, it was to his alliance that Philip owed the grand success of 1189. But the friendliness of the young princes could not survive Richard's elevation to the crown; and with his father's and his mother's lands Richard inherited the traditional hostility of the king at Paris.

Other special grounds of quarrel there were between Richard and Philip which had not existed between Henry and Louis. After long dallying, Richard had repudiated his engagement to Philip's half-sister Alice; and though the French king could stoop to accept compensation in money, he can hardly have put out of mind the insulting reason which

Richard gave for his refusal. Cupidity also had its share in the quarrel; the two kings had sworn to divide all the spoils of their conquests; but both had with more or less of reason found occasion to recede from this engagement. Moreover while yet in Sicily they had quarrelled openly; for Tancred had shown to Richard certain letters which he professed to have received from Philip, and which invited his assistance in a treacherous attack on the English. Philip denied all knowledge of the letters, but it was only with great difficulty that the Count of Flanders contrived to effect a seeming reconciliation.

Nor were personal dissensions the only troubles with which the two kings had to contend. National rivalry, which had nearly wrecked the First Crusade, was destined to be the ruin of the Third. Richard's coming to Acre had been hailed as the "coming of the desired of all nations;" but the joy was of short duration, for soon the old jealousies broke out, and it was found necessary to forbid the two nations even to fight side by side. "The two kings and peoples," says the English chronicler, "did less together than they would have done separately, and each set but light store by the other." So it was agreed that when the knights of one nation advanced against the city, the others should remain to keep ward in the trenches.

But a yet more serious rock of offence lay in the struggle for the kingship of Jerusalem. Sibylla and her infant children had died in the latter part of 1190. Their death encouraged some of the native nobles to dispute Guy's title once more. According to the normal rules of the land Henfrid IV. of Toron should have governed in the name of his wife Isabella, Sibylla's younger sister. But the great nobles had never forgiven Henfrid for his refusal to join in their rebellion four years before; they therefore sought another candidate in Conrad of Montferrat, whose vigour had saved Tyre for the Christians, and whose brother William had been Sibylla's first husband and the father of their last accepted king. Conrad was a man of resource and action, who, both for his birth and his personal merit, ought to satisfy even the proud barons of Syria. The one obstacle was Isabella's previous marriage; but with the lady's consent a divorce was procured on the plea that she had been married to Henfrid against her wish. The attitude of Philip and Richard was foreshadowed in the action of their followers, for Baldwin of Canterbury was foremost in opposing the divorce, whilst the new marriage was celebrated by Philip of Beauvais, cousin to the king of France.

Guy could not be expected to acquiesce in the loss of his title and power; naturally enough he had sought in Cyprus the aid of his former overlord, King Richard, who had there promised him his support. Before the siege of Acre was over the quarrel had culminated in open violence; Guy's brother Geoffrey bluntly accused Conrad of treachery, and Conrad rather than maintain his innocence by gage of battle withdrew to Tyre; nevertheless, Philip Augustus took that noble under his protection, and openly declared his opposition to the wishes of the King of England. However, at the end of July, after a formal trial, a compromise was arranged, under which Guy retained the title of king, but shared the royal revenues with Conrad, who was to be hereditary lord of Tyre, Sidon, and Beyrout; at Guy's death the crown was to pass to Conrad and his children by Isabella.

By this time Philip had already wearied of the Crusade, and a little later he rejected Richard's proposal that they should both bind themselves to stay in the land for three years. Soon he went even further, and begged Richard's sanction for his return, pleading that his health was bad and that he had sufficiently performed his oath. The remonstrances of Richard and of his own followers had no weight with Philip, who on July 31st set out for Tyre. Before his departure the French king swore neither actively nor passively to do any wrong to the King of England's men or lands in Europe. "How faithfully he kept his oath the whole world knows. For directly he reached home he stirred up the whole land, and threw Normandy into confusion. What need for further words! Amid the curses of all he departed, leaving his army at Acre."

Richard waited for Saladin to pay the agreed ransom; but August 14th arrived and the Mohammedans had not completed their engagement. So on the Eve of the Assumption Richard left Acre and pitched his tents beyond the eastern trenches; here he waited again six days more, till, on the afternoon of August 20th, the king and his knights advanced into the plain. Then the captives were brought out and massacred in full view of their countrymen; it was in vain that the Saracens threw themselves upon the murderers of their kinsfolk, and in all five thousand prisoners are said to have been thus slain, the more notable only being preserved for ransom. The massacre was not, perhaps, so gratuitous and unwarrantable as would at first sight appear; Roger Howden asserts distinctly that Saladin had slain his Christian captives two days before, an assertion which the words of Baha-ed-din seem to countenance; Richard may also have felt the danger and difficulty of keeping so many prisoners, and have honestly doubted the good faith of Saladin as to the stipulated ransom.

On August 23rd Richard started for Ascalon; the army marched along the shore, whilst the fleet accompanied them at a little distance from the land. Every evening, when the tents were pitched, the herald took his stand in the midst of the host, and thrice cried aloud: "Aid us, Holy Sepulchre!" As he cried the whole army took up the shout with tears. "Who would not have wept, seeing that the mere recital moves all that hear to sorrow?"

Inland on the low hills to the left Saladin's host followed and harassed the Crusaders. Despite the enemy, and the terrible heat, which caused many to fall dead by the way, the Christians marched on past Haifa and Caesarea, till on September 1st they reached the Dead River, where the coast became so bad for marching that Richard struck inland by the mountain road. On September 3rd a fierce attack was made on the Templars in the rear; the arrows flew so fast that there was not a yard of the army's march where they did not lie; Richard himself was among the wounded. But still the host pressed on, till on the 6th they rested by the Nahr Falaik, or River of the Cleft, some sixteen miles from Caesarea. Here they learnt that Saladin was awaiting their approach with an army of three hundred thousand men, three times the estimated number of the Crusading host. With the early dawn of the 7th of September the Christians resumed their march in five divisions. First went the Templars; then the Bretons and men of Anjou; next the Poitevins under Guy; fourth came the Normans and English with the royal banner; in the rear were the Hospitallers. The Christian army, marshalled in close array, filled the whole space between the hills and the sea. Richard and the Duke of Burgundy with a band of chosen knights rode up and down the lines keeping a wary eye on the order of their troops.

About nine o'clock the battle began with an attack by Saladin's negro troops and Bedouins—pestilent footmen with bows and round targes; in their rear the heavier Turkish troops kept up an incessant din with their drums and cymbals. Again and again the Turks rushed down on the rear of the Christians; at last the Hospitallers could bear up no longer, and begged Richard to let them make but one charge. Richard, however, would permit no deviation from his plans. The heavy horses of his cavalry with their armoured riders were no match for the swift-footed Arab steeds of the lightly-clad Saracens; it would be worse than useless to charge till the enemy was well within their grasp. When the decisive moment arrived six trumpets were to give the signal; then the footmen were to open wide their ranks, and let the knights pass through to the attack.

So the Hospitallers endeavoured to still endure the renewed onset of the foe; one knight in despair invoked the great warrior-saint of the

231

Crusaders, who perhaps from this period tended to become the patron saint of England: "Oh, St. George! Why dost thou leave us to be destroyed? Christendom perisheth, because we strive not against this accursed race." Then the Grand Master petitioned the king in person, but Richard still replied: "It must be borne." Most of the Hospitallers murmured but obeyed; two knights, however—the marshal of the order, and Baldwin de Carew, "a right good warrior, bold as a lion"—burst from the ranks and overthrew each his man; the remaining Hospitallers could be no longer restrained and out they charged to their comrades' aid. The battle soon became general and for a time threatened to go ill for the Crusaders; but when Richard himself came up on his Cyprian bay, the Turks fell back before him as he clove his way into their ranks with his sword. The Christians then resumed their march, and were already encamping outside the walls of Arsuf when the enemy attacked once more; but again the Turks turned in headlong flight as Richard galloped up to the rescue thundering out his war-cry: "God and the Holy Sepulchre aid us!"

The Christians counted two-and-thirty emirs dead upon the field of battle, besides seven thousand corpses of meaner folk. They boasted that their own loss was not as many hundred. But one death in particular they had to mourn; the heroic James of Avesnes was surrounded and slain by the Turks. On the morrow his corpse was found with fifteen of the enemy lying dead around him.

On Monday, September 9th, the march was renewed, and next day, just three weeks after leaving Acre, the Crusaders encamped in pleasant quarters amid the orchards outside Jaffa. At the same time the fleet arrived bringing an abundance of food.

Past experience had taught the Crusaders that until they held Ascalon and Jaffa they could not hope to maintain themselves in the Holy City, even if they should succeed in capturing it at once. Worse still would be their position if they had to conduct a prolonged siege with all the seaboard, from Caesarea to Damietta, in the hands of the foe. To all this Saladin was not less alive than Richard himself; but he was too weak to hold Ascalon, and so ordered it to be dismantled in haste, before the Crusaders could come up. The Christians, however, were as busy with the restoration of Jaffa as the Saracens were with the destruction of Ascalon. Not that Richard was blind to the importance of the latter city, which he would have attacked before but for the supineness of Philip; but now as then French opposition compelled him to postpone the advance, and this delay perhaps ruined the expedition.

Six weeks of precious time were lost at Jaffa, and it was only in the end of October that Richard renewed his march towards Jerusalem. Even then he had to stay at the Casal of the Plains and Casal Maen, between Ramleh and Lydda, for two months. At the end of the year he advanced to Beit-Nuba, some ten miles nearer the Holy City, but was there once more detained by the violence of the winter storms. The wind tore up the tents, and the wet rotted the store of provisions, whilst sickness played havoc both with the men and their horses. Yet in the midst of their misfortunes the Crusaders were glad in heart with the hope of reaching the Lord's Sepulchre, and the thought that nothing should now prevent the accomplishment of their pilgrimage. But the military orders and the Syrian Franks knew the dangers of a winter campaign, and feared that ever success would have no other result than to shut up the host in a city which they could not defend. In a council held on January 13th their opinion prevailed, and the order was given for a retreat to Ramleh. Many of the French then withdrew to Jaffa, or elsewhere; but Richard, full of wrath at the turn affairs had taken, determined to lead his diminished army to Ascalon. Two days of weary marching through snow and rain brought them at last to the ruined town on January 20th. After a little the French were induced to rejoin the host, and pledged themselves to obey Richard's orders till Easter. All then set about the task of restoring Ascalon; nobles, knights, squires, and men-at-arms working together with their own hands, and with one will. But the main glory of the work belonged to the king; he was everywhere directing, exhorting, and even working. His eloquence heartened the great lords to fresh efforts and larger liberality. Where means were lacking he supplied them, till when at last Ascalon was restored, it was said that Richard had paid for three-quarters of the work.

The previous autumn had witnessed some lengthy, if not perhaps very genuine negotiations between Richard and Saladin. Richard at first demanded the restoration of the whole kingdom as it existed under Baldwin IV. When this was refused he suggested a marriage between El-Adel or Saphadin, the Sultan's brother, and his own sister Joanna, who might then rule together in a new kingdom of Palestine." The proposal flattered El-Adel, who visited Richard in or near the Crusaders' camp; the king had just undergone his autumn bleeding and could not receive his visitor in person, but had him entertained at a great banquet. This was followed next day by an interview and the exchange of costly presents, from which there sprung up a warm friendship between the two princes. The negotiations, however, fell through, according to the Saracens, because Joanna refused to wed a Mohammedan. The Christian account makes no mention of the marriage, and ascribes the failure to Saladin's refusal to dismantle Kerak. Perhaps, indeed, the chief object of both parties had been to gain time—Richard that he might complete the fortification of Jaffa, Saladin that he might postpone hostilities till winter had made a serious campaign impracticable. At the same time both parties may have found good reasons to wish for peace—Richard in his suspicions of Philip Augustus, and Saladin in his fears of the descendants of Zangi.

Richard, moreover, was at this time much hampered by the behaviour of Conrad of Montferrat. The marquis had not only held aloof from the main enterprise, but had also a party among the Syrian

Franks, with Balian of Ibelin and Reginald of Sidon for his chief supporters. Conrad and his party, like Richard, had opened negotiations with Saladin, but the Sultan's council had declared against them on the ground that there could be no sincere friendship between the Saracens and the Syrian Franks. When in February, 1192, Richard called Conrad to his aid at Ascalon, the marquis found occasion to excuse himself. The Duke of Burgundy had about the same time withdrawn from the army because Richard refused him any further loans of money.

The French now went to Acre, where they took up the cause of the Genoese against the Pisans, who were partisans of Guy. The Genoese called on Conrad, whilst the Pisans sent word to Richard, on whose approach the marquis went back to Tyre, taking Burgundy with him.

Despite a personal interview the breach between Conrad and Richard grew wider, and the latter presently renewed his negotiations with Saladin. So friendly did the King and Sultan become that, on Palm Sunday, Richard knighted El-Adel's son at Acre in great state. However, some hostilities of the Franks near Darum inclined Saladin to turn once more to Conrad, who agreed to join in open war with his fellow Crusaders. Richard, who by this time had returned to Ascalon, was now forced to let the French, who had thus far remained with him, depart to their compatriots at Tyre. The news of troubles in England which arrived about this time, made Richard himself anxious to go home. Some settlement of the kingdom was now imperative, and Richard rather reluctantly consented to the recognition of Conrad as king.

Hardly had the marquis thus attained the object of his ambitions, when he was cut off by a mysterious fate. On Monday, April 27th, so runs the story in the Franco-Syrian chronicles, Conrad, weary of waiting for his queen, who had stayed late at the bath, went out to dine with Philip of Beauvais. Finding that the bishop had already dined, Conrad turned home. As he came out of the bishop's house into the

235

narrow road, two men advanced to meet him; one of the two offered him a letter, and whilst Conrad was thus off his guard they stabbed him with their knives. Conrad fell dead on the spot; of his murderers one was instantly slain, and the other was captured soon after. When put to torture this man confessed that he and his comrade had been despatched by the Old Man of the Mountain to take vengeance for the ˙ robbery of one of his merchant vessels.

Queen Isabella now declared that she would hold Tyre for Richard, but the French clamoured for the city to be surrendered to them on behalf of their king. But as it happened Richard's nephew, Henry of Champagne, had hurried to Tyre on the news of Conrad's death; the people at once hailed him as lord, and begged him to marry Isabella. Richard readily assented to the proposal, and so Palestine once more had a king, whose claim was supported not only by the French and English, but also by the Syrian Franks. With these brighter prospects before him Richard once more postponed his departure. Like a true knight-errant, he was more attracted by the hope of conquering a new kingdom from the Saracen, than by the prospect of merely preserving the one which God had given him.

Richard did not when assenting to his nephew's elevation forget the deposed king for whom he had struggled so long. Cyprus was bestowed on Guy, whose family ruled in that island for more than two centuries after the last remnants of the Christian kingdom on the mainland fell into the hands of the Moslem.

In the middle of May Richard, who was anxious to strike a blow whilst Saladin was still troubled with the threatened revolt on the Euphrates, left Ascalon with a small force to besiege Darum. That fortress was very strong, but the fleet soon arrived with the siege train, and on the 22nd of May Darum surrendered after only four days' siege. Hardly was the fortress taken when King Henry arrived with the French, and received Darum from his uncle as the first-fruits of his new realm. Very shortly afterwards fresh news of a disquieting nature from England made Richard think once more of returning home. But after some hesitation he pledged himself to stay till the following Easter, and ordered preparations to be made for an immediate advance to Jerusalem. At this news, "all began to rejoice as a bird at dawn of day," and forthwith made themselves ready for the journey, crying out: "We thank Thee, O God! because we shall now behold Thy city, where the Turks have dwelt so long."

On Sunday, June 7th, the Crusaders marched out from Ascalon, and after a few days' journey, once more pitched their tents at Beit-Nuba. Here they had to stay a month till King Henry brought reinforcements from Acre. This delay was unfortunate for the Christians, for there seems little doubt that if they had pushed on at once they could have taken the city. Whether they could have held it for long is another matter. Probably most of the Crusaders, after paying their vows at the Holy Sepulchre, would have returned home, without further care for the land they had so hardly won.

Two incidents in the desultory warfare of this tedious month deserve notice. One day in June Richard came upon a party of Turks near the fountain of Emmaus unawares, and slew twenty of them. In his pursuit of the remainder along the hills he advanced so far that as he chanced to raise his eyes, he caught a glimpse of the Holy City from afar. A little latter there came news of a great caravan on its way up from Egypt. Richard with characteristic generosity invited the Duke of Burgundy and the French to share in the spoil. Marching by moonlight, the king's force of five hundred knights and a thousand serving men came out to Keratiyeh, where during a short halt they learnt that one caravan was already marching past the "Round Cistern." The report was confirmed by Richard's own spies, who were sent out in disguise as Bedouins. Another night's march brought the Crusaders within a short distance of the caravan. At dawn the bowmen were sent out in advance, and the

237

king with his knights followed in the rear. The caravan was surprised while resting, and its escort fled before the charge of the Crusaders like hares before the hounds. Besides a very rich spoil of spices, gold, silver, silks, robes, and arms of every kind, there were captured no less than four thousand seven hundred camels, besides mules and asses beyond number.

The loss of this caravan "was an event most shameful to us," writes Baha-ed din; "not for a long time past had such a disaster befallen Islam. Never did any news so trouble the Sultan." Saladin was, indeed, in no small alarm lest the Crusaders should advance forthwith on Jerusalem. But after a few days there came the welcome news that the Franks were in retreat.

The causes of this retreat are more or less of a mystery. It would seem that about a fortnight previously, before the arrival of King Henry with the reinforcements, the Franks were very eager for an immediate advance. Richard declared that the idea was impossible, and that he would not take the responsibility for an enterprise which would expose him to the censure of his enemies. If others saw fit to attack Jerusalem, he would not desert them; but in that case he would follow, and not lead. He pointed out the dangers of their present position, and urged that the Crusaders should follow the advice of the native lords as to whether it was wiser to besiege Jerusalem, or march against Cairo, Beyrout, or Damascus. So at Richard's suggestion the plan of campaign was referred to a committee of twenty sworn jurors. The twenty decided in favour of attacking Cairo. At this the French cried out, declaring that they would march only against Jerusalem; Richard in vain offered the assistance of his fleet which lay at Acre, and promised a liberal contribution towards their expenses; his efforts were without avail, and on the 4th of July he ordered a retreat towards Ramleh.

Richard now withdrew to Acre, and reopened negotiations with Saladin. But the Sultan, hearing of an intended expedition against

Beyrout, determined to divert the attack, and on July 26th appeared before Jaffa. After a five days' siege the town was captured, and the remainder of the garrison in the tower promised to surrender if aid did not come by the following day. But Richard had been well informed of the danger, and though the French would lend him no assistance, had already left Acre with a few galleys. Through contrary winds he only reached Jaffa at midnight on the 31st. When day dawned it seemed that he had arrived too late, for Saladin's banners were already flying on the walls. Richard was in doubt what to do, until a priest swam out to the ships with news of the peril to which those in the tower were exposed. The king delayed no longer, but ordered his galleys to be rowed towards the shore, and himself led the Christians as they waded through the water to the land. The Turks fled before them, and the royal banner was soon waving from the walls. Richard himself was foremost in the fight: "never did warrior bear himself so nobly, as did the king that day; Saladin fled before him like a hunted hare." For more than two miles the English cross-bowmen pursued the Turks with terrible carnage, and at night Richard pitched his tent on the very spot where Saladin's had lately stood. Richard's position was still one of considerable peril. He had with him but fifty knights, and only fifteen horses good or bad. An attempt at a surprise was only frustrated by a happy accident. At dawn on the 5th of August a Genoese, who was out in search of fodder, heard the tramp of men and caught sight of their helmets gleaming in the eastern sky. Hurrying back he roused the sleeping camp, but hardly was there time to arm or even dress before the Turks were upon them. Richard was marshalling his little army, when a messenger came up crying out that they were all lost, and that the enemy had seized the town. Sternly ordering the man to hold his peace, Richard bade his followers be of good cheer, and to show his own confidence rode off with half-a-dozen knights to discover what had actually taken place in Jaffa. The Saracens who had gained the town fled before the king as he forced his way into the streets, and Richard could soon rejoin his army outside. There the enemy, though they continually charged close up to the Christian line, would not venture to attack. At last in the afternoon Richard advanced, and after a fierce engagement put the Saracens to flight. It was on this day that, according to the romantic tale, El-Adel, hearing Richard had no horse, sent him two Arab steeds; a generous gift, which the king accepted in a like spirit, and afterwards splendidly recompensed.

After this battle negotiations were once more resumed. The French would render no help, and sickness was playing havoc with the Christian host. Richard himself fell ill, and thought it better to ask for a truce than to go away leaving the whole land to be laid waste, as did others who departed by crowds in their ships. By the mediation of El-Adel terms were at length arranged on the 2nd of September. Ascalon was to be left unoccupied for three years, during which time the Christians were to have peaceful possession of Jaffa, and free access to the Holy Sepulchre; commerce was to be carried on over the whole land.

Richard warned the Sultan frankly of his intention to return and renew the war. If, replied Saladin, he was to lose the land, he would rather it was to Richard than to any other prince he had ever seen. To the Christians the king's departure brought great grief, and when the day (October 9th) arrived, the people cried aloud: "O Jerusalem, now art thou indeed helpless! Who will protect thee when Richard is away?" Richard's own last words, as the Holy Land faded from his sight, were a prayer that he might yet return to its aid. Of that other fate which awaited him, of his captivity, of his warfare with his treacherous ally, and of his death, this is not the place to speak.

Before their departure many of the Crusaders had availed themselves of the truce to go up to Jerusalem. Richard himself would not visit as a pilgrim the city which he could not rescue as a conqueror. The pilgrims, chief among whom was Hubert Walter, were treated generously. To the bishop Saladin showed much courtesy, and, besides inquiring many things concerning his master, granted him permission for Latin priests to celebrate divine service at the Holy Sepulchre, and in Bethlehem and Nazareth.

Romance has invested the Third Crusade with a halo of glory, altogether incommensurate with its direct results, which, if less disastrous than those of the Second, were in no wise to be compared with the splendid achievements of the First Crusade. As of old, the failure of the Western Crusaders was due more to divisions amongst themselves than to the prowess of the enemy. Richard alone of the great princes who took part in the war had his heart in the cause, and, save for Acre, the whole of the acquisitions of the Christians were due to his efforts. The French were more anxious to thwart the English king than to further the Holy War, and Richard would probably have benefited if Philip had taken all his subjects back with him. As things went, a three years' truce, and a narrow strip of coast from Acre to Ascalon were the sole results of an expedition that had drained the wealth and nobility of Western Europe. Never again did the Syrian Franks behold so great an army, under so valiant a leader come to their aid from the West; but the mutual jealousies and personal ambitions that had wrought the ruin of the Third Crusade remained with them always as the most persistent and dangerous foes of the Latin kingdom of Jerusalem.

XXIII.

ARMS, ARMOUR, AND ARMAMENTS.

"And higher on the walls,
Betwixt the monstrous horns of elk and deer,
His own forefathers' arms and armour hung.
And, 'this,' he said, 'was Hugh's at Agincourt,
And that was old Sir Ralph's at Ascalon.' "

TENNYSON, *The Princess.*

INASMUCH as the Crusades were in a sense the greatest military achievement of the Middle Ages, and since they influenced profoundly the progress of the art of war during that period, the present volume would be incomplete if it did not attempt some description of the mediaeval warrior's equipment. Yet at the same time it is impossible here to more than briefly discuss a subject which might readily occupy an entire work.

Siege operations formed so large a part of Crusading warfare, that it does not seem improper to commence with some description of them. The engineering science of the Crusaders was, for the most part, a development of Byzantine methods. The most formidable weapons of attack were machines for hurling huge stones against the walls, known as petrariae or stone-casters, mangonels, and, most formidable of all, the trebuchet. Mangonels and stone-casters were used by the Crusaders in their earliest siege operations, as at Nicaea in 1097. Yet the experience requisite for their successful use cannot have been very common, for at Tyre in 1124 it was found necessary to call in the aid of an Armenian engineer from Antioch. But much of a great leader's reputation for military skill depended upon his capacity to construct and direct these formidable machines, and even kings did not think it beneath their dignity to give this branch of warfare their personal attention. At the siege of Acre Philip Augustus had a famous stone-

242

caster, "The Bad Neighbour," which the Saracens destroyed by means of alike engine called "The Bad Kinsman." Richard, too, had stone-casters, which discharged day and night a store of polished Sicilian flints, that had been brought on purpose from Messina; these stones were of such size, that one which was sent out of the city for Saladin's inspection is said to have killed twelve men. How Richard rose from his sick-bed to superintend the use of these engines has been already described. When the walls of a fortress had been sufficiently battered by such engines, the besiegers would approach them under cover of a "testudo" or shed, sometimes called a "sow," which was made of wickerwork protected with hides. Under this shelter the moat would be filled up with stones and earth, and thus access was obtained to the walls. The "testudo" was often used to cover the men who brought up the "aries" or ram, a heavy beam with which they battered the walls, as did Bohemond's men at Durazzo. At other times the besiegers, under cover of the "testudo," would undermine the walls by picking out the loosened stones. To such labours the men were encouraged by the promise of abundant rewards; Raymond of Toulouse offered a denarius for every three stones cast into the moat at Jerusalem, and Richard two gold pieces for every stone dislodged from the walls of Acre. Where the defence was stubborn the besiegers would sap the walls, propping them up for a time with wooden beams, which, when a sufficient distance had been excavated, were fired, and by this means a breach was created.

But the crowning achievement of mediaeval offensive engineering was the "belfry" or siege-castle. This was a movable tower, built of wood, and of such a height as to overtop the walls of the town which was being attacked. It was constructed in several stories, which were called "coenacula" or "solaria." Godfrey's great "Machina" at the taking of Jerusalem had three stories, while that used by Amalric I. at the siege of Damietta had seven. The "belfry" was moved on wheels, sometimes worked by men from the inside—sometimes moved from the

243

outside on rollers. On one story there was often a ram, in a higher story were fitted bridges, which could be lowered on to the wall, and at the top were the archers, the mangonels, and other missile engines. The besieged would attempt to keep this machine from approaching the walls, by affixing iron-pointed beams to resist it, and if this proved futile they could, as a last resource, pour down the deadly Greek fire upon the enemy, or with flaming arrows set the dreaded construction ablaze. Time after time at the siege of Arsuf did Baldwin I. find himself baffled in this way. At the siege of Damietta in 1219 the Saracens menaced the Christian floating siege-castle with five mangonels, or similar engines, from the wall. To guard against the effects of fire or stones, the machine was covered with hides steeped in vinegar, and with a network of rope, or with stuffed sacks. These huge constructions, costly and difficult though they must have been to erect, were not in any sense permanent engines, but seem to have been built when occasion required from whatever material was procurable. The famous Matte Griffin, which Richard had made in Sicily, and brought with him to Acre, was, however, an exception.

From the military engines we turn to the equipment of the soldier himself. During the Crusading age and the following half-century, armour underwent a development more important and more marked than in any other period of the world's history. It passed from the *broigne*, a loose-fitting mail-coat of steel-rings, or small closely set plates of iron, through the grand hauberk to the mail plate of the fourteenth century. Originally the Teutonic warrior went to battle in the tunic of ring-mail. It was in such array, a war corslet, whose "polished iron rang in its meshes"—that, according to the primaeval English battle-song, Beowulf entered Hrothgar's hall to do battle with the fiend Grendal. At the time of the First Crusade we may picture the accoutrements of Western Europe from the pictures given in the Bayeux Tapestry and from the "Song of Roland." At this period armour seems to

244

have been made either of linked chains or of plates sewn upon a leather back-ground, or welded close together. If made of plates the garment was generally long and often sleeveless, if of chains it fitted closely to the body and generally covered the arms, while short, armoured breeches protected the thighs. In a very few cases the Norman knight seems to have worn iron shoes and leggings distinct from his upper tunic, and it is thus that William I. is represented in the Bayeux Tapestry.

Soon after the First Crusade a change set in which did not become universal for nearly a century. This consisted in the introduction of the hauberk, which, in its final form as the grand hauberk, was composed of two parts, a closely fitting chain tunic that covered the whole body to the knees, with an under garment protecting the legs and reaching as far upwards as the waist. This grand hauberk was not sewn upon any ground, but simply formed of interlocking rings; it was cloven behind so as to facilitate horsemanship. In most cases the grand hauberk seems to have been fitted with a ring-mail hood to protect the neck and head, and the whole accoutrement was crowned with a pointed conical helm, laced on to the rest of the armour. In the twelfth century the small conical helmet, which appears everywhere in the Bayeux Tapestry, began to give way to one of cylindrical shape and much larger proportions, which covered the whole head and face, leaving, when the visor was down, but one or two apertures for seeing and breathing. In such helmets it was impossible to recognise friend or leader, and hence it is no wonder that Baldwin I. was refused admission to Arsuf, and that the later chanson represents William of Orange as shut out from his castle by his warder and wife till he had unbared his head.

Just as the Crusades are ending we may trace the faint beginnings of plate armour, when the links were displaced by large pieces of metal. Gradually the two simple garments gave way to a multitude of

245

detachable pieces, each with its own particular use and special name. But this development does not fall within our period.

The mediaeval warrior's defensive equipment was completed by his shield. This from the earliest days had been made of linden-wood. Such was the "yellow linden shield," with which Wiglaf went to aid his lord Beowulf against the dragon. It was behind the shield-wall of linden-wood that the Danes ranged themselves in vain against Athelstan at Brunanburgh. In the twelfth century the best shields seem to have been made of elm, and it is only very rarely that we read as in Beowulf of an iron buckler. The mediaeval shield was generally kite shaped as in the Bayeux Tapestry, but sometimes almost oblong or circular. It was covered with leather and generally had a raised knob in the centre, whence bands of metal ran out in all directions. When not in use it was carried on the back, but during a single combat, when the lance was in rest, was slung round the neck in front as an extra protection.

The offensive weapons most in use were the sword, the lance, and the axe. Early English poets sing with rapture of the "sword-play," and invested this weapon with something of a human personality. All the great heroes of romance have names for their swords as though they were something more than senseless metal. Roland's sword was Durendal, Charlemagne's Montjoie, Arthur's Excalibur. So far was this worship carried that we find the rusty weapon furnished to Huon of Bordeaux for his combat with Galofre described as Durendal's sister. The mediaeval sword was sometimes long and sometimes short, from three to four, or from two to three feet, as the case might be.

The spear was generally of ash-wood, but an alternative was the wood of the apple. "Ashtimber with tip of grey, seamen's artillery, stood stacked together" in Hrothgar's hall. Of ash too was Charlemagne's spear in the "Chanson de Roland." The head was of various shapes—leaf-like, as it appears in the Bayeux Tapestry, or "squared," as it is often designated in mediaeval poems. Shaft and tip together, the

246

weapon seems to have measured some eight feet. When used overhand as a kind of missile, the shaft must have been rather slender, and hence in the Tapestry is represented by a single thread. But with the custom of tilting lance in rest it must have assumed larger proportions, and so in most mediaeval poetry the appropriate epithets are "stout" or "thick."

The axe plays but a small part in the Crusades, though at Constantinople, in 1203, it was still the weapon of the English in the Varangian guard, and, nearly fifty years later, Joinville tells us it was carried by the soldiers of the Old Man of the Mountain.

The one other weapon of the first importance was the bow in its various forms. At the time of the First Crusade the Westerns seem to have used the short bow alone. The cross-bow or arbalest is, however, of indefinite antiquity, and under the latter name figures in the "Chanson de Roland." Bohemond's soldiers used it at Durazzo, for Anna Comnena refers to it as "a thoroughly diabolical device." The use of the arbalest rapidly spread among the Crusaders. It was a favourite weapon with Richard, who was very skilful in its use, and who is said to have re-introduced it to Western warfare to be himself slain by an arrow from one. Of the English longbow there seems to be no trace throughout the whole period under review.

Three animals divided the attentions and shared the affections of the mediaeval knight—his hawk, his hound, and his horse. Skill in hawking and the chace was the chief boast of Huon of Bordeaux, and a main part of the education of Richard of Normandy. Nor does art fail to support the evidence of mediaeval song and history. The Bayeux Tapestry shows us Harold riding out with his hawks upon his wrist, while his servants may be seen carrying the dogs on board the ship which was to bear the Saxon earl into the hands of the Norman duke. Even in the supreme moment of life the passion for the chace did not leave the mediaeval knight. We have seen how Roger of Antioch went out to hunt on the very morning of his last fatal fight. Of the kings of Jerusalem, Fulk died

247

from a hunting accident, and Baldwin I. received the wound which eventually hastened his death whilst in the pursuit of his favourite sport. Even in death the mediaeval sculptor would depict the armour-clad knight with his feet resting on the effigy of the faithful hound that had been his comrade in life.

But the horse was the knight's peculiar friend. " 'O my steed,' cries William of Orange, in the old Romance, 'thou art weary; right willingly would I charge the Saracens again, but I see thou canst not help me. Yet I may not blame thee, for well hast thou served me all the day long. . . . Couldst thou only bear me to Orange, none should saddle thee for twenty days, thou shouldst feed on sifted barley and choicest hay, drinking from vessels of gold, and clad in fine silks.' And his horse hears its master's words; its nostrils quiver, and it understands what is said as though it were a man." The horse is indeed almost the hero of one mediaeval song, "Renaud de Montauban"—where Bayard, the offspring of a fairy ancestry, bears Renaud and his brothers from the court of Charlemagne to the forest of Ardennes. The twelfth-century horse had, however, but little in common with our modern racer. Now and again we do find allusion to the horse's speed as in the "Chanson de Roland," where horses are spoken of as swifter than sparrow or swallow, and in some incidents of Crusading history, as Baldwin I.'s swift mare Farisia, and the intended rescue of the young Baldwin III. on the steed of John Goman in 1145; but for the most part strength was preferred to beauty or speed. Archbishop Turpin's horse was light footed, but its legs were thick and short, its breast broad and its flanks long: "With its yellow mane, little ears, and tawny head, there was no beast like unto it." In another romance we are told, "with his short head and gleaming eyes, small ears and large nostrils, the horse was strong and stout, a better steed you would nowhere see." So also Richard I.'s Spanish horse, though of graceful form, with pricked-up ears, and high neck, was also of great height, with broad breast, solid haunches, and wide hoofs. In contrast to the ideal knightly steed, broad breasted, thick ribbed, and short flanked, we have the sorry beast furnished by the Saracens to Huon of Bordeaux for his combat with Galofre, thin ribbed and scraggy necked that had not tasted oat or wheat for seven years.

From the equipment of the engineer and the knight, we must turn for a little to the fortress, which was at once the Crusader's bulwark against the enemy and his home. The fortification of cities and towns was regarded as of less importance than that of isolated castles or the citadels which protected the towns, and, indeed, the warfare of the age did not well lend itself to the defence of an extensive system of fortifications. So though the walls of the important towns and the great ports was a matter of particular care, and especially in the last age of Crusading history, it is in the great castles like Kerak or Krak des Chevaliers and Markab that we find the most stupendous monuments of Frankish enterprise. The care of the kings and military orders lined the Christian frontiers with numerous powerful fortresses from Kerak and Montreal on the south-east, Darum, Ibelin, and Blanche Garde on the south; to Beaufort, Chateauneuf, Safed, Chastellet, and Belvoir, which guarded the Lebanon; and the famous Kerak des Chevaliers, Markab, Tortosa, and others in the territory of Tripoli. The Frankish castles in Palestine followed two main types, of which the first had for their model the French castles of the eleventh and twelfth centuries, whilst the other class borrowed more from the Byzantines and Arabs. Of the first the finest examples are found in the castles of the Hospitallers, and especially at Kerak des Chevaliers and Markab; to the latter class belong the buildings of the Templars as Safed and Tortosa. Even in the first class there were certain Eastern characteristics as the double enceinte which was borrowed from the Byzantines, and the huge mass of masonry specially adapted to meet the possibility of earthquake. Markab had a site of extraordinary grandeur overlooking the Mediterranean, and from its position, on a jutting spur of the mountains, impregnable on all sides but one. Kerak des Chevaliers preserves to this day all its main features intact as they were when the Hospitallers abandoned it in 1271. But the illustrations will give a more adequate idea of their grandeur than is possible in a brief description.

The fortified towns of Syria were many of them girt with twofold walls, and the space between was given up, at all events in large measure, to gardens. On the highest ground there usually stood a castle of surpassing strength, to which the inhabitants could retire if the defences of the town proper were forced. The walls were generally broken by frequent towers; of these the fortifications of Antioch boasted no less four hundred and fifty, which were eighty feet high.

For the protection of all these towns and fortresses, the Assizes of Jerusalem recorded a most elaborate system of military organisation. Every fief, every city town or castle was bound to furnish so many knights and so many men-at-arms for the war. The lordships of Galilee and Sidon had to supply one hundred knights in case of need; from such smaller fiefs as Toron and Maron fifteen and three were demanded respectively. Among the towns and cities we find Jerusalem assessed at forty knights, Acre at eighty; whilst a small place like Darum had to supply two only. In addition, they had to furnish a fixed number of men-at-arms from the five hundred of Acre and Jerusalem to the fifty of Caesarea and Haifa. Not even the prelates and great ecclesiastical corporations were exempt, but had each to furnish their fixed quota. To these forces we must add the troops of the military orders, the Turcoples and mercenaries in the royal pay, and the European knights who came with every spring and autumn to fight for Christ and the Holy Sepulchre. Still, with it all, if we may trust William of Tyre, the largest army ever mustered in Palestine since the days of Godfrey was only twenty thousand strong.

If in many respects the Crusades mark an epoch in military progress, they are of hardly less interest in naval history. In the First Crusade the fleet had been supplied by the Italian republics, and during the early days of the kingdom in particular, valuable service was rendered by the seamen of Venice, Pisa, and Genoa. The Latin kings, however, established a naval service of their own, and maintained arsenals at Tyre and Acre. But it may be that they still chiefly depended on the fleets of the Italian republics, of northern pilgrims like Sigurd, or whatever other assistance chance might afford; at any rate, there is no mention of the office of admiral in the history of the Cypriote kingdom till towards the end of the thirteenth century. Still, in 1153, we find Gerard of Sidon commanding the royal fleet at Ascalon, when he had fifteen swift vessels; and when Saladin threatened Beyrout in 1182, Baldwin IV. was able to assemble thirty-three galleys within seven days. The two great orders also maintained galleys of their own, and the Count of Tripoli and Prince of Antioch had each their own fleet. So in 1187 Tripoli could muster twenty galleys for the relief of Tyre; and even as early as 1127 Bohemond II. had ten galleys and twelve transports. In addition to the Mediterranean fleet thus maintained, there was, at least for a short time, also a Christian armament on the Red Sea. The Franks held Elim from 1116 to 1170, and again in 1182-3; at the later date, Reginald of Châtillon equipped five galleys and a large number of smaller vessels with which he ravaged the whole coast of the Hedjaz, and, in the absence of any Mussulman fleet that could oppose him, even threatened the pilgrims on their way to Mecca. This success was, however, shortlived, for Saladin had a fleet prepared which, in the early months of 1183, totally destroyed Reginald's armament.

The most important class of ships used for purposes of war were galleys; these vessels were from a hundred to a hundred and twenty feet long, and about six feet wide, with but a single bank of oars and a crew of one hundred men. Other vessels of war were "safeties" or scouts, "colombels," "gamells," all of them small, swift vessels for scouting purposes. The trading and transport vessels were known as dromonds, busses, salandres, and huissiers. The dromond was the largest of all, and was used to carry pilgrims—as the great vessel wrecked in Egypt in 1182, which had fifteen hundred persons on board—or merchandise. Richard's rich prize, after leaving Cyprus in 1191, was a Saracen dromond. In war the dromond was used to carry arms, food, and the military machines. Busses and salandres were smaller vessels. The huissiers were horse-transports; those in Manuel's fleet, in 1169, had large open castles in the poop for the carriage of the horses, with gangways for their embarkation.

None of these vessels were very fast sailing, nor did they often venture far from land. The swiftest voyage from Marseilles to Acre took from fifteen to twenty days, but was indefinitely lengthened when made by the Italian coast to Messina, then successively to Crete and Cyprus, and so to Syria. For the longer voyage from Northern Europe, Richard's fleet took nearly six months to reach Messina, whilst Sigurd's piratical expedition extended over three or four years. As for equipment, one of Richard's chief ships had "three rudders, thirteen anchors, thirty oars, two sails, and triple ropes of every kind. Moreover, it had everything that a ship can want in pairs—saving only the mast and boat. This ship was laden with forty horses of price, with all kinds of arms for as many riders, for fourteen footmen and fifteen sailors. Moreover, it had a year's food for all these men and horses."

XXIV

THE KINGDOM OF ACRE—THE STRUGGLE FOR RECOVERY.
(1192-1244.)

"A brave man struggling with the storms of fate,
And greatly falling with a falling state."

POPE.

SALADIN did not long survive the conclusion of the Third Crusade. Early in November, 1192, he left Palestine for Damascus, where, despite ill health, he spent the winter in hunting. When Baha-ed-din rejoined him in February, he remarked that his master had lost his old elasticity of spirit. On February 19th the illness took a serious form, and a fortnight later terminated fatally. "Never since the death of the first four Caliphs," writes Baha-ed-din, "had religion and the faithful received such a blow." Saladin had won the respectful admiration of Christian and Moslem alike. Both in history and romance his name has always been coupled with that of his great rival Richard. "Could each," said Hubert Walter, "be endowed with the faculties of the other, the whole world could not furnish two such princes." A Western legend, of somewhat later date, is so eminently characteristic of Saladin that it deserves repetition. When Saladin lay dying he charged his standard-bearer, saying: "As thou didst bear my banner in war, bear also my banner of death. And let it be a vile rag, which thou must bear through all Damascus set upon a lance, crying, 'Lo! at his death the lord of the East could take nothing with him save this cloth only.'"

Saladin's dominions were divided at his death. His sons, El-Afdal, El-Aziz, and Ez-Zahir, became lords of Damascus, Egypt, and Aleppo. His brother, El-Adel, ruled at Kerak, and his great-nephews, Shirkuh and El-Mansur, at Emesa and Hamah. But this arrangement did not long subsist, for El-Adel first expelled El-Afdal from Damascus, and afterwards, in February, 1200, from Egypt, where the latter prince had become guardian for his infant nephew, El-Mansur. Two years later, by the subjection of Ez-Zahir, El-Adel became, like his brother before him, lord supreme of Syria, Mesopotamia, and Egypt. At his death, on August 31, 1218, the Moslem lands were once more divided, but his descendants reigned as sultans of Egypt with more or less power for thirty years afterwards.

For the Franks the years that followed on the death of Saladin were disturbed only by disputes between the military orders and the warfare of Bohemond of Antioch with the Christian prince of Armenia. But if the Syrian Franks were content to enjoy what they still possessed, the opportunity afforded by the death of Saladin did not pass unheeded in Western Europe. Pope Celestine III. renewed his endeavours in the cause of the Holy War. In France and England he met with little success; Philip was too intent on his ambitious projects, and Richard too busy counteracting them, whilst their subjects had too lively a recollection of their recent sufferings. But in Germany the Pope's appeal accorded with the Emperor's designs on Sicily and Constantinople. In 1196 Henry entered Italy at the head of forty thousand men, intending to proceed by sea to Palestine as soon as he had secured his authority in his wife's kingdom. He was destined to accomplish only the first part of his plan, but a large contingent of German Crusaders came to Acre late in 1197, under the leadership of Conrad of Wurzburg. Somewhat against the will of the native lords, the war was renewed; El-Adel at once retaliated by an attack on Jaffa; before the Franks could come to the rescue from Acre, Henry of Champagne was killed by a fall, and during the confusion consequent on his death, Jaffa was taken by the Saracen.

Isabella now bestowed her hand and kingdom on Amalric de Lusignan, who two years previously had succeeded his brother Guy as ruler of Cyprus, Encouraged by the arrival of a fresh force of Crusaders from Northern Germany, the new king resolved to attack Beyrout. The Saracens abandoned the city in panic, and about the same time a Crusading army won a great victory over El-Adel between Tyre and Sidon. These successes were followed by the recovery of all the coast towns, and the Crusaders had laid siege to Toron, when in December, 1197, the news of the Emperor's death called the Germans home. The partial success of this Crusade was thus marred by its hasty termination, which left the recovered territory without defenders in the face of an embittered foe.

Next year (1198) the preaching of a French priest, Fulk of Neuilly, stirred up a new Crusade. Fulk was credited with strangely miraculous powers; he cured the blind and the lame, at his bidding the prostitute forsook her calling and the usurer his treasure. Even before kings he was not ashamed, and in God's name bade Richard of England provide for his three daughters. "Liar!" said the angry king, "I have no daughter." "Nay! thou hast three evil daughters—Pride, Lust, and Luxury." With mocking words Richard turned to his courtiers: "He bids me marry my daughters. I give Pride to the Templars, Lust to the Cistercians, and Luxury to the prelates." Fulk's efforts were aided by the new Pope, Innocent III., who mourned over the return of the Germans after such slight achievements, and endeavoured to make peace between the kings of France and England.

The kings turned a deaf ear to priest and pope alike, but many of the great French nobles did under Fulk's influence, take the Cross. Foremost were Baldwin of Flanders and his brother Henry, Theobald of Champagne and his cousin Louis of Blois, the Count of St. Pol, Simon de Montfort, and John de Nesles. But the expedition was long delayed, and only started in 1202. Fulk meantime had died of grief, and though the treasure he had collected was sent over sea to Palestine, his projected Crusade proved, so far as the Holy Land was concerned, a miserable failure. The great part of the Crusaders allowed themselves to be diverted from their proper aim, and after conquering Zara for the Venetians, sailed against Constantinople. How they captured that city, chose Baldwin for emperor, and portioned out the European lands of the Eastern Empire amongst themselves, belongs to another story.

A smaller force, however, passed through the Straits of Gibraltar, and under the leadership of Reginald de Dampierre reached Palestine in 1203. Some plundering raids were followed by concessions on the part of El-Adel, who surrendered Nazareth and concluded peace. Reginald, in wrath, went off to join Bohemond of Antioch; on his way he fell into an ambush, and of all his army only a single knight escaped. When, a little later, John de Nesles reached Acre with a further contingent, he also went north to aid the Prince of Antioch in his warfare with Armenia.

During the last years of the twelfth century the power of the Christian princes of Armenia had much increased. After long disputes between the kinsmen of Thoros, a prince called Rupin secured the throne about 1175. Rupin acquired Tarsus from Bohemond III., and ruled on the whole prosperously till 1188. His successor and brother, Leo, though married to a niece of Bohemond, sought to secure the independence of his country, which up to this time had been subject to the princes of Antioch. Bohemond treacherously endeavoured to capture Leo at a conference, but the Armenian, suspicious of his host, had taken such precautions that it was Bohemond, and not Leo, who became the prisoner. As the price of Bohemond's release, Leo was confirmed in his conquests and independence, and a few years later, in 1198, was anointed king by the German chancellor, Conrad of Wurzburg. The death of Bohemond III. in 1201 was followed by further wars, for Leo supported the claims of his nephew Rupin, the child of the late prince's elder son, Raymond, against the new prince, Bohemond IV. It was to aid in this warfare that John de Nesles went north in 1203.

The close of the twelfth century had been grievous for the East. Egypt was vexed with a sore famine, and the consequent pestilence spread into Syria, so that all the lands from the Euphrates to the Nile were filled with mourning and desolation. Next year a terrible earthquake ruined almost all the cities of Palestine, with the exception of Jerusalem. The treasure collected by Fulk of Neuilly now proved of timely service for the rebuilding of the walls of Acre.

The pressure of these calamities did not avail to enforce observance of the truce. Amalric's Cypriote subjects were vexed by piratical Egyptian galleys, and when El-Adel would make no restitution, the king retaliated by a series of raids, which extended even to the east of Jordan. But eventually the truce was renewed for five years. A little later, in 1205, Amalric died, leaving an infant son, Amalric III.; but the youthful king and his mother both died within the year. The throne then passed to Mary, Isabella's eldest daughter by Conrad of Montferrat. John of Ibelin was made bailiff for the little queen, and Philip of France was asked to recommend a suitable husband. His choice fell on John de Brienne—an experienced warrior, but not a man of any great rank. John, accepted the proposal, and after some delay, with the aid of money lent him by the French king and the Pope, equipped three hundred knights, with which little force he reached Acre on September 14, 1210. On the following day he was married to the young Queen Mary, and a week later was crowned with his wife at Tyre.

Before John's arrival in Palestine the Christians had refused to renew the truce. But though the new king took the field with courage, he presently found himself unable to cope with his powerful foe, the more so as most of his own knights had soon returned to Europe. Accordingly, in 1212, he appealed to the Pope to send him fresh succour from the West.

Innocent III. had long desired to make good the unhappy Crusade of 1203, but the intervening years had not been propitious. The death of Henry VI. had left Sicily with a child ruler, and Germany with a disputed succession. Both in France and England the Pope was involved in a serious quarrel with the royal power. But although these troubles hampered the execution of Innocent's projects, he did not abandon them. At the Lateran Council, which met in November, 1215, and had been summoned over two years previously, four hundred and twelve bishops were present, including the Latin patriarchs of Jerusalem and Constantinople. Through Innocent's influence the project of a new Crusade was adopted, and preached with vigour; James de Vitry, the future bishop of Acre and historian of the Holy Land, and the English Cardinal, Robert de Curzon, who died in 1218 at Damietta, being foremost in the work. Chief amongst those who took the Cross were Andrew, King of Hungary; Leopold, Duke of Austria; William, Count of Holland; and the English Earl Ranulf of Chester.

So towards the autumn of 1217 there were gathered at Acre the four kings of Hungary, Armenia, Cyprus, and Jerusalem, besides many nobles and men of lesser degree. A great foray was made to Bethshan and the Saracen castle on Mount Tabor besieged; but the Sultan would not permit his son Corradin to offer battle, and the Crusaders were at length forced to retire after effecting but little. The kings of Hungary and Armenia then returned to their own land, whilst Hugh of Cyprus went to Tripoli, where he soon fell ill and died.

During the winter many Crusaders who had made the long sea voyage from Northern Europe arrived at Acre. John de Brienne now proposed an expedition to Damietta, and accordingly in May, 1218, the great host set sail with a fair wind for Egypt. Damietta was well fortified with towers and walls, and protected by the river and a moat. In mid-stream rose an immense tower of great strength, which was the first point for attack. An assault was made on July 1st, but without success, and many of the Crusaders were drowned. On August 24th (St. Bartholomew's Day), the attack was renewed; the Saracens poured down fire and sulphur on their assailants, so that the ladders were set ablaze, and the Crusaders reduced to despair. Suddenly it seemed that the fire was extinguished, and the Christians saw the banner of the Holy Cross waving from the tower. With fresh vigour they returned to the attack, and now their efforts were crowned with success. Men soon fabled that this was due to no earthly prowess, but to a band of heavenly knights in white armour, the brilliancy whereof had dazzled the eyes of the Saracens, whilst their leader, clad in red, was hailed as none other than St. Bartholomew himself.

In September the papal legate, Cardinal Pelagius, reached the camp. A little later there came many French and English knights—the former under the Counts of Nevers, and Marche; the latter under the earls of Chester, Winchester, and Arundel. But winter was now coming on, the camp was flooded, provisions destroyed, and many ships lost. With the spring, however, the Crusaders renewed their efforts; by crossing the river on February 5th, they secured a better position for the attack, and then prepared their engines for an assault.

Meantime El-Adel had been succeeded by his son, El-Kamil. The new Sultan was in such despair that he meditated a retreat to Yemen; but on Palm Sunday, after reinforcements had come from Syria, he made a fierce though unsuccessful attack on the Christian camp. In May, Leopold of Austria went home, whilst on the other side, on Feb. 7, El-Kamil's brother, El-Muazzam, or, as the Crusaders called him, Corradin, prince of Damascus, arrived with a great army of Saracens. But Pelagius and King John had made a Lombard "caroccio" to bear the Christian banner, and the sight of this novel engine with its mysterious emblem scared Corradin from a fresh attack. During the summer famine and disease raged within the city, and in the Saracen camp outside. Nor were the Crusaders in much better plight; for if many

Saracens sought relief and baptism in the Christian camp, certain evil Spaniards and English fled to the Moslem and denied Christ. At last the Saracens sent envoys offering to deliver up the land, "because the power of God was against them." But meantime El-Kamil succeeded in throwing reinforcements into the town, thanks to the departure of the Count of Nevers, whose name became a by-word among the Christians. The Crusaders then broke off the negotiations, and on November 5th, at midnight—the hour when, according to the mediaeval belief, Christ harrowed Hell, the Crusaders forced their way within the walls. The credit of this achievement belongs to certain "Latins and Romans," who, taking one of the towers by stealth, thundered out the "Kyrie Eleeson," as a sign of success to their comrades below. Then the Templars and Hospitallers forced their way into the city, and so Damietta was captured.

Scarcely was the city taken when a quarrel broke out between John and Pelagius. John was angry because the legate had lordship over him, and seeing that Leo of Armenia was now dead, departed to prosecute his wife's rights to that kingdom. John was absent for a whole year, during which time Pelagius vainly endeavoured to keep the Christian host from melting away. The Saracens in their despair offered extravagant terms for the recovery of Damietta—the whole land of Jerusalem excepting Kerak, and all their Christian prisoners. This the Crusaders refused because they hoped that if the Emperor Frederick came on his long-promised expedition, they might then conquer all Egypt. Thus in their folly they threw away the best chance of recovering the Holy City. Philip of France said with reason that they must have been daft to prefer a town to a kingdom.

When, however, Frederick did not come, it was decided to advance against Cairo. Pelagius was reduced to appeal to John de Brienne for his assistance, but the king would not leave his own land till a liberal sum had been promised for his services. When John arrived, June 29,

1221, the Crusaders had already started. Two months later he found the host in a perilous position, for the Saracen galleys prevented provisions from being brought up from the sea, whilst the Nile was already rising. The Sultan ordered the dykes to be cut, and the waters rose so high that it was impossible to advance or to retreat. The Crusaders were at the mercy of the Saracens, and John had to make the best terms he could. El-Kamil, in pity for the Christians, offered to let them go free if Damietta was restored. There was no alternative but to consent, and the Sultan further promised to release all his prisoners, restore the Holy Cross, and grant a truce for eight years. John de Brienne and James de Vitry became hostages for the fulfilment of the treaty. It is related that as John sat before the Sultan he wept for thought of his starving companions. El-Kamil, on learning the cause of his tears, was moved to compassion, and sent enough store of food for all the people.

After his release John appointed Eudes de Montbeliard his bailiff at Acre, and went over sea to ask aid for his unhappy kingdom. He visited Rome, France, England, and Spain, where he married the King of Castile's sister. Later he joined the Emperor in Apulia, and gave his daughter, Isabella or Yolande, in marriage to Frederick. After a time John quarrelled with the Emperor, and took service with the Pope; but he does not again appear in Crusading history.

The Emperor Frederick, who, by this marriage became lord of Palestine, was certainly the greatest prince, and in some respects also the most remarkable man of his time; it was not without justice that an English chronicler called him the "Wonder of the World." His natural gifts and acquired accomplishments were alike extraordinary; he was not only a great ruler, but a poet, and lover of art and all intellectual pursuits; the many tongues of his wide dominions—German, Italian, Greek, Latin, and Saracen—were alike familiar to him. But among men of the next generation he was remembered best as the foe of the papacy, and as the rumoured scoffer at all things holy. His relations with the Roman see can hardly have disposed him to reverence for the faith of which it was the centre, and his attitude to religion was no doubt one of indifference. It was even fabled that he had written a book of extreme blasphemy on the Three Impostors—Moses, Christ, and Mohammed. False though this accusation was, there is something almost grotesque in the fate which made him the leader of Christendom in its Holy War.

After his coronation by Honorius III. in 1220, Frederick publicly renewed his vow of a Crusade. Year after year the Christians had hoped for his coming, and still he had never come—not even on the conquest of Damietta, when it would seem that the very rumour of his coming would suffice to lay the whole East at his mercy. Four months before his marriage to Yolande, in November, 1225, Frederick once more promised to cross the sea for two years; if he failed to fulfil his covenant he would fall under the interdict of the Church. Before the appointed time had elapsed, Honorius III. had been succeeded by Frederick's destined foe Gregory IX. But although one of Gregory's earliest acts was to urge Frederick in a somewhat imperative letter to fulfil his vow, the relations of the new Pope with the Emperor were not at first unfriendly. Frederick, indeed, had made his preparations in all sincerity, and in the appointed month of August, 1227, a large host had assembled at Brindisi. The Emperor embarked, and the fleet set sail; but three days later the former entered the harbour of Otranto, whilst the latter dispersed. Frederick pleaded sickness as the excuse for his return, but Gregory nevertheless pronounced the excommunication which the Emperor had incurred under his oath two years before. The sentence and its subsequent confirmations were treated with contempt by Frederick, who determined to prove his sincerity by starting on the Crusade in the spring.

The hostility of the Pope caused the desertion of many who had intended to join the Crusade. But Frederick probably counted more on the negotiations, which for some time past he had maintained with El-Kamil, than on the strength of his arms. So it was with only six hundred knights—more like a pirate than a great king, as Gregory declared—that he landed at Acre on September 7, 1228. Frederick was received with hostility not only by the clergy, but also by the military orders, who presently refused to serve under his commands. El-Kamil, not unaware of the Emperor's difficulties, endeavoured to renew their old amity, and made overtures for a compromise. The negotiations proceeded slowly, but meanwhile there was much friendly intercourse between the two monarchs. Frederick's first demands were for the restoration of the kingdom in its fullest extent, together with liberal privileges for his merchants in the ports of Alexandria and Rosetta. But El-Kamil would not surrender Jerusalem entirely since the Saracens held the Temple in no less esteem than did the Christians the Holy Sepulchre. At first Frederick was disposed to war, but the news that Gregory and John de Brienne were capturing his Italian cities made him anxious to return at any cost. He therefore came to terms with El-Kamil, who agreed to surrender Jerusalem, Bethlehem, and Nazareth, if the site of the Temple, whereon stood the Mosque of Omar, was left to the Saracens. As soon as the treaty was arranged Frederick and his Germans went up to Jerusalem on March 18, 1229. Next day—it was Sunday in Mid-Lent—he took the crown from the high altar in the Church of the Holy Sepulchre, and with his own hands placed it on his head; "but there was no prelate, nor priest, nor clerk, to sing or speak." His pilgrimage to the Sepulchre over, and his coronation accomplished, Frederick displayed his strange catholicity by visiting the Mosque of Omar also. So, likewise, when the Cadi out of regard to the Emperor's feelings, forbade the muezzin to give the usual call for prayer, Frederick rebuked him: "You were wrong to fail in duty to your religion for my sake. God knows, if you were to come to my country, you would find no such respectful deference."

After a pretence of refortifying Jerusalem, Frederick suddenly went back to Acre, and thence set sail for Europe. The peace which he had secured was extremely distasteful to his foes the Templars, whose great church at Jerusalem was left in the hands of the Moslem. Frederick announced his treaty in Western Europe as a great achievement. Gerold the Patriarch, on his part, wrote a letter condemning it as a betrayal of religion and the Church. Gregory had already described it as a monstrous reconciliation of Christ and Belial. But with the effect of this treaty on its author's subsequent fortunes we have nothing to do. Frederick did not again visit his Oriental kingdom. He died in 1250 the victim of a strange and novel crusade. By his will he left a large sum of money for the succour of the Holy Land.

On his way to Palestine Frederick had stopped at Cyprus. The king of the island, Henry I, was then a child of eleven; the Emperor claimed the right of wardship, and forced the bailiff, John of Ibelin, to do him homage. John accompanied Frederick to Palestine, but after his departure returned to Cyprus in June, 1229, and besieged the Emperor's officers in the fortress of Dieudamour. His enterprise had just met with success when the arrival of a German fleet led to a new series of troubles.

The Saracens had not long kept the peace. Within little over a year they began to harass the pilgrims, and declaring that they would no longer suffer the Holy City to remain in Christian hands, broke into Jerusalem itself. Frederick's representatives were able to expel the intruders, and the Emperor on hearing of the violation of the truce at once despatched a fleet to Palestine under Richard Filangier, whom he appointed bailiff of the kingdom. An order to Henry de Lusignan to dismiss John of Ibelin was met with a refusal, and an attempt to dispossess that noble of Beyrout was no more successful. The native lords declared that Frederick was violating the ancestral customs of their land, and together with John of Ibelin appealed to the king of

Cyprus for assistance. Henry and his lords responded readily; but even with their aid John could not venture to take the field against the bailiff Richard, who was besieging Beyrout.

Some time later, on May 3, 1232, Richard surprised the Cypriot lords near Casal Imbert, whilst John of Ibelin chanced to be absent at Acre. Though the young king managed to escape, his followers were utterly routed, and the disaster was fatal to John's ambitions. Richard was even able to carry the war into Cyprus, and for a time held possession of the greater part of that island, until John expelled him in 1233. The Imperial power on the mainland did not last much longer, and when John of Ibelin died in 1236, Queen Alice of Cyprus persuaded the barons to accept her third husband, Ralph of Soissons as bailiff, since Yolande had long been dead and Frederick would not send her young son Conrad to take her place.

Whilst these feuds weakened the Christian cause in the kingdom, similar troubles were working mischief in the principalities further north, where the Prince of Antioch endeavoured to reap advantage from the weakness of the infant daughter of Leo the Armenian. Such a state of affairs gradually wore away whatever powers of resistance the Syrian Franks might yet possess, and so when a new source of danger made its appearance they proved quite incapable to cope with it.

Meantime there had been great changes in the lands of the Ayubites. At the death of El-Adel on August 31, 1218, his son El-Kamil had succeeded him at Cairo, with the title of Sultan and some kind of supremacy over his brothers who ruled in the various cities of Syria. El-Kamil reaped some advantage from the dissensions of his kinsfolk, but his rule in Syria was not altogether prosperous, and his last years were troubled by the dangers which threatened from the Turks of Iconium in the north, and the advancing Tartars to the east. His sudden death at the beginning of 1238 was the signal for general warfare amongst the Ayubite princes of Syria. Eventually Es-Saleh Ayub, El-Kamil's eldest son, became lord of Damascus; with the support of his cousin Dawud, the son of Corradin, he invaded Egypt and overthrew his brother El-Adel, in May, 1240. But the new Sultan soon quarrelled with his powerful kinsman Dawud, and the troubles of the Ayubites were still unsettled, when the landing of a new Crusade marked the termination of the ten years' truce concluded by the Emperor Frederick.

In the midst of his conflict with Frederick II., Gregory IX was not unmindful of his fellow Christians in the East. As the conclusion of the ten years' truce made by Frederick II. drew near he issued a summons to a new Crusade. The time was opportune for a fresh effort; the feuds of the Ayubites within, and the pressure of the Tartars from without, had much shaken the power of Islam. The chief response to Gregory's appeal came from France and Spain. King Louis being unable to go in person sent his constable Amalric, Count of Montfort; other French nobles were the Duke of Burgundy and the Counts of Bar and Nevers, whilst the leader of the expedition was Theobald, King of Navarre. The host mustered at Marseilles, and refusing to wait a year for the Emperor to join them, sailed for Palestine in August, 1239. After landing at Acre they resolved on an expedition for the recovery of Ascalon, and with this purpose marched out towards Jaffa on the 2nd of November. Whilst halting in this town, the Count of Brittany made a successful raid on the Saracens. Emulous of this good fortune the Count of Bar and other nobles determined to make a raid towards Ascalon. Theobald expostulated, but to no purpose; the knights, bent on gain, declared that at least they would ride to Gaza and return on the morrow. So they went along the coast till they reached the brook that divided the kingdom of Jerusalem from Egypt. Here Count Walter of Jaffa advised that they should rest, but his comrades insisted on proceeding further. At length they halted in a place shut in by mountains, and prepared to feast on the delicate provisions they had brought with them. Whilst thus engaged the Saracens of Gaza came

266

upon them. Count Walter, at their approach, rode off with the Duke of Burgundy, knowing that it was hopeless to fight in such a position. But the Counts of Bar and Montfort persisted in giving battle; they and all their followers were captured or slain before Theobald, who had now advanced to Ascalon, could come to their aid. On the news of this disaster Theobald withdrew in haste to Acre. Next year he sought for the release of the prisoners by making a truce with the Sultan, but before the treaty was completed went home by stealth and most of his host with him. Shortly afterwards Earl Richard of Cornwall reached Acre, and the release of the prisoners was finally secured through the assistance of his wealth. With Richard came Simon de Montfort, Amalric's more famous brother, whom a year or two later the Syrian barons begged Frederick to appoint as bailiff of the kingdom during the minority of Conrad. The quarrels of the military orders rendered any active warfare impracticable, and the English earls shortly went home after accomplishing no more than the release of the prisoners.

The Christians soon found that the Sultan had only granted a truce to gain time for the conquest of his rivals. So in 1243 or 1244 they negotiated with the lords of Kerak and Damascus, who promised the Franks all the land west of Jordan save Hebron, Nablûs, and Bethshan. By this means Jerusalem was restored to the Christians, and in the words of a letter of the time, "all the Saracens were expelled, and the sacred mysteries celebrated daily in all the holy places, wherein for fifty-six years the name of God had not been invoked." But hardly had the Christians in Europe time to rejoice over this news, when they heard that Jerusalem was lost again.

Es-Saleh Ayub, in need of aid to reassert his power, called in strangers from outside. His new allies were the Charismians, an eastern tribe, who, driven from their own land by Genghis Khan, had conquered themselves a new home on the Euphrates. They offered their services to the highest bidder, and so fought first for one and then for another of the Ayubite princes. As the Charismians marched south to join Es-Saleh they fell upon the city of Jerusalem, and slew its inhabitants, men, women, and children, to the number of thirty thousand. Mohammedans and Christians united in face of a common danger. Ismail of Damascus sent an army under El-Mansur of Hamah to help the muster of the military orders, which had marched out from Acre. Count Walter de Brienne joined them at Jaffa, and by the time the army reached Ascalon it mustered six thousand knights without counting the men-at-arms, both horse and foot. El-Mansur advised that they should abide safely in a place well stored with food till the inevitable time when a savage horde with no settled base must melt away. Some of the Christians approved, but others distrusted an infidel's advice. The latter prevailed, and the army marched out to encounter the Charismians near Gaza on October 14, 1244. The battle was short but fierce; El-Mansur and his host fled from the field; the Christian army was almost annihilated. Of the Templars, who numbered three hundred, only four knights survived, and of the Hospitallers only nineteen, and but three men-at-arms of the Teutonic order. The grand masters of the Temple and Hospital, and Count Walter were taken prisoners—the last two died in captivity. This disaster was fatal to the power of the Franks in Palestine, and from this moment even the semblance of the Christian kingdom began to fade away.

XXV.

THE CRUSADES OF ST. LOUIS AND EDWARD I.

"Some grey Crusading knight austere
Who bore St. Louis company."

M. ARNOLD.

IT might have been expected that the destruction of Jerusalem would send a shock of horror throughout Christendom, and rouse all Christians to the reconquest of the Holy Land. Just one hundred years previously the loss of Edessa, far removed as that city was from the interests of the European west, had been a trumpet call to king and noble and peasant. But things were not in the thirteenth century as they had been in the twelfth. The new era had different ideals, different hopes, and different aims; the political energy of the West was being transfused into new channels. The great cities were winning privileges at the expense of lords and Emperor; new kingdoms were rising into prominence or developing into strength. Here the king was gathering all power more and more into his own hands; there the nobles were asserting their rights to his detriment. But in the fervour and industry of a new age, that was building the noblest churches ever seen, inventing fresh heresies, opening out new studies, there was little place for true religious enthusiasm. The age of Roger Bacon and Albertus Magnus was beginning, that of Anselm and Peter the Hermit dying out. Religion was no longer a matter for the emotions only; but was more and more a thing for philosophers to wrangle over, not one that a practical man need trouble himself about.

But above all else the thirteenth century had no St. Bernard to rouse it to the service of God. Such religious zeal as remained was frittered away in internecine crusades against the Albigeois and a heretic emperor, or diverted its energies from warfare with the infidel abroad,

269

to the rescue of afflicted Christians at home. The Templar and Hospitaller had warred in Palestine for the Holy Sepulchre, the followers of St. Francis and St. Dominic toiled in the crowded cities for the poor, the friendless, and the sick.

Europe was, moreover, confronted by a danger unknown for many centuries past. The Tartars threatened to sweep away all civilisation from the Volga to the Atlantic. Frederick, even had he not been excommunicate, was too busy with this grave trouble to undertake a new Crusade. In the west the kings of Spain were still waging their perpetual crusade with the Saracens of their own peninsula, and the King of England in the pressure of incident at home could spare no time for Jerusalem and the East Italy was distracted by the feuds of emperor and pope. To France alone could the Latin Christians of the East look for help.

Louis IX. of France was now about twenty-seven years old. The great-grandson of our English Henry II. and the grandson of Philip Augustus, he had been left an orphan at the age of ten, but through the prudence of his mother Blanche the troubles of his minority had been averted. About the end of 1244 Louis fell so ill that his life was despaired of; as he lay unconscious, his nurse thinking all was over, was about to draw the sheet across his face, when a companion stayed her hand. At the sound of their voices the king roused from his trance, and calling for a cross vowed himself to God's service for the recovery of Jerusalem. It was not, however, for more than three years that Louis sailed from Marseilles on the 25th of August, 1248.

Louis was perhaps the most truly religious king that ever lived. His whole life was a prayer; his whole aim to do God's will. His horror of sin was deep and unaffected. "Would you rather be a leper, or commit a deadly sin?" he once asked Joinville. The seneschal bluntly blurted out that he would rather commit thirty deadly sins than have his body covered with leprosy. Louis reproved his choice: for the leprosy of the body would disappear at death, but the leprosy of sin last hereafter. Everything about the king is charming from the "As-you-Like-it" scene where he administered justice beneath the great oak at Vincennes, to his washing of the feet of the poor in imitation of Christ. Nor was he regardless of learning, even though he commended the knight who closed an unsuccessful disputation with a Jew by a blow from his stick. He had a great library of books at Royaumont, was the patron of Robert of Sorbonne, and chose Vincent of Beauvais, the greatest scholar of his day, to be his reader and the teacher of his sons. But with all this he was no weakling or do-nothing. All men trusted him, and the English barons accepted him as arbiter in their disputes with Henry, knowing that he would never seek his own advantage from quarrels among his neighbours. But that which most struck his contemporaries was his extreme sobriety of language; Joinville, who was with him constantly for two and twenty years, declares that he never heard him utter a word of blasphemy though this was the commonest fault of that age.

Such was the king who now started on the last Crusade but one. With him though not in his immediate following, went Jean de Joinville his biographer. All history might be racked in vain for a passage of more simple pathos than that in which the great French noble tells how on his way to Marseilles he passed beneath the walls of his own castle, and dared not cast a look upon them lest his heart should melt at the thought of his little children, who there lay all unconscious of the perils on which their father was embarking. Louis reached Cyprus towards the end of 1248, and remained there till the following May. Great preparations had been made in the island long beforehand, and Joinville remarks on the great heaps of corn that were turning green upon the top where the grain was sprouting into active life, with the wine casks piled up into "houses" as it seemed—all in readiness for the start to Syria or Egypt.

Joinville, whose own money was now spent, took service with the king, and on the 21st of May the French host set forth in eighteen hundred vessels, whose white sails made a very fair sight. A sudden storm, however, dispersed the fleet; but on Whit-Monday the wind fell, and Louis reached Damietta three days later on the 27th of May with seven hundred ships. He had scarcely landed when the Saracens fled in terror from the city, and the French became masters of this great port without striking a serious blow.

For six months the army lay in or near Damietta, until the remainder of the fleet under the king's brother, the Count of Poitiers, could arrive from Syria. This was not till October, and then a council determined to waste no time in attacking Alexandria, but to push on boldly for Cairo itself; for said the Count of Artois it were better if they wished to kill the serpent to crush him on the head. Accordingly, at the end of November, the army marched south; but at the Delta, or to use the mediaeval expression "The Island," formed by the Damietta branch of the Nile and one of the other numerous river channels, their further advance was stayed; for they could not cross the river in the face of the great army that opposed them on the southern side. The French determined to construct a causeway to enable them to pass over, but whenever the work seemed to be making progress the enemy managed to destroy it. The Saracen stone-casters, and other military engines troubled the labourers incessantly, whilst the wooden towers or belfrys which the Crusaders had erected for their protection were twice destroyed by Greek fire. Louis was now in a most perilous position, for a hostile force which had crossed the Damietta branch into "the Island" threatened his rear. In this emergency he accepted the offer of a Bedouin who agreed for five hundred besants to guide the French to a secret ford. On Shrove Tuesday, February 8, 1250, Louis marched out for the ford, leaving the Duke of Burgundy to guard the camp. In the van went the Templars, with the Count of Artois in the centre, and the king in the rear.

Amongst the few English who took part in this Crusade, the most distinguished was William Longsword, second earl of Salisbury, the grandson of Henry II., and in all probability of Rosamond Clifford. Though the king's cousin and titular earl of Salisbury he was a poor man, and had been obliged to collect money for his expedition to the East, by what practically amounted to the sale of dispensations to the timid or the old, who at the last moment lacked courage for the journey. In the earlier days of the expedition he had succeeded in capturing an Egyptian caravan on its way with spices to Alexandria. Of this spoil, however, so says a contemporary English writer, the French had robbed him; William appealed to Louis for justice, but the king though admitting his wrong declared himself powerless to grant redress. The angry earl forswore the authority of so weak a prince and withdrew to Acre. There he awaited the coming of the main body of the English, but in vain, for the Pope at King Henry's request forbade their passage. Eventually at Louis' wish, probably when the army was marching on Cairo, Earl William returned to Egypt, and was thus present on this fatal day.

The Templars and the Count of Artois crossed the river with such ease that the count was for moving on Mansurah in the first flush of their success. To this rash project the Master of the Templars objected, advising that they should wait for the king. But the fiery temper of the French prince would brook no delay. He accused the Grand Master roundly of treachery, and of a desire to avoid any decisive victory since the power of the military orders depended on the preservation of something like equality between the Eastern Christians and the Saracens. The intervention of the Earl of Salisbury only aggravated the dispute. "See how timid are these tailed English!" cried the angry count; "it would be well if the army were purged of such folk." This taunt stung the English earl to the quick. "At least," he retorted, "we English to-day will be where you will not dare to touch our horses' tails."

All prudent thoughts were now cast aside, and the whole van charged into Mansurah. The wisdom of the Templar and the boast of Longsword were alike justified. The earl was slain refusing to fly, while the Count of Artois, in his endeavour to escape, was either killed or drowned in the river. The French were only saved from annihilation by the arrival of the king, and by the valour of Joinville, who held, at all hazards, a small bridge that led from Mansurah.

After this battle Louis remained on the south bank of the stream for several weeks, till the news came that the Saracens had blocked the Damietta stream. As he was now on the verge of starvation he reluctantly ordered a retreat into "the Island," and commenced negotiations with the Sultan for the exchange of Damietta against the kingdom of Jerusalem. But on the 29th of March matters had become so intolerable that the order was given for a further retreat towards Damietta. Then the Saracens seeing what plight the French were in, refused to abide by the terms they had been discussing. They threw themselves on the sick, and began to murder them as they were warming themselves by the fires. Louis himself, despite the desperate valour of his attendant, Sir Geoffrey de Sergines, was taken prisoner as he was attempting to guard the river. Joinville had already gone on board his ship, and reached the place where the Sultan's galleys blocked the river. Four of these Saracen vessels bore down on him, and his life vas only saved by the generous deceit of a Saracen, who swore that he was the king's cousin. The good knight, though he would not tell a lie himself, did not scruple to take advantage of his protector's falsehood. Nor is it unpleasing to find that afterwards the same Saracen, as he led Joinville away, slipt into his hand that of a little lad, Bartholomew de Montfaucon, bidding him never let himself be parted from him, or the child's life would be sacrificed.

Such was the end of the French army. After protracted negotiations Louis was set free. In spite of many tortures with which he was threatened the king refused to surrender the Christian fortresses in Palestine, or to forswear his faith, but agreed to purchase his freedom and that of his army by the payment of one hundred thousand livres and the surrender of Damietta. In the midst of the negotiations the Sultan Turan Shah was murdered by his Mamluks on the 4th of May, and Louis had once more to display his constancy in the presence of danger. But after the payment of an increased ransom, Louis and the remains of his host were able to sail for Acre in the middle of the month.

After the murder of Turan Shah the power in Egypt fell into the hands of the widow of Es-Saleh, who ruled in the name of her son Khalil; but after a little the emirs displaced her in favour of Musa, a great-grandson of El-Kamil. The Mohammedan princes of Aleppo and Damascus were offended at the ransom of Louis; such a prince, they said, should have been kept in perpetual captivity and not set free for money. They placed themselves at the head of a great league, and marched against Musa, to be utterly routed on February 3, 1251. Musa, in the stress of his contest with his kinsmen entered into communications with the French king, and concluded a truce for fifteen years. In the West men spoke of Musa as a possible convert, and whispered that Louis had sworn to spend the remainder of his life in the Holy Land. The king had sent home his brothers to collect the remainder of his ransom; they had urged the Pope to compose his quarrel with the Emperor in the interests of Christendom, and lend them his aid; but Innocent remained immovable in the pursuit of his feud with Frederick and his sons. So the time wore on with nothing done, for though Henry of England took the cross his motives were seemingly sinister. A little later the regent of France, Louis' mother Blanche, died, and this event appears to have called the king home. Louis had spent nearly four years in the Holy Land, busy with the fortification of the great seaports. Caesarea, Jaffa, Sidon, were all rebuilt during these years, and it was not till the spring of 1254 that the king departed reaching his own country about July 11th.

Sixteen years later King Louis embarked upon a second Crusade. In the interval he had always remained a Crusader at heart, and amidst all the troubles of his home life his real ambition was set upon the Holy Land, though the duties of his position forced him to remain in France. It was not till July, 1270, that the king started on his second expedition from Aigues Mortes. Despite Louis's earnest request Joinville would not accompany him, pleading that his first duty was to his own vassals, who suffered so many wrongs during his absence on the previous Crusade.

Louis, who was accompanied by his eldest son Philip, and the kings of Navarre and Aragon, was induced to turn aside to Tunis in the hope of converting its ruler to Christianity. Whilst encamped near this city he was seized with dysentery. On Sunday, the 24th of August, he crept from bed to confess his sins and receive the last sacrament from the hands of Geoffrey de Beaulieu, to whom we owe most of our knowledge of this expedition. In the night as he lay on his ash-sprinkled couch the words "Jerusalem! Jerusalem!" showed in what direction his thoughts were turning. As morning drew on the watchers caught fragments of the good king's prayer for his people, and a little later heard his last cry, "Domine in manus tuas animam meam commendavi;" shortly afterwards, about the hour of nones, St. Louis expired. With him may be said to have perished the last hope of the Latin kingdom in the East. For over a century the French kings had been the recognised defenders of this outpost of the Christian religion and French culture. But the old spirit of piety was dying out; the new king, an illiterate warrior, had little care for a distant land, and after a few years the complex problems of a new age forced the grandson of St. Louis into a very different line of policy. In his life St. Louis afforded the most perfect illustration of the aspiration of two centuries towards an impossible ideal, and his death

276

tolled the knell of hopes, which if essentially futile were no less essentially sublime. The good king did not leave his peer behind, and the dream of a united Christendom mustering its forces for the subjugation of a common foe was destined to fade away among the ruder visions of national integrity and feudal dissolution.

Amongst those who had taken the cross at the same time as St. Louis was Edward, the eldest son of Henry of England. In his company went many of the great English nobles—especially those of the younger generation, whom he is said to have taken with him to divert them from the wars at home. Edward reached Tunis about the 9th of October with his cousin Henry of Almaine. He found the French barons, who had been victorious in more than one engagement, bent on enforcing the tribute which they said was due from Tunis to the King of Sicily. After exacting a great treasure the Crusading host set sail for Sicily, meaning to winter there; but a storm fell upon them outside the harbour of Trapani, and the tribute of the Mohammedan prince was lost in the sea. Next spring Edward, finding the French princes unwilling to accompany him, set sail with his English followers and reached Acre fifteen days after Easter, just in time to save the city from the Saracens. After a month's rest he made a raid to the casal of S. George between Acre and Safed, and at the end of November led another expedition as far as Chaco (Kakoun), and Castle Pilgrim or Athlit on the south. These trifling successes were probably intended to pave the way to greater achievements. At his request the barons of Cyprus, who had refused the summons of their own lord, the King of Jerusalem, came over with a great following and declared themselves the faithful servants of the English king, whose predecessor had won their island for the Latin Church; it was only on their coming that Edward had ventured so far afield. After his return to Acre Edward commenced negotiations with a Saracen emir who professed himself ready to become a Christian. His messenger was admitted time after time to Edward's presence and all suspicion was lulled asleep. At last, on his fifth visit, on June 18, 1272, the assassin found his opportunity. After a cursory examination for arms he was permitted to pass into the prince's presence. The day was hot and Edward, clad in a tunic only, was resting on a couch; he took the emir's letter from the messenger who, as he bent in Eastern fashion to answer the prince's questions, drew a knife from his belt and struck a blow at his intended victim. Edward caught the blow on his arm, and tripping the villain to the ground with his foot wrenched the dagger from his grasp and stabbed him as he lay. The English servants coming in found the would-be murderer dead, but to make assurance doubly sure, battered out his brains with a footstool. Edward's life was in much danger, for the weapon was poisoned, and though the Master of the Temple gave him what was declared to be a certain antidote, the wound grew daily worse. At last, an English doctor pledged himself to effect a perfect cure. He bade the nobles lead the weeping Eleanor from her husband's presence; then he cut away the poisoned flesh, and thus, under his care, Edward was within fifteen days able to appear on his horse in public. Very shortly afterwards Edward concluded a ten years' truce with the Sultan. His departure was accelerated by a letter from King Henry urging his son to return immediately since his health was failing, Edward left Palestine on the 14th of September, but did not reach England till two years later, long after his father's death. Throughout his life he cherished the hope of completing the exploits of his earlier manhood, and at the very close of his career vowed himself once more to the service of God, if He would but grant him vengeance on his enemy Bruce.

XXVI.

THE KINGDOM OF ACRE—ITS DECAY AND DESTRUCTION.
(1244-1291.)

ὡς οὐδέν ἔστιν οὔτε πύργος οὔτε ναῦς

ἔρημος ἀνδρῶν μὴ ξυνοικούντων ἔσω.

SOPHOCLES.

("Worthless each tower and worthless every ship,
Reft of the people that should dwell therein.")

WE must now turn back thirty years to trace the last fortunes of the Latin colonies in Syria. After the departure of Frederick II. Jerusalem was to all intents and purposes a kingless realm, and during the greater part of this period even the bare tenure of the title of king was not allowed to go undisputed. It may seem strange that under such circumstances the Frankish rule should have dragged out even a moribund existence for so many years. But a variety of circumstances contributed to delay its dissolution. Chief among these we must place the extreme weakness of the Ayubite Sultans during the sixteen years that elapsed between the death of El-Kamil and the final destruction of their power by the Mamluks in 1254; and, in the second place, we have the fact that the very existence of a Mussulman empire was threatened by the rise of a new power in the person of the Tartar Khans. No credit can be placed to the continuance of any vitality in the Franks themselves; for saddest of all features in these fifty years of Crusading history is the presence of perpetual feuds among the Christians in the East.

After Frederick's death in 1250 his rights should have passed to Yolande's son Conrad, but the Emperor, in bequeathing his own dominions to his eldest son, expressly stipulated that Jerusalem should go to Henry, the offspring of his marriage with Isabella of England. But both Conrad and Henry died within a few years, and the title passed to Conradin, the youthful son of the former, on whose tragic death in 1267 the line of Yolande came to an end. Meantime in Palestine the office of bailiff was held for the most part by one member or another of the house of Ibelin. Henry of Cyprus died in 1253, leaving an infant son Hugh by his wife Plaisance of Antioch. The claims of this child were asserted by his uncle Bohemond VI. of Antioch in 1258, but resisted by the Hospitallers and Genoese, who supported Conradin. Hugh died in 1267, and his cousin and namesake, who had been warden of Cyprus in the boy-king's name, then asserted his right to succeed him both in Cyprus and Jerusalem. Hugh III. of Cyprus was actually crowned King of Jerusalem at Tyre on September 24, 1269; but though he maintained a more or less shadowy authority on part of the mainland during seven years, his claims were disputed by his aunt Mary of Antioch. At last, in 1276, the opposition of the Templars drove Hugh to leave Acre; the knights of the other orders and the Genoese would have supported him, and were anxious for his return. But the Templars declared: "If he wants to come he can come, and if he does not, let him stay away." Hugh contented himself with a declaration to the Western Powers that he could not maintain justice or order in the strife of contending parties at Acre; whilst Mary, his opponent, went to Europe in person, and there sold her rights to Charles of Anjou, whom the Pope had made king of Sicily. Charles sent Roger of St. Severin as his bailiff to Acre next year, but though Roger had the support of the Templars there was no longer any pretence of a supreme authority in the Frankish possessions.

The divisions among the Latins in the East had a twofold origin; on the one side, there was the commercial rivalry of the Venetians, the Pisans, and the Genoese; on the other, the military jealousy of the two great orders. In 1249 the Pisans and Genoese had fought against one another at Acre for eight and twenty days with two and twenty kinds of engines, stonecasters, tribuchets, and mangonels. Louis IX., during the four years of his residence in Palestine, was able through the preponderance of his authority to maintain some sort of peace. At his departure he left Geoffrey de Sergines as his lieutenant with a force of one hundred knights. Geoffrey fought with some success before Jaffa, which was excepted from the truce, but it was not long before these old jealousies broke out with new force, and "the Christians waged war with each other villainously." On the one side, were the Venetians, the Pisans, and Pullani, or Syrian Franks, supported as it would seem by the Templars; on the other side, the Genoese, the Spaniards, and the Hospitallers. It was in the midst of this war in 1258 that Bohemond VI. paid his visit to Acre, and endeavoured without success to make peace. The struggle continued during two years till at last, in a great sea fight off Acre, a fleet of fifty Genoese galleys was defeated by forty Venetians with a loss of seventeen hundred men. A little later the Templars were disastrously defeated in a pitched battle with their rivals. Much of this warfare had been conducted in the streets of Acre, where the contending parties battered each other's quarters and towers till a great portion of the city was utterly destroyed. In the end the Genoese had to abandon their quarter and withdraw to Tyre. There was no such open and prolonged war after this, but the continued dissensions of the Christians lasted till the very day when Acre was taken.

It was at the time of this warfare among the Christians that the Tartars began to threaten Syria. In the early years of the thirteenth century Genghis Khan had established his authority over the Mongols and laid the foundations of an empire, which within a few years extended from the most eastern confines of Asia to the borders of Germany. The sons of Genghis held rule in China, Persia, and Russia; Europe was with difficulty preserved by the valour of Conrad; and when at length in 1258, Bagdad was taken and the orthodox Caliphate extinguished by Hulagu Khan, the son of Genghis, it seemed as though

281

the very existence of Islam was at stake. Despite the terror which the first invasions of the Tartars had inspired, the eyes of the Christians had already been turned towards the new power as a possible ally for the destruction of the Moslem. From the council of Lyons, in 1245, Innocent IV. despatched Dominicans on a mission to the great Khan; and four years later Louis IX. received at Cyprus an embassy from Ilchikadai, a Tartar Khan, with promises of assistance. In response the king sent certain friars, who, returning after an absence of two years, found Louis at Caesarea; afterwards Louis despatched the Franciscan Rubruquis, who has left us a graphic account of his long journey, and of the court of the great Khan. It was no doubt, therefore, with mingled feelings of hope and dread that the Franks beheld the Tartars enter Syria in the year after the fall of Bagdad. Aleppo, Hamah, and Damascus fell before them. The Sultan appealed to the Franks for assistance, but through the counsel of the Hospitallers and Teutonic knights the proffered alliance was refused. On September 3, 1260, the Sultan Kutuz met and defeated the Tartar host at Ain Talut; it was one of the decisive battles in the world's history, for not only was the tide of Tartar conquest stemmed, but the fate of Palestine was settled. The fruits of the victory did not, however, fall to Kutuz, for as he was returning to Cairo he was murdered on October 24th by his Mamluks, and the throne of Egypt passed to Bibars Bendocdar.

Bibars was the true founder of the Mamluk rule in Egypt, and was the most formidable and relentless foe that the Christians had had to encounter since the death of Saladin. The first year of his reign was signalised by the discomfiture of the Tartars in a second battle near Emesa; from this moment Bibars was able to turn his arms against the Franks, and win for himself the titles of the Pillar of Religion and Father of Victories.

The lax authority among the Franks gave Bibars an easy opportunity to disregard the truce, which nominally subsisted between the

Christians and Mohammedans in Syria. In 1263, he appeared for the first time before the walls of Acre, and two years later commenced his career of conquest by the capture of Arsûf. The next year was marked by the fall of Safed and massacre of all its defenders, and in 1267, whilst the Venetians and Genoese were contending for the mastery outside the harbour of Acre, Bibars was plundering the gardens beneath its very walls. In 1268, the victorious Sultan appeared once more in Palestine, Jaffa was taken on March 2nd, and then passing northwards the Mohammedans laid siege to Antioch in May. The prince was absent at Tripoli, and this great city, which 170 years previously had resisted the Crusaders for over six months, fell once more beneath the sway of the Mohammedans after a siege that had not lasted so many days. The fall of Antioch led to the Crusade of Edward, but that enterprise as we have seen, did little to check the progress of Bibars. It were tedious to trace in detail the steps by which the last poor remnants of the Latin colonies perished. One by one the strong castles of the military orders were captured, until the Franks were confined to a few isolated cities on the coast, which were separated yet more by mutual jealousy or discord. Bibars died, perhaps of wounds received in battle with the Tartars, in 1277, but his death brought no relief to the Franks. His successor, Malek El-Mansur or Kalaún, took Markab in 1285, and the great and rich city of Tripoli in 1289. As one by one the different towns were taken, their inhabitants were either put to the sword, or suffered to escape with their lives to Acre. Thus the population of that city was much increased, and within its walls there were gathered representatives from every nation in Christendom. For every one there was a separate commune, and the various lords of the land, the masters of the great orders, the representatives of the kings of France, England, and Jerusalem, each exercised separate authority, so that there were in one city seventeen independent powers, "whence there sprang much confusion." It is not strange that under such circumstances the city became, as it were, the sink into which all the vileness of Christendom found its way. Over its mixed population many ruled but none had authority; within its walls the precepts of religion, law, and morality were alike void, so that in its last days Acre became a byword in all Christian lands for the luxury, turbulence, and vice of its inhabitants. Popes did not cease to preach with more or less sincerity the duty of a new Crusade, but the spirit of self-denial and heroism which inspired the warriors of the Cross in an earlier age was now extinct. Such assistance as the West afforded came in the shape of mercenary troops, and it was the dissolute violence of some of these mis-called Crusaders that precipitated the end of the Christian rule in Syria.

Pope Nicholas IV., in his zeal for the Eastern Christians, had sent, as it is said, no less than seventeen hundred mercenaries at his own cost to Acre. These men, being left without pay and in lack of means of subsistence, fell to plundering the Saracen merchants, who, under cover of a truce, had come to Acre for the purpose of peaceful trade. The Sultan appealed to the rulers of Acre for redress, but it was in vain that the Templars urged the justice and prudence of concession. Malek El-Ashraf or Khalil, who just at this time succeeded Kalaún as Sultan, then had resort to arms, and on the 25th of March, 1291, his troops appeared before the walls of Acre. There were not wanting enough soldiers to have successfully defended the city; but even in this the last hour of their extremity, its inhabitants were more intent upon feasting than upon fighting, and when the trumpet called them to battle, could not tear themselves from the pleasures of love. Cowardice and discord also played their part in ruining the hopes of a successful defence. Many at the first threat of danger made haste to flee oversea; whilst others who stayed for a time departed when the prospects of success grew desperate. Among these latter, to his shame, went the Burgundian knight, Otho de Grandison, whom Edward of England had sent with treasure and men to the assistance of the Christians in the East. Not even when the whole purpose of their existence was in peril could the Templars and Hospitallers lay aside their mutual jealousy; and so the defence, if conducted with valour in parts, lacked that general unity of purpose which could alone have made it successful. At length on Friday, the 18th of May, Khalil's engines had wrought such a breach in the walls, that the moat being filled with the stones and the bodies of the dead, his army forced its way into the city. The people fled before him to the towers, the palaces of the nobles, or the great house of the Templars. Others, making their way to the harbour, crowded on board the ships in such numbers, that some vessels were swamped as they lay at anchor. Henry II. of Cyprus, who had played a not unworthy part in the early days of the siege, had already escaped to his island kingdom, whither the Grand Master of the Hospital and a number of other fugitives now followed him. But there yet remained sixty thousand Christians whose fate was slavery, or the sword, or worse. The Templars and those who had taken refuge with them met the noblest end; for, resisting to the last, they succumbed only when their fortress was undermined, and together with numbers of their assailants perished in its ruins. Thus almost exactly a century after its recovery by the soldiers of the Third Crusade was Acre finally lost to the Christians; and since Tyre and the few other places that still remained to the Franks could offer no effectual resistance, the last vestiges of the Latin kingdom of Jerusalem were swept away.

XXVII.

THE CLOSE OF THE CRUSADES.

"For now I see the true old times are dead,
And now the whole Round Table is dissolved."

TENNYSON.

IT would be wrong to suppose that the feelings of Western Europe were not deeply excited by the fall of Acre. Pope Nicholas in particular was eager that this loss should be made the occasion of a new Crusade. But neither his influence, nor the feelings of princes and people themselves, were strong enough to bring about the serious undertaking of such an enterprise. The century that had elapsed between the capture of Jerusalem by Saladin, and that of Acre by Khalil had witnessed great and marvellous changes in Europe. In a mis-called Crusade the papacy had crushed the power of the Empire, and destroyed the semblance of unity in the Western world. The triumph of the papacy had fostered the growing seed of the principle of separate and independent nationalities. It had been fatal also to its own authority. When the popes debased their spiritual office for the furtherance of their political aims, they lost the substance which they possessed, and obtained but the shadow of what they clutched at. The coming century was filled with the national warfare of the French and English, and with a divided papacy and a nerveless empire there was no central authority that might have rallied the nations of the West to a new Crusade.

Yet in a half-hearted way popes preached and princes talked of renewed warfare for the Church against the Infidel. Nicholas IV. spent his last days in calling on the rulers of Germany, France, and England to take the Cross; but he did not survive the fall of Acre by a twelvemonth, and after his death the papacy was vacant over two years.

286

Of his successors, Boniface VIII. was too full of his schemes for papal aggrandisement; Clement V. too much the tool of the French king to seriously resume the initiative. John XXII. took up once more the cause of Christendom, and obtained from Philip of Valois and Edward III. a promise to go on the Crusade. But in the midst of his labours John was cut off by death, and within a few years his two allies had involved their countries in a war that was to last with but little intermission for over a hundred years.

Meantime the power of the Ottoman Turks was growing yearly, at the expense of the Greek Empire in the East. At the end of the fourteenth century the victorious Bayazid had overwhelmed Bulgaria and Servia, and threatened to destroy Hungary also. The imminence of the danger stirred the chivalry of the West to take up arms against the common foe of Christendom. In 1396 a goodly band of French knights, under the Comte de Nevers, went to aid Sigismund in his warfare with the Turks, but only to share in his defeat at Nicopolis. If Bayazid failed to accomplish the conquest of Constantinople, it was due, not to the valour of Christendom, but to the might of Timur the Tartar. The Greek Empire was further preserved by the quarrel of Bayazid's sons, and it was only in 1453 that the capture of Constantinople by Mohammed II. stirred a pope to proclaim once more to the princes of the West the duty of a Crusade. For another two centuries the Turks hung as a storm-cloud over Eastern Europe, and in one sense the victories of Don John at Lepanto in 1571, and of Sobieski at Vienna in 1683, may be counted amongst the Triumphs of the Cross. Yet these exploits cannot, any more than the frequent wars with the Algerine corsairs from the fourteenth to the nineteenth centuries, properly be counted as Crusades; for though politically speaking they aimed at averting what was substantially the same danger, they did not possess that religious characteristic which is essential to the idea of a Holy War.

It is indeed to the decay of that spirit of enthusiasm which had imparted to the Crusades their religious characteristic, that we must attribute the discontinuance of the attempt to preserve the Holy Places under Christian rule. Some instances we do, however, find of men who were to all appearance fired with the true Crusading fervour. Such was our own king, Henry V., who died with these words on his lips: "Good Lord, Thou knowest that mine intent hath been, and yet is, if I may live, to rebuild the walls of Jerusalem." Henry's intention seems to have been sincere, and only a short time previously he had despatched the Burgundian knight Gilbert de Lannoy to Egypt and Syria to report on the practicability of a fresh Crusade. So too Columbus dreamt of a new war for the faith in the East, before he took up that marvellous enterprise in the West, which, by diverting the course of commerce, made a new Crusade more than ever unlikely. But these men stand out as solitary exceptions, and with the changing spirit of the times it was impossible that the world should witness again such strange scenes of enthusiasm as had marked the early days of the First Crusade, or as that perhaps still stranger delusion which in the years 1212 and 1213 sent numbers of children wandering off, in the belief that by their means should be accomplished that which had been beyond the power of kings.

But if the Crusading spirit had run its course in Europe the Latin kings of Cyprus and the knights of St. John at Rhodes maintained during two centuries a gallant struggle in defence of the Cross. The latter were avowedly dependent on recruits from Europe; the former no doubt also benefited by the aid of soldiers, who had left their homes for this purpose, or who, during a pilgrimage to the Holy Sepulchre, landed at Cyprus, and for a time gave their services to the king. Amongst these warrior pilgrims who came from our own land were Henry of Lancaster, father in-law of John of Gaunt; William, Lord Roos of Hamlake, who died in the East in 1352; and John, Lord Grey of Codnor, who, after serving his own sovereign with distinction in France, fought for Peter de Lusignan, King of Cyprus, with other English knights, at Alexandria in 1365. Peter may in some sense not unfairly be called the last of the Crusaders, and had made an endeavour to rouse the flagging interest of the West, in the course of which he paid a visit to England and was handsomely entertained by Edward III. But his fight at Alexandria had no practical result, and the city was abandoned almost as soon as it was taken. Still it was the last notable achievement of Western chivalry in the East, and it is perhaps in this spirit that Chaucer says of his perfect knight—

"At Alisaundre he was whan it was wonne."

If, however, military enthusiasm had declined, there was no falling off in pilgrim zeal. From John of Wurzburg and Theoderic, in the days of the kingdom, to Burcard and Felix Fabri, in the latter years of the fifteenth century, the pilgrim record runs on in an unbroken line. So numerous were the pilgrims that a regular system was organised for their conveyance under the superintendence of the Venetian senate. An "Information for Pilgryms," by William Wey, Fellow of Eton, was of sufficient interest to be printed by Caxton. Wey gives the would-be pilgrim careful directions for his journey to Venice, and details of various excursions to be made in Palestine, together with such useful advice as where to buy a bed for the voyage in Venice; how it was well to avoid the lowest stage in the vessel, "for it is ryglit evyll and smouldryng hote and stynkynge"; how Famagosta was unhealthy for Englishmen; how there was "good wine and dear" to be had in Jerusalem, and what payments it would be right to make in the Holy Land.

But the zeal which has maintained the stream of pilgrims to the present day was a thing apart from that enthusiasm for the Holy War which made the Crusades possible. Though in a sense the age of the

Crusades was not closed till the dawn of the Renaissance, their interest as a living force came to an end when the last visible sign of the kingdom of Jerusalem perished with the fall of Acre.

XXVIII.

CONCLUSION.

"The old order changeth, yielding place to new,
And God fulfils Himself in many ways,
Lest one good custom should corrupt the world."

TENNYSON.

It is always difficult to estimate with precision the exact limits of any great upheaval of human thought and action, or to trace with certainty the true relations of cause and effect amidst the multitude of historic facts. Nowhere is this difficulty more apparent than in the Crusading epoch, when so many forces were at work, so many countries in connection, so many creeds and races in strange antagonism or yet stranger alliance. But with it all some broad facts seems to stare us in the face. Contrast the Europe of the eleventh century with the Europe of the fourteenth, the age that preceded the capture of Jerusalem with the age that succeeded the fall of Acre, and in a rough way we can suggest limits within which the Crusades have affected the world's history. Still we cannot be sure that the changes which we perceive are due to the Crusades alone. Thus nothing seems more clear than that the growth of the great Italian seaports was fostered by the Crusades; but that growth had already begun when the First Crusade started, and would doubtless have continued had no armed pilgrim ever set foot in Palestine. Such an example serves to show the difficulty of assigning a specific cause to any of the great changes wrought during our epoch. Historically speaking, no one influence ever acts singly, and if we are justified in attributing any particular results to the Crusades, it can only be in a very loose and general way. But subject to such limitations it seems proper to indicate, however tentatively, the modes wherein Western life—political, ecclesiastical, social, commercial, and

291

intellectual—was affected by so great an upheaval as was involved in the Crusades.

In the political, or perhaps to speak more accurately the national, life of Europe the Crusades acted both as a combining and a disintegrating force. The continued absence of the petty baronage in the East, and its perpetual decimation under the pressure of debt and travel, battle and disease, helped to concentrate authority in the hands of the royal officers. Each nation, too, had brought home to it a consciousness of unity such as it had never felt before. Community of danger in the toilsome plains of Hungary, the pathless Bulgarian forest, the rugged depths of Asia, or the burning Syrian desert, drew together all men of kindred race and speech. So in the First Crusade there were the two opposing factions of Provençals and Franco-Germans, nominally divided as to the genuineness of the Holy Lance, but in truth by mutual jealousy. A like discord between Franks and Teutons was perhaps the rock on which the Second Crusade split; and again in the Third Crusade it was jealousy of English valour that sent the French king home before the work of the war was well begun. Later Crusades showed similar features on somewhat different lines; the feud was now between adherents of pope and emperor, but as the one included the French, and the other the Germans, here also the quarrel tended to assume a national aspect.

It was in France that the combining forces of the Crusades were most felt. There one by one the petty fiefs were swallowed up in the greater lordships, and the greater lordships in the royal power. In the eleventh century the kings of France ruled only in a narrow strip of territory with Paris as its centre, but by the time of the fall of Acre France had already put on much of its present form. It might thus in a sense be said that modern France is a creation of the Crusades; and though such a statement would involve the disregard of other important factors, it must not be forgotten, as we shall see later on, that the Crusades did much for the consolidation of French national sentiment by the spread of French culture and the French speech over a wide area.

In the other countries of Europe the growth of national sentiment was also fostered during the Crusading epoch, but there was no such spectacle of political consolidation as is afforded in France. We are here more struck by the process of disintegration; for before the Crusades the Empire gave Europe a semblance of unity which had nearly disappeared by the time that they came to a close. The power which the Crusades threw into the hands of the popes aided them materially in their struggle with the Empire, and it was indeed in a so-called Crusade towards the close of our own period that the true authority of the Empire was destroyed. The disintegration of the Imperial power was followed directly by the destruction of true political unity alike in Germany and in Italy. In the latter country the power of the cities was fostered through the development of commerce, whilst at the same time such central authority as was possessed by the emperors disappeared. The process of disintegration was further assisted by the policy of the popes in Southern Italy, where the union of the crowns of Sicily and Jerusalem in the person of Frederick II. was turned to his ruin by Gregory IX. and Innocent IV. It is only in our own time that Germany and Italy have recovered from the havoc that was wrought by the network of Crusading politics.

In England we can trace no direct influence of equal importance. But it must not be forgotten that the warfare which led to the loss of the Angevin dominions in Northern France originated in a Crusading quarrel, and that it was in the Crusades that the antagonism of France and England was developed, if not actually created. In this way the circumstances of the Third Crusade contributed not a little to the growth of English liberty in the thirteenth century. The other countries of Europe had but a slight share in the Crusades. Yet Spain and Portugal were created through the process of their own warfare with the infidel, and the foundations of modern Prussia were laid through the Crusading enterprise of the Teutonic knights in Lithuania.

Outside the limits of the Latin world it is important to note that the Crusades led to a political intercourse, and to semi-political relationships of a kind that had not been witnessed since Otho II. married his Greek wife. Let alone the alliances of the Frank princes of Syria with the Imperial house of Constantinople, we find the sister of Philip Augustus wedded to the Emperor Alexius; Italian nobles, the dukes of Austria and kings of Sicily, sought alliance in the same direction, and even Philip of Swabia, the son of Barbarossa, and claimant of the Imperial throne, did not hesitate to take a Greek wife. Of no great importance in themselves, such incidents point to an enlargement of the political horizon, which was of considerable moment to Western Europe. The same tendency finds a rather ludicrous illustration in the proposal gravely made to Edward I., that European princesses should be brought up to speak Eastern tongues, that thus by marrying Tartar kings and Saracen emirs they might through the grace of God and their own beauty win over their husbands to the faith.

On the vast importance of the Crusades for ecclesiastical history, there can be but one opinion; yet here also exists the difficulty of tracing simple relations of cause and effect. Thus we are confronted with diverse opinions; some holding that the Crusades were the foreign policy of the papacy and the source of its preponderant power; whilst others argue that by widening the intellectual horizon of mankind they paved the way for the Reformation, and were an essentially false move on the part of the popes. As a retrospective judgment there is much truth in either statement; but in so far as they attribute a conscious motive to Roman policy, both appear mistaken. For though the Crusades were turned very much to the advantage of the Roman see, they did not owe their origin to the popes, who were powerless to promote them when enthusiasm had flagged. Still less could the popes have foreseen the dangers that were to result from the breaking down of old barriers of thought and intercourse.

To turn, however, to particulars. In the first place, there can be no question that the authority of the popes was much increased through the preaching of the Crusades under their auspices. On the other hand, it was no small thing that, whether from forethought or good fortune, the popes avoided those dangers which the actual direction of a Crusade entailed. No other Western power was equally happy. The union of Western Europe in a common effort on behalf of the faith gave the papal see an opportunity to assert for itself a position as the centre and mainspring of the politics of Latin Christendom. Those, moreover, who took the Cross, put themselves in the power of the Pope, who could alone remit their vows. In each of the great kingdoms of the West the sovereign at one time or another assumed the Cross, either from religious enthusiasm or to propitiate papal favour. The vow once taken, it mattered little whether the prince went or whether he went not, whichsoever course he adopted must turn to the advantage of Rome. If he went he acknowledged the Pope's headship, if he went not he incurred his anathema. With what fatal effect the papal see could use the power thus obtained is best illustrated in the history of Frederick II. In England, also, the power which the popes acquired in the thirteenth century sprang directly from those troubles which had their occasion in the Crusade of Richard.

If the Crusades contributed to elevate the ecclesiastical over the civil power, within the Church itself they favoured the assertion of papal supremacy. The preaching of the Crusades gave rise to constant legations, which afforded the popes a useful opportunity for asserting their position as the head of the Church in every country of the Latin obedience. The absence of Western bishops in the East gave from time to time further opportunities for the assertion of papal authority, whilst the establishment of Eastern bishoprics led in the end to the creation of those bishops *in partibus infidelium*, who have in later ages filled a not unimportant part in the polity of the Church. More than this the Crusades led directly to the creation of the entirely novel military orders. The knights of the Temple, in particular, were a powerful prop of papal policy, and under different auspices might have become a veritable militia of the Church in Western Europe. A more religious, but less direct product of the Crusades, were the orders of Friars, of whom the Dominicans sprang immediately from the pseudo crusade against the Albigenses. Yet, again, the Crusades were the pretext for frequent levies on the clergy, by which means both the power and wealth of the papacy were much increased. If, however, the clergy were taxed in the cause of the Church, they themselves could well afford it. The Crusading knight or noble had to sell or mortgage his estates at a sacrifice to procure the money for his journey. When all were in turn so anxious to sell, the ecclesiastical corporations alone had the power and desire to buy. The wealth thus amassed was never alienated, and by this means was brought about that concentration of landed property in ecclesiastical hands, which, politically speaking, was in great measure to cause and to justify the Reformation. Yet a further source of wealth was found in the sale of immunities to those who desired exemption from a vow which they had taken in thoughtless enthusiasm. So far did this practice proceed that it was even customary for the aged and infirm to be given the Cross for the express purpose of being made to pay for exemption. It was in this custom that there originated the sale of indulgences for other purposes, which in the course of time was to become the immediate cause of the Reformation.

If, however, the Crusades brought to the Church both wealth and power, these advantages were inevitably followed by the reaction of covetousness and discontent. Thus the age of the Crusades was also the age of heresies, to combat which the intolerance natural in minds accustomed to religious warfare called into being the Holy Inquisition.

The Albigensians were in a sense the precursors of the Reformers, and Dominic himself the prototype of Torquemada. But in the heresies of the twelfth and thirteenth centuries there was this further peculiarity, that they appear to have originated in part from intercourse with the East. There is grave reason to regard the Albigensians as tainted with Manicheism, the doctrines of which were no doubt brought home by returning Crusaders. Be this as it may, there can be no doubt that the doctrinal, political, and social causes which led to the Reformation all sprang from seed that was sown in the times of the Crusades.

Probably few ages of the world's history have witnessed a greater amelioration in the conditions of social life than took place in Western Europe during the period of the Crusades. The tenth and eleventh centuries were acquiescent under a regime of almost hopeless anarchy, the fourteenth was through the widespread existence of social discontent pregnant with promise for the future. But the causes which underlie any great change of social condition are usually so complex and so obscure that it is hazardous to speak with any certainty. In the present case, however, the changes are most marked pt the top of the social scale, and it is here that the influence exerted by the Crusades can be most clearly traced. Politically, as we have seen, the Crusades were fatal to the power of the feudal nobility; but this loss of power was in the end to turn out to the good both of the order as a part and of society as a whole. The misdirected activity, which found its vent in the waste bickerings of feudal despotism and anarchy, was through the Crusades turned into a well-ordered channel. On the one hand, those turbulent spirits, who made all progress at home impossible, were drawn away to a distant and harmless enterprise; on the other hand, a high and noble ideal was substituted for the base and petty motives of personal aggrandisement. The lust of warfare was sated by the Crusades, whilst at the same time it was purified by the inspiration of religious enthusiasm. This in itself would have contributed not a little

297

to the general improvement of morals and manners. It was further supplemented by the growth of luxury and culture consequent on the commercial and intellectual expansion, which resulted from the Crusades. These influences, combined with the growth of royal authority, transformed the feudal nobility from the curse of the West, into a settled and orderly member of the body politic.

Such a change was of the utmost importance to the inferior orders of society, and the consequent amelioration of manners could not but make its influence more and more widely felt as time went on. The people of the towns were the first to reap the benefit. The displacement of feudal anarchy by settled order under a strong central authority, enabled the townsfolk to profit to the full from the growth of commerce. With increased wealth came larger notions of liberty, and the power to assert them. Thus it is to these centuries that in every country of the West we can trace under diverse circumstances the revival of an organised and vigorous civic life. It is indeed true, so far as we can judge, that the change must in any case have come; but, at the same time, the Crusades and all that was involved in them did beyond question contribute in a marked degree to that development of town life which is one of the most striking characteristics of Western Europe during our period.

Of the changes that took place in the condition of the country folk it is more difficult to speak. Their elevation from a condition of serfdom did not come till the age of the Crusades had passed away, and was then, as it would appear, due to the operation of other causes. But over and above the softening influences consequent on the general improvement of manners, there are some respects in which the Crusades were directly beneficial to the peasant class. It was not that those who took the Cross became free, for, numerous as these may have been, those who survived to return were but relatively few. More important were the better social order and the milder rule of the new times. To the peasants it must have been an additional boon that, through the transfer of property, many came under the rule of ecclesiastics, who, if harsh taskmasters, were still preferable to the turbulent nobles they displaced. Yet, again, the growth of larger ideas was favourable to freedom, and at least made the future hopeful. But so far as the mass of the population is concerned perhaps the most that can be said, is—that the widening of the bounds of human knowledge through the Crusades helped to make a better order possible.

One of the greatest of the benefits conferred on society by the Crusades was the raising of the standard of comfort through the spread of luxury. The expansion of commerce in the Middle Ages is from one point of view that change which we can attribute most safely to the influence of the Crusades. It was the need of the Crusaders for transport, and the traffic necessary to supply the wants of those Franks who had settled in Syria, that gave the requisite stimulus to the infant commerce of Italy, and effectually opened up the East to the West. By this means the cities of Italy were brought into close commercial relations with the Greeks and Saracens, and less directly with even more distant nations. The establishment of the Latin Empire at Constantinople paved the way for the creation of the Venetian colonial system in the Levant; and the fall of that Empire led to the success of the Genoese under Greek patronage in the Euxine. The latter people thus established a caravan trade with Persia from Trebizond; whilst about the same time the Venetians entered into friendly relations with the Saracens of Alexandria, and thus secured the profitable trade of the Nile and the Red Sea. The caravan trade of the Euphrates valley had already been tapped from the ports of the Syrian coast. By the side of this wider commerce the actual trade with the Latin colonies of Syria was of comparatively slight importance, and it is this which explains the fact that the loss of those colonies and the cessation of the Crusades were not detrimental to Italian commerce. Indeed the same motives of self-interest, which made the Italian cities favourable to the Crusades at the start, made them lukewarm, if not hostile, when the continuance of the warfare threatened to jeopardise the commerce which it had created.

The commercial benefits of the Crusades were not confined to Italy. Marseilles enjoyed like privileges with her Italian rivals in Palestine, and shared in the profits arising from the transport of pilgrims and soldiers, as notably in the Crusade of Richard I. Nor was this all, for during the twelfth century English, Flemish, North German, and even Danish and Norwegian fleets appeared in the Mediterranean. The commercial influence of the Crusades on Northern Europe was, however, for the most part either less direct or of later growth. Venice as the chief distributing mart of the Middle Ages became in the fourteenth century the southern terminus of a great land trade-route. It was on this continental traffic that the wealth of the German and Flemish cities largely depended, and thus the Hanseatic League owed its prosperity if not its origin to the Crusades. It is noteworthy also that the other great line of Hanseatic development was aided by the Crusading enterprise of the Teutonic knights in Prussia and Lithuania.

The commerce which the Crusades assisted to create was purely "thalassic" or "potamic"; when, through the discoveries of Columbus and Vasco da Gama, the trade of the world assumed an "oceanic" phase, the commercial influence of the Crusades came to an end. We could have no clearer evidence of the close relation between the Crusades and mediaeval commerce than the fact that the Crusading epoch was only definitely closed when commerce was diverted into a new course.

In other points, however, the commercial influence of the Crusades, if less direct, was more enduring. It is not, perhaps, too much to say that the discoveries of the fifteenth and sixteenth centuries were the outcome of the maritime energy that was fostered by the Crusades. At any rate, these discoveries would probably have been deferred had the

300

commerce of Europe pursued a more sluggish course in the early Middle Ages. Yet again, it was to the Crusades that we owe the first beginnings of maritime law; Crusading princes, like Richard of England, made ordinances for the rule of their fleets at sea, and the Assize of Jerusalem includes regulations which contain the germ of a maritime code. Other indispensable adjuncts of a commercial system which owe their origin, in part at least, to the Crusades are banking and exchange. The financial needs of Crusaders and merchants in the East gave occasion for the practice of the elementary principles of commercial finance. The Jews and great Italian merchants had regular banking agents in Syria, and made the advance of money to Crusaders a formal part of their business. The military orders were not above sharing in such profits, and the Templars in particular undertook financial transactions, and were entrusted frequently with the care of treasure by Western princes and nobles. The extension of papal taxation through the Crusades was also important in this connection. The true development of commercial finance belongs, however, to a later age.

One result of the expansion of commerce was to bring into common use the spices, perfumes, and other products of the East, which, before the Crusades, had been the luxury of the few. Bede, for instance, on his death-bed divided his little store of pepper and incense amongst his friends as something very precious. But in the thirteenth century pepper was an article of such common use that, according to a rumour recorded by Matthew Paris, the Saracens plotted to destroy their Christian enemies in the West, by poisoning their spices. Pass over a hundred years, and we find in the vivid picture of a country inn in "Piers Plowman," that even the wife of Beton the Brewster has "pepper and pionys, and a pound of garlike," to spice her ale with. Various industries also, such as dyeing and glassblowing, profited much from intercourse with the East. Silk-weaving was introduced to Sicily from Greece by King Roger, in 1148, and the sugar cane was brought to that island about the same time. The Latin kings of Jerusalem gave special care in their legislation to commerce, and in the trading cities of their kingdom, the merchants of the West could find not only the cotton and silken goods of Syria, but perfumes from Persia, spices and jewels from India, and even precious pottery from China.

The previous pages will have indicated that in some respects it is for their intellectual results that the Crusades are most important, and that it was their effect on the mental environment of mankind which determined their influence within the more limited spheres of action. It will be most profitable to dwell on some particular phases of the extension of human knowledge and understanding, which will sufficiently illustrate the general aspect of intellectual development.

In the First Crusade Europe was, one may almost say for the first time since the days of Thucydides, confronted by an event of stupendous importance, and yet one which, like the struggle between Athens and Sparta, lent itself to a strictly artistic treatment. So unique an occasion was not lost, and the history of the Holy War is told by ten or twelve almost contemporary historians. But the fame of all was overshadowed by the great work of William of Tyre, which may perhaps fairly be called the first historical work of the Middle Ages that is not a mere chronicle of events. If Herodotus is called the Father of History, William may be styled the Father of Modern History. Such a title he deserves for his well-ordered and artistic treatment of a great and worthy subject, for his judicious, and not slavish use of earlier authorities, and for his vivid narrative of those events which came within the wide range of his own knowledge. The growth of the historic sense is shown also by the change that comes over Western historians. In the twelfth century our English writers not only concern themselves in an unwonted way with continental politics, but actually begin to be somewhat of authorities for events abroad. Among the historians of the later Crusades there is no single name of such note as William of Tyre; but, for another characteristic, they are even more important. William's great work was probably translated into French soon after his own death, and within fifty years a continuation was written in France by Ernoul who, as a young man, had been squire to the famous Balian of Ibelin. Ernoul was the first to tell the story of one of the great kingdoms of Latin Christianity in its own speech, and without the aid of rhyme. Bernard the Treasurer, and others, composed further continuations which carry on the history almost to the fall of Acre. The whole narrative, including the French translation of William of Tyre, was known as the *Chronique d'Outremer,* or *Estoire d'Eracles;* it enjoyed great popularity, and is well worthy to rank with the works of Villehardouin and Joinville. Ernoul, like these two writers, describes events in which he had himself taken part, and it was no small thing for literature that history had thus begun to be written by laymen in the common speech for popular perusal.

History, in the literary sense, owed much to the Crusades, but geography was still more deeply indebted. Geographical knowledge and science had indeed retrograded in Western Europe since the days of Ptolemy. With the First Crusade, however, a new era commences; not only was the knowledge of Eastern lands revived in the West, but a far more intimate acquaintance was established as to the intervening countries and seas. Every spring and autumn witnessed the departure of the fleets for Syria, and the stages of the journey were marked with such precision, that Roger Howden can give the distances from port to port in regular order from England to Palestine. A further extension soon followed, for in Syria merchants and pilgrims came into contact with those whose knowledge reached to the most eastern and southern confines of Asia. The next step was for Europeans to acquire a firsthand acquaintance with the far East; this they did through the relations which were established during the thirteenth century between the princes of Latin Christendom and the rulers of the Mongol Empire.

Most famous of these early travellers was the Franciscan William Rubruquis, whom Louis IX. sent as his envoy to the great Khan, in 1253. Of still more importance are the Venetian Marco Polo, and the Franciscan Odoric, who, early in the next century, travelled through Persia, India, and China. These travellers first made common in Europe a real acquaintance with the far East, and it was through them that geographical knowledge once more began to advance. More than this, it was their discoveries which inspired the enterprise that culminated in the achievements of Columbus and Vasco da Gama.

If the Crusades thus extended man's knowledge of other peoples and lands, they extended no less the limits of his own understanding. Not, it is true, altogether in those directions that might most naturally have been expected. Intercourse with the Empire of the East caused no such revival of classical learning as was to come about three centuries later. Nor did contact with Syrian Christians or Mohammedans confer any special benefit on medicine or philosophy. The treasures of Arabic skill and science were imparted to Latin Christendom from another quarter, and in so far as they contributed to the advance of medicine and philosophy the debt is due to the doctors not of Damascus but of Salerno and Toledo. Nor even was such knowledge of Eastern languages as existed due specially to the Crusades, and the Koran itself was translated about 1144 by an Englishman, Robert, who had gone to study astronomy in Spain, and probably never set foot in Palestine at all. From the same quarter came also the revived knowledge of Aristotle, which paved the way for mediaeval philosophy and scholasticism.

But if we turn from science to literature we find that the influence exerted by the Crusades was great and manifest. The Crusades were the creation of French-speaking peoples, and, above all, of those adventurous Normans who carried the language of their adoption wheresoever they settled. Never did Christendom come so near having a

304

common speech; for several centuries French was the most universal medium of intercourse from the Atlantic to the Jordan and the Golden Horn. If French thus became the speech of princes, lawyers, and merchants, yet more important was it that it became the recognised language of literature. The great Italian, Arnault Daniel, used it for his famous poem on Lancelot—which Dante has immortalised. Dante's own tutor, Brunetto Latino, adopted it for his *Tesauro*, boldly declaring that he chose French in preference to his native tongue "because it is more delectable and more widely diffused."

Mediaeval poetry was indeed the creation of Frenchmen and the Crusades. Only one chanson—that of Roland—is certainly of earlier date, but from the moment of the Crusades the world of romance wakes into new life. Religious enthusiasm, warlike gallantry, and the mystery of the East, all combined to inspire the minstrel with themes for his song. Jerusalem was hardly captured before French poets began to tell of the achievements of French knights in French verse. Soon every great chanson has its Eastern element; Huon of Bordeaux has many adventures in Babylon and the East; Renaud de Montauban, in his later years, performs no mean exploits in the Holy Land; Bevis of Hamptoun visits Jerusalem and Damascus and weds an emir's daughter; Richard Coeur de Lion's mother, like Thomas a Becket's, is in legend a Saracen princess. Even when the scene is not laid in the East we have fighting with Saracens nearer home, as in the romance of "Doon de Mayence."

If the Crusades created a new poetical literature, they also created the long historical poem as distinct from the short "cantilena." Geoffrey Bechada, early in the twelfth century, sang in French the story of the First Crusade, in which he had himself taken part; though his work has now perished it was well known to Geoffrey of Vigeois fifty years later. Richard the Pilgrim, even earlier, composed what was probably the oldest form of the "Chanson d'Antioch," which was afterwards the favourite theme with Crusaders, and was perhaps the foundation of the

305

Latin poem of our own Joseph of Exeter. Another early writer was William IX. of Poitiers, who used to amuse his friends with songs of his adventures in Palestine. The historical narratives thus composed were transformed by later minstrels, who embellished them with romantic additions of their own, such as the legend of the "Knight of the Swan," and the wondrous descent of Godfrey of Bouillon. In the process there was created a new romantic literature of pure imagination, wherein the bare facts of the older writers were lost in a wealth of legendary fable, fancy, and folly.

Of all that was entailed for literature in this creation of romance, and of its still abiding influence, we cannot now speak. Perhaps, indeed, it is of more value here to dwell on its importance for the mediaeval world; on the new element of brightness that it brought into man's life; on the inspiration of nobler ideas that it afforded; and on the quickening of the human intellect, of which it was the first and not the least hopeful evidence.

But from the discussion of the results of the Crusades we must now turn away to consider for a little their true character, and how far they were successful in achieving the objects that they aimed at. If the consequences of the Crusades are puzzling in their complexity, no less complex are the motives to which they owed their origin. The enthusiasm of religion, the spirit of adventure, the lust of power, the desire of gain, all, no doubt, contributed in their degree. Probably it is true to say that only of a few Crusaders, as of Godfrey and St. Louis, can we predicate absolute purity of motive. But after all detractions are made, there will still remain the overmastering fact that the Crusades were the outcome of an enthusiasm more deep and enduring than any other that the world has witnessed. They were no mere popular delusion; for principles of sound reason overruled the ungoverned excitement of the mob. No deep-laid plot of papal policy; for neither Gregory VII. when he projected, nor Urban II. when he preached the

Holy War, could have foretold the purposes to which their successors would, half unconsciously, turn it. Not the savage outbreak of warlike barbarism; for they entailed a patient endurance which only the inspiration of a noble ideal made possible. The Crusades were then primarily wars of an idea, and it is this which sets them apart from all other wars of religion; for into the Crusades proper the spirit of religious intolerance or sectarian jealousy hardly entered. The going on the Crusade was the "Way of God," not to be lightly taken up or lightly laid aside like the common affairs of men. The war was God's warfare, to be waged in His behalf for the recovery of the Heritage of Christ, the land which Our Blessed Lord Himself had trod. If this idea was not present to all when they took the Cross, yet it is safe to say that the great mass of the Crusaders came at some time under its spell. It is hard always for the men of one age to comprehend the enthusiasms of another. We can only marvel at the strange infection which for nearly two centuries ran riot through the West of Europe. It is easier for us to recognise the epic grandeur of the enterprise, in which was concentrated all that was noblest in the mediaeval spirit. The Crusades were the first united effort of Western Christendom. They raised mankind above the ignoble sphere of petty ambitions to seek after an ideal that was neither sordid nor selfish. They called forth all that was most heroic in human nature, and filled the world with the inspiration of noble thoughts and noble deeds. Of the manifold consequences that were to spring from this inspiration, the higher ideals of life, the wider range of understanding, enough has been said already to show that the Crusades were as beneficial in their general results as they were undoubtedly sincere in their original undertaking.

From the consideration of ideals which inspired the Crusaders, we pass naturally to the practical purpose which they endeavoured to achieve. Two principal objects presented themselves to the promoters of the First Crusade. The chief was no doubt the restoration of the Holy

Places to Christian rule; the secondary object—but to such leaders at least as Gregory VII. and Urban II. a no less clear one—was the defence of the Eastern Empire against the danger of Turkish conquest. The first was based on a sentiment, but on a sentiment which with some change of form still survives; the second, on an urgent necessity, the pressure of which was yet felt two centuries ago. The first object was within a few years achieved by the establishment of the kingdom of Jerusalem. But the success was barely complete before the process of decay commenced. With the causes of that decay, the narrow limits and ineffectual frontier of the kingdom, the jealousies of Crusaders for the Syrian Franks and for one another, the rival policies of the military orders and the native baronage, the deterioration of energy amongst those who settled in the East, and the waning enthusiasm amongst those who remained in the West, we have already in their several places dealt. A failure in this sense the Crusades no doubt were; but with it all we cannot regard as entirely fruitless an enterprise which maintained a fairly vigorous life for one century, and prolonged its death struggle for another.

The success of the second great object of the Crusades is best regarded from a twofold point of view—firstly, as concerns the Empire of the East; and secondly, as concerns the history of the world at large. In the former case, it seems clear that but for the First Crusade the Empire of the Comneni must have succumbed to the Seljukian Turks. Certainly the twelfth century witnessed a great recovery both of territory and power on the part of the Eastern Empire. But, at the same time, it must be remembered that the constant passage of huge and disorderly hosts was the source of serious harm, and that the destruction of the true Empire of the East was the work of a so-called Crusade. Perhaps it is not too much to say that whatever benefit was wrought by the First Crusade was more than undone by the Fourth. From the time of the latter enterprise there was no strong united power to guard the East, and the success of the Turks was probably due as much to this as to their own prowess. Certainly the political and religious dissensions of East and West were aggravated by the Crusades, but, above all, by the Fourth Crusade, and the power of resistance in Christendom was so far weakened. From this standpoint, therefore, the eventual failure of the Crusades to achieve their second great object was hardly less complete than it was in the case of the first.

Looking at the Crusades, however, from the more general standpoint of the world's history, we can pass a more favourable judgment. It was an imperative necessity for the welfare of Christendom that the advance of the Turks—which during the eleventh century had made such rapid progress—should be stayed. The First Crusade rolled back the tide of conquest from the walls of Constantinople, and the wars of the next two centuries gave full employment to the superfluous energies of Islam. Even after Acre had fallen, the Latin kingdom of Cyprus, the knights of St. John at Rhodes, and the maritime power of Venice—all creations of the Crusades—combined to delay, if they could not stop, the advance of Mohammedanism. The importance of this for Western civilisation cannot be over-estimated. Had the capture of Constantinople by Mohammed II. been anticipated by three centuries it is impossible that the Turkish conquests should have been confined to the peninsula of the Balkans and the valley of the Lower Danube. A new influx of barbarism, at the very moment when the gloom of the Dark Ages was breaking, might have been as ruinous to the social and political life of Western Europe as it was to that of Western Asia. At the least it must have put back the progress of civilisation in Europe by centuries, if it had not altered utterly the course of the world's history.

We of the present day who live under the shadow of the Revolution, and still feel the effects of the Reformation, are too apt to regard all that went before as matters of purely archaeological interest, or as furnishing only the foundation for a romantic tale. It is easy to contrast the glories of the Renaissance with the wreck of Mediaevalism, and to feel that between the two there is a great gulf fixed. But the mediaeval world had had its own glories, which, as they faded, let fall the seeds of future prosperity. The processes of decay and new birth are as natural to the historical as to the physical world, and there is no justice in the taunt of failure; for it is in the failures and half-successes of one age that there are sown the seeds of the glories of another. The Middle Ages were, in their way, as important and fruitful for mankind as any other epoch of the world's history. The Crusades were their crowning glory of political achievement, the central drama to which all other incidents were in some degree subordinate. If the enthusiasm which produced them perished, it was not until it had borne good fruit: we may perhaps contrast the age of the Crusades with the age of the Early Renaissance, which succeeded it, in some respects to the disadvantage of the former; but when all is said and written this much at least must be admitted: it was not altogether a change from the worse to the better that gave France a Louis the Treacherous for a Louis the Saint, and England a Richard of the Subtle Brain for a Richard of the Lion Heart.

"The old order changeth, yielding place to new,
And God fulfils Himself in many ways,
Lest one good custom should corrupt the world."

END.

310

Printed in Poland
by Amazon Fulfillment
Poland Sp. z o.o., Wrocław